APPREHENDING THE CRIMINAL

For Dino,

with admiration and friendship

Christine

POST-CONTEMPORARY

INTERVENTIONS

Series Editors:

Stanley Fish

Fredric Jameson

APPREHENDING THE CRIMINAL

The Production of Deviance in Nineteenth-Century Discourse

◆

Marie-Christine Leps

Duke University Press   Durham and London 1992

©1992 Duke University Press
All rights reserved
Printed in the United States of America
on acid-free paper ∞
Library of Congress Cataloging-in-Publication Data
appear on the last printed page of this book.

For Anne Marjorie and Paul-Emile Comtois
my parents and great friends

[Historians] will soon come to realize
that Western history cannot be dissociated from
the way "truth" is produced and inscribes its
effects.—Michel Foucault

Contents

◆

Figures

◆

Acknowledgments

◆

Without the direction and inspiration provided by the work of Marc Angenot, a leader in discourse analysis and a superb teacher, this book would not have been possible. I am also greatly indebted to the writing, teaching, and friendship of George Szanto, who undertook the task of encouraging and clarifying my project from beginning to end. Over the years, the writings of Timothy Reiss and Wlad Godzich have been crucial; their support for my work invaluable. Darko Suvin and Paisley Livingston helped with their readings of earlier versions, and Reynolds Smith guided me through the final form with judiciousness and generosity. Stephen Barber masterminded the index. A fellowship from the Social Sciences and Humanities Research Council of Canada provided me with the much needed time to complete this work.

For their friendship, judgement, and unfailing sense of humor, I would like to thank my colleagues Lesley Higgins, from York University, and Linda Hutcheon. Finally, my family has been wonderful, as always.

Introduction

♦

During the course of the nineteenth century, Western ways of perceiving and processing criminals underwent radical transformations. Criminal laws were modified to handle new forms of urban and industrial crime; modes of punishment were redefined and imprisonment became the almost universal means of social retribution; police forces were reshaped into national networks, progressively extended through international cooperation. Variously pursued and opposed by legislators and magistrates, landowners and businessmen, philanthropists, reformers, and a wide variety of experts (in medicine, commerce, and architecture), such alterations took place only gradually, through heated debates, and often in reaction to chance or circumstance. Nonetheless, during the last third of the century, integrated systems of criminal justice crystallized a new perception of crime and its perpetrators. Earlier, turn-of-the-century apprehensions of crime as a symptom of severe and threatening social trauma were replaced by a general acceptance of crime and criminals as normal, inevitable occurrences to be faced with rational methods of control. How this new conception came about, to what effects, and in answer to what economic, political, and social pressures will be the general questions investigated in this study.

Previous researchers have amply demonstrated how the new systems of criminal justice were structured to meet the requirements of industrial capitalism. Codes establishing the equality of all before the law were necessary to abolish aristocratic privileges and protect the rising middle classes from royal power. The widespread use of police forces for the preservation of order and the recourse to imprisonment as punishment for crime were needed by the industrial and commercial factions who lacked the time, resources, or inclination to protect themselves directly from property offenses. Landed interests had exercised their authority through a taut system of vertical integration, where traditions of deference, personal benevolence, and exemplary repression had promoted obedience and order. The new propertied classes preferred to interpose a police force between them and the thieves, strikers, or rioters who threatened their positions of wealth and authority, as "it [the police] would draw attack and animosity upon itself and would separate the assertion of constitutional authority from that of social and economic dominance."[1] The general adoption of penitentiaries as the obvious means for the punishment and reformation of criminals has been analyzed by Michel Foucault in *Discipline and Punish* as one instance of the general deployment of disciplinary processes characterizing the development of industrial capitalism: to equal rights in the face of the law, schools, factories, hospitals, and prisons oppose the nonrights of discipline, where power is exercised in the very production of its object (the submissive subject) through mechanisms of classification, examination, and normalization.[2] This study begins where Foucault's ends, with the social dissemination of texts, in order to investigate the discursive practices which transformed the phenomenon of crime and the existence of criminals into "simple facts of life" near the end of the nineteenth century. How was this new knowledge produced? From what institutional—and common—places?

Three major developments in the contemporary discourse on crime and criminals can readily be singled out as contributory factors in this remarkable feat of social integration. The emergence of criminology as a human science established the criminal as an object of scientific investigation, thereby aligning criminality with other social problems like poverty or disease, which, according to the positivistic belief in progress, could be grasped, contained, and ameliorated by scientific advances. The rise of mass journalism turned crime stories into ordinary commodities made for daily consumption as news items. Finally, an ever expanding mass of crime literature began to move from mysterious and faraway crimes to familiar, local situations; specialized products such as the detective novel or the French "police novel" (*roman policier*) emerged as extremely popular genres, and the study of crime became fashionable as "high literature" material, with authors like Charles Dickens, Feodor Mikhailovich Dostoevsky, and Emile Zola. The elaboration and circulation of discourse on crime thus gained prominence in social discourse as a whole, if only by virtue of its ubiquitous presence.

Rather than search for debts or influences between different discourses on the criminal (through an approach considering scientific discourse as representing a primary "truth" of the criminal, and press and literary discourses as derivative products), this study will focus on intertextual modes of knowledge production; its purpose is to outline common cognitive models, shared methods of discovery and analysis (such as measurement, the compilation of details, the recourse to narrative realism, and the use of types), and preferred argumentative strategies (rhetorical devices, topoï, and modes of reasoning). Such analyses will trace the convergence of local discursive tactics into the general production of the recognized "nature" or reality of the criminal. However, the points of diffraction and divergence between these discourses on the criminal will also be investigated. A curious distribution of objects between these discursive practices can be noted from the outset: the scientific discourse of criminology virtually excluded discussions of theory and methodology (notwithstanding vague references to scientific objectivity, the value of facts, and the truth of positivism) and concentrated on the description and tabulation of the physical, physiological, and moral characteristics of "criminal man"; conversely, detective novels practically excluded criminals who served as mere pre-texts for lengthy discussions on the science of deduction and analysis, generally accompanied by spirited diatribes against the blindness of institutional knowledge; and day after day all the details of the latest crimes were being packaged and sold for one penny on city streets. Intertextual analyses allow such distributions to be noticed and thus lead to an investigation of the relation between the status of a discursive practice (as scientific, informative, or entertaining discourse), its mandate in the social production of knowledge, and the limits of its sayable.

Two primary hypotheses direct this research. Stated in the broadest possible terms, the first is that the exercise of power and the production of hegemonic or "true" knowledge are inextricably linked in discourse. In this sense, the truth of a period corresponds not to the closest perception of a primary reality, but rather to the sets of information which, having been legitimized by institutions, organize the mode of being, the social arrangement, the historic reality of people and products. Thus, power is not a thing one can acquire or maintain by force, or at least, not by force alone; rather, power is both the result and the support of a complex system of production and distribution of knowledge which, once in circulation, acquires a truth value placing it in a position of domination. The second working hypothesis is that there exists an interreferential network between institutions producing hegemonic knowledge: power does not originate in a specific locus—such as the legal, penitentiary, or police systems, or schools, families, or armies—but in the web of reciprocal validation and authentication existing between these various institutions.[3] From this perspective, it would be wrong to assume that within social discourse, certain institutions "count" more than others in the establishment of power and knowledge. When magistrates at the end of the nineteenth century condemned beggars and vagabonds to imprisonment with hard labor, it was certainly important that they *know* that paupers were generally defective, lazy, and unintelligent, neither clean nor moral, and their families, schools, newspapers, and literature had provided them with this indispensable knowledge since childhood— but it was equally important that masses of paupers *learn* to recognize the authority of institutions, at home, at school, at the factory, and in prisons. The powers of the politician or the industrial head, the magistrate, police officer, or general derive from this production and distribution of knowledge. However, within the totality of social discourse, each institution possesses its mandate and status which determine the limits of its investigations: while there exists an intertextual circulation of objects of knowledge, ideological maxims, methodological precepts, and epistemological presuppositions, each institution must integrate them in the sense of its particular relation of domination, and reduce to silence all elements heterogeneous to its position. Thus, while knowledge is produced intertextually, each discursive practice retains a relative autonomy within social discourse.[4]

Consider the following descriptions, taken from a scientific treatise, a newspaper, and a detective novel of the end of the last century:

> Habitual homicides have glassy eyes, cold, immobile, at times sanguinary and injected; the nose is often aquiline, crooked or rather hawk-like, always voluminous; the jaws are robust, the ears long, the cheek-bones large, the beard scarce, the teeth canine and very developed, the lips thin, frequently curled up on one side by nystagmus or contractions, almost in a sneer or a threat; the hair is frizzy, abundant, and dark.[5]

The White-Chapel [*sic*] district in London is sinister. . . . Some
of these caves give shelter to families that wallow in mould and
manure. All day these pariahs stay crouched at the bottom of their
dens. At night, they go out, naked, throw themselves like animals
on refuse, fighting with the dogs for bones and bits of bread. They
seem like birds of prey.[6]

This malignant and terrible contortion, combined with the low
forehead, blunt nose, and prognathous jaw, gave the dead man a
singularly simious and ape-like appearance, which was increased
by his writhing, unnatural posture.[7]

In these passages describing habitual homicides, the inhabitants of
Whitechapel, and a character in a novel, the same images (birds of
prey, animals, and dogs) are utilized to imply a threatening nature,
embodied in immediately recognizable features: receding foreheads,
prognathous jaws, crooked noses, and voracious teeth. This transmi-
gration of similar and often identical images and descriptions from
contemporary scientific to informative and fictional texts shows that
while it is necessary to study the evolution of scientific and literary
knowledge within the restricted areas of specialized fields of investigation, it is indispensable to consider the position of any text within
the general discourse of its time. Without anticipating the results of
the analyses to follow, it can be assumed that the necessary conditions for the emergence of a science describing the criminal as an
atavistic resurgence of "prehistoric man" would include a widespread
circulation of descriptions of the "laboring and dangerous classes" as
a separate race, primitive, animal-like and threatening, throughout
social discourse, in novels, newspapers, political and economic treatises, reports of commissioned inquiries, and religious tracts. A new
human science is not simply constituted by the progressive refinement
of previous research: its emergence and development require the arrangement of an institutional locus, the determination of its object
and mandate, and these are in large part derived from social systems
of verisimilitude. Similarly, if the affiliation between the works of Sir
Arthur Conan Doyle, Emile Gaboriau, and Edgar Allen Poe need to be
considered and further related to earlier adventure stories, the New-
gate Calendars and broadsheets, it is equally important to examine the
detective novel's position in relation to informative and scientific texts,
in order to discover its role in the social production of knowledge.
Intertextual analyses inevitably raise the question of the truth value of

discourse. Indeed, a modern reader finds it difficult to classify these extracts: do they show a science which fictionalizes its object, or science fiction, a romantic report, or a scientific novel? Where does the make-believe start, and where does it end? Paradoxically, only the literary text remains readable for us, while the criminological and journalistic texts, which claimed to provide objective truth, have become largely unthinkable, neither true nor false: current social discourse provides different conditions of acceptability for the definition of the criminal.

The simple juxtaposition of similar descriptions taken from radically different contemporary discourses (by their origin, position, and audience) indicates the interest of an intertextual analysis of knowledge production. This kind of study could have focused on any number of objects of knowledge, such as the working classes, revolution, evolution, elites, or children.[8] However, "criminal man" seems to constitute a particularly useful object for an examination of the production of knowledge and power because it is often through the discussion of deviance that norms are established. The very choice of criminal *man* as the primary object of scientific investigation signals a will to normalize using "man" as standard measurement (or more specifically, as further analyses will show, the white, middle- to upper-class version) and considering all other social groups (defined by class, gender, race) as somehow secondary or deviant phenomena. Analyzing the apprehension of "criminal man" can therefore serve to uncover the modes of production and dissemination of hegemonic truths in social discourse, and to trace the exclusions which they operate (the means through which such truths can be denied, by the reaffirmation of difference in resistance and conflict, will have to be the object of other studies).[9] My corpus will be limited geographically to England and France, and will include:

(1) The major criminological works circulated in these countries between 1876 and 1913, the nominal dates of the birth and death of criminal anthropology, corresponding respectively to the publication of *Criminal Man* by Cesare Lombroso, the so-called "father of criminology," and *The English Convict*, by Charles Goring;

(2) The press coverage of crime during the same period and more specifically, the reporting of the Jack the Ripper murders (1888) in four newspapers representing both the prestige and mass press: *The Times* (London) and the *Daily Telegraph*, the Paris *Le Temps* and *Le Petit Parisien*;

(3) A selection of novels and short stories dealing with crime and criminals, from three different perspectives: "scientific" and "experimental" investigations in the naturalist novels *La bête humaine* (1889–90) by Emile Zola, and *Dans les rues* (1913) by J.-H. Rosny Aîné, a popular imitator of the master of the school; psychological explorations in *Le Disciple* (1889) by Paul Bourget; entertaining accounts of the pursuit of criminals in the ever popular Sherlock Holmes stories by Arthur Conan Doyle and in the romance *Strange Case of Dr Jekyll and Mr Hyde* (1886), by Robert Louis Stevenson.

Thus, while covering the period extending from the last quarter of the nineteenth century up to the beginning of the First World War, this research will focus on a shorter time span, between 1885 and 1892, when developments in the three discursive practices under study displayed great momentum.[10]

Usually labeled discourse analysis or discursive criticism, this kind of work follows Michel Foucault's groundbreaking research on how knowledge and power are articulated in discourse. Foucault insists that "power and knowledge directly imply one another; that there is no power relation without the correlative constitution of a field of knowledge, nor any knowledge that does not presuppose and constitute at the same time power relations."[11] Power-knowledge matrices are established in discourse, that is, in the total network of conflicting, converging, contradictory, and intervalidating discursive practices constituting reality.[12] Thus, discourse does not express or result from power relations established elsewhere, nor does it exist in a superstructural relation to economic forces of production. Rather, as argued by Timothy Reiss in "Project for a Discursive Criticism":

> The word *episteme* marks an abstraction whose concrete side is named by the word *society*: the use and practice of a given *class* of discourse. . . . "Together" (but they can perhaps not be conceived of at all as being apart or separated) they compose what may be called the sociocultural environment. Discourse and society are a total praxis, "society" designating a kind of concrete anchorage of discourse, "discourse" designating the way in which society makes itself meaningful to itself.[13]

The analysis of any discursive practice (understood as the conjunction of institutional bases, qualified members, and normalized discursive productions) therefore entails its correlation to economic, social, and political relations. Foucault illustrates this point in *The Archaeology of Knowledge* by correlating the establishment of clinical medicine at the end of the eighteenth century to contemporary political practice: he outlines how the political and administrative discovery of the "population" opened new fields of objects for medical discourse; how it attributed a new status and exclusive authority to physicians not only in the exercise and teaching of medicine but also in their extended role as judges in administrative decisions and arbiters in the establishment of social norms; how finally the discourse of medicine then served to translate other social conflicts as natural phenomena.[14]

In keeping with these premises, the phrase "apprehending the criminal" refers to a complex power-knowledge matrix which gradually developed in the nineteenth century, gaining strength and increasing its influence with the establishment of new discursive practices (a science of "criminal man," a mass press thriving on crime stories, and the circulation of fictional crime narratives in unprecedented numbers), with the implementation of new methods of repressing criminal deviance (with police forces and penitentiaries), and with broad economic, political, and social developments often understood in terms of a general, incipient criminality (urban slums, for example, leading to fears of a criminal population). The elaboration of this power-knowledge matrix entailed the articulation of the scientific knowledge of an emerging criminology to common knowledge, the accepted truths which go without saying and are therefore constantly reiterated in the totality of social discourse, in press and literary narratives of crime, in parliamentary speeches, and in the reports of philanthropic organizations, in tracts of every description, religious, reformist, radical; these discourses in turn invested the institution of processes ensuring the physical apprehension of individuals by the police, court, and penitentiary systems (as well as their own rapidly developing branches of expertise, the police and penitentiary sciences, forensic medicine). The apprehension of "criminal man," a mixture of fear and fascination confirmed by scientific conceptions, assuaged by the exercise of legal and penitentiary means of capture, and ultimately consumed in the form of public opinion as constructed in the press, was the resultant of these multiple processes of knowledge and power, articulated in discourse.

In order to outline the historical development of the main discursive practices under study and account for their eventual position in the totality of social discourse, each will be examined from three perspectives:

(1) Broad and necessarily schematic outlines situated at the level of social discourse as a whole will identify the *preconditions of emergence* of the discursive practices by tracing the economic, political, and social developments which prepared the grounds for their general acceptability and determined their objects, status, and mandates;

(2) The analysis will then focus more specifically on the *conditions of emergence* of the practices in order to identify the main groups participating in their elaboration, to articulate their political and economic positions, and consider the stakes involved in the establishment of their institutional bases;

(3) An analysis of their *textual construction* will then survey the theoretical, enthymematical, and narrative techniques which were used to produce knowledge about "criminal man," and examine the extensions and effects of such knowledge.

Although the discursive practices will be examined separately for the purposes of clarity and convenience of analysis, the theoretical premises of this study consider the development of each practice to be dependent on that of all others, as the totality of social discourse takes precedence over the elaboration of any of its constituent practices.[15] Similarly, each of the three perspectives adopted in the following analyses will implicate all others: the final close study of textual construction will lead back to the initial considerations of the preconditions of emergence in the totality of social discourse, as specific arguments, topoï, and even short narratives are shared by various discursive practices, and thus trace a more general pattern of knowledge production; textual analyses will also allow the specification of the limits of the sayable of individual discursive practices, as first outlined in the conditions of emergence. The end result will be a grid of intelligibility whose progressively finer mesh will ultimately sketch the negative totality of social discourse.

The theoretical and methodological principles of discourse analysis outlined above will be complemented in this study with recent linguistic and semiotic research on the notion of *presupposition*, as it applies to the logico-semantic, ideological, and epistemological levels of textual construction. A brief explanation of the different extensions of the notion of presupposition seems necessary at this point, to clarify the general orientation of the work to follow.

Interest in the notion of presupposition is sparked by the observation that words, utterances, texts, or discursive formations can mean and do much more than they actually say. This capacity derives not only from the semantic richness of language (a single word with several meanings can have various extensions) but also from the rules governing discourse in social organization: the rights to speak of certain subjects, give orders, request permissions, declare wars, or even end conversations are strictly distributed according to relative positions of authority. These phenomena have given rise to a multitude of philosophic, linguistic, and sociological inquiries into the ways in which power is inscribed in discourse.

The most rigorous definition of this notion applies to its logico-semantic forms: presuppositions are those elements of an utterance which, although unsaid, form part of its *literal meaning*. A now classic example of presupposition was given by Bertrand Russell in 1905:

> The present king of France is bald.
> presupposes: There is a king of France.[16]

Logico-semantic presuppositions provide textual coherence: surface propositions construct and elaborate arguments within the context of correlated presuppositions. Therefore, one of the most important functions of these presuppositions is to determine the limits of discourse: for example, a question can only be answered by propositions which assume its own presuppositions. Affirmative or negative answers to the question, "Is the present king of France bald?" will always presuppose: "There is a king of France." To reject this presupposition, the question itself must be questioned, as well as its author's knowledge or intentions. The strategic value of presuppositions in argumentation is immediately apparent: as what is stated can always be criticized or opposed, it is often preferable to presuppose certain parts of an argument in order to impose their acceptance as condition for the pursuit of the exchange.[17]

Aristotle in his *Topics* had studied the presence of unsaid maxims, or topoï, in argumentation: he described them as general propositions from which an infinite number of specific arguments could be drawn. Arguments derived from topoï (enthymemes) would win recognition not because they necessarily expressed an essential truth, but because they were approved of by everyone, or, as outlined by Aristotle, by those who represented enlightened opinion, and were recognized as authorities by the community.[18] Truth and power are correlated in discourse. Semioticians studying verisimilitude have recently followed this analytical line and proposed that narrative texts also construct their meaning from unsaid ideological maxims (ideologemes). As suggested by Marc Angenot, narremes (the minimal units of a narrative sequence, usually consisting of a subject and predicate) hold a presuppositional relation to ideologemes which is similar to that held by enthymemes and topoï (Narremes : Ideologemes :: Enthymemes : Topoï).[19] These presupposed maxims belong to common opinion (the doxa) and form the basis for the social construction of reality: they can be traced throughout the intertext where they establish both the internal coherence and outer limits of discourse. Perhaps the clearest illustration of the presence of such ideological maxims is provided when two topically unrelated propositions are united in a single sentence, as in the following extract from Rosny's novel, *Dans les rues*: "Sure to be stronger than Jacques, he feared something indefinable; falcons and kites avoid a sparrow of mediocre size, but of disconcerting audacity."[20] This sentence juxtaposes two diverse statements, the first dealing with a character's emotions, the second describing the behavior of certain birds of prey. The narrative sequence only becomes intelligible through the presupposition of an ideological maxim uniting animal and human behavior: "(it is likely) that street dwellers live as animals live, by instinct." By presupposing the animal nature of the working class, Rosny establishes it as a fact which "goes without saying," and need not be justified. Several narrative events can thus manifest the truth of a maxim which *remains indisputable because it is presupposed* by the text. Sets of correlated ideologemes produce objects of knowledge: "the workers" in Rosny's text are defined by such a set, which includes presuppositions on their instincts, intelligence, physical appearance, and natural criminality.

Preconstructs are broader cognitive categorizations already available in social discourse as means of ordering experience and apprehending reality. The immediate relevance of such categorizations, their apparent naturalness render them so obvious that their inclusion in textual construction is never justified and remains largely unthought. In the second half of the nineteenth century, physical measurements served as preconstruct for many emerging sciences of "man." Sociologists, anthropologists, and criminologists "naturally" measured their objects to *know* what they were talking about. The cephalic index was particularly prized, and used to demonstrate almost any mental or moral trait (the inferiority of blacks or women, the criminality of the working class, and the intelligence of the white male bourgeois Parisian) without recourse to any contextual theorization. The phrase "the struggle for life" served a similar function, as it could apply indiscriminately to any situation (moral, psychological, economic, political, racial, sexual, and religious), and immediately endow the argument with a scientific tone, or at least a high credibility. Preconstructs literally *make sense* wherever they appear, because their intertextual circulation gives them a very high truth value. By connecting a text to a specific field (scientific, artistic, or popular), they provide it with authority. Finally, preconstructs allow texts to bypass necessary and often unavailable theoretical explanations, and thus authorize a freer production of ideological knowledge. According to J. J. Courtine, preconstructs (which he describes as the invariant kernel statements of networks of modulating formulations) constitute the "memory" of a discursive formation and institute the place from which a universal subject can say "everyone knows that. . . ."21 Epistemological presuppositions provide the basis for knowledge production, circumscribing the general, abstract relation between the subject and object of understanding, and the nature of the cognitive process; they are the primary propositions from which all elaborations are derived. When in a position of authority, they serve to disqualify texts which hold different epistemological presuppositions from the "truth" of the period—and thus draw the dividing line between truth/falsehood, reason/madness, sense/nonsense. Although these four levels of presuppositional phenomena vary in their nature (logico-semantic, ideological, and epistemological) and their connection to textual formation (either through single words or through phrases, syntagmatic construction, or argumentation), all are related in that their assumption is required for the immediate understanding of textual meaning. Their association provides the heuristic model for the analysis of social discourse given in figure 1. Presuppositional analyses thus allow textual phenomena (such as enthymematic and narrative development, logico-semantic and syntactic construction, and rhetorical devices) of widely divergent texts (from scientific treatises to press reports and romances) to be correlated to the ideological struggles and epistemological configuration of their time.

The power-knowledge matrices so discerned are both intentional

Figure 1   Grid for an Intertextual Analysis of Discourse

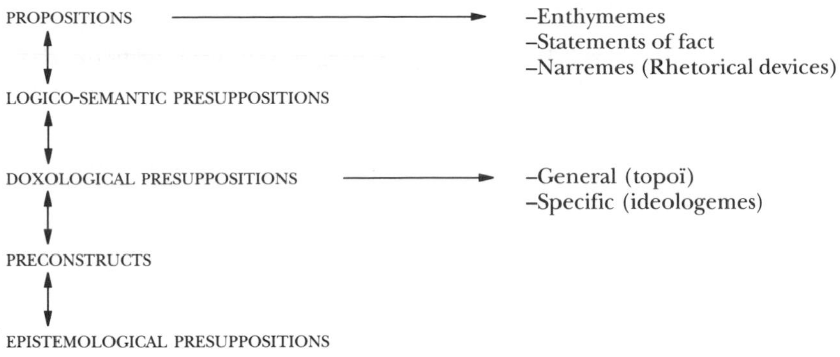

PROPOSITIONS ⟶ –Enthymemes
–Statements of fact
–Narremes (Rhetorical devices)

↑
↓

LOGICO-SEMANTIC PRESUPPOSITIONS

↑
↓

DOXOLOGICAL PRESUPPOSITIONS ⟶ –General (topoï)
–Specific (ideologemes)

↑
↓

PRECONSTRUCTS

↑
↓

EPISTEMOLOGICAL PRESUPPOSITIONS

and nonsubjective, as demonstrated by Foucault.[22] Relations of power are intentional, as they are actively sought by individuals with immediate goals and objectives in mind, as any textual analysis of a discursive practice immediately reveals. However, these maneuvers are nonsubjective in that the individuals involved have interiorized their positions of enunciation and their objects of knowledge, and have come to recognize as their own the topics, modes of argumentation, and rules of validation imposed by the discursive practices in which they participate. Social discourse necessarily predates the individual's entry; Foucault continually insists on the presence of an enveloping discourse, a *grand murmure* from which any enunciation must arise.[23] Power relations "are to be analyzed, therefore, not on the basis of a subject of knowledge who is or is not free in relation to the power system, but, on the contrary, the subject who knows, the objects to be known and the modalities of knowledge must be regarded as so many effects of these fundamental implications of power-knowledge and their historical transformations."[24]

The end result is that power is exercised through an impersonal process in modern disciplinary societies, in a network of forces on which no claims of ownership or control can be made. Foucault asserts this in his study of the Panopticon as emblematic of disciplinary power: its intricate organization of surveillance establishes it as a *dispositif* or mechanism which "automatizes and disindividualizes power. . . . There is a machinery that assures dissymmetry, disequilibrium, difference. Consequently, it does not matter who exercises power. Any individual, taken almost at random, can operate the machine."[25] This analysis retains the notion of class domination in an altered frame-work: Foucault demonstrates that power is not a homogeneous entity that can be held by a concerted group, that power is "exercised rather than possessed," that "it is not the 'privilege', acquired or preserved, of the dominant class, *but the overall effect of its strategic positions.*" [26] Dif-fused in a multitude of power-knowledge matrices, exercised every-where, in the diverse tactical and dynamic arrangements of families, schools, factories, offices, and prisons, power relations interconnect into an overall strategy ensuring the hegemony of a certain knowledge and the authority of a certain class; this process Foucault terms the "double conditioning" of power.[27] Thus, discourse analysis is a form of historical materialism, but one which recognizes the materiality of discourse and its effects on the constitution of the subjects and objects of knowledge.[28]

1 CRIMINOLOGY

The origins of criminology are usually traced to the Italian School of Criminal Anthropology, founded by Cesare Lombroso during the last quarter of the nineteenth century, and counting Enrico Ferri and Raffaele Garofalo as two of its most prominent members. This science emerged as the first to place "criminal man" at the center of its investigations, a choice constantly justified in reference to the earlier works of the Classical School, which had concentrated on the study of crime and punishment as legal entities. Criminologists rejected this perspective elaborated by penal philosophers such as Cesare Beccaria and Jeremy Bentham, regarding it as metaphysical at best, misguided and socially harmful at worst; determined not to err as their predecessors had done, they claimed to follow the unmistakable path of facts alone: criminals as they could be scientifically measured and examined.

As noted by Marx in the introduction to the *Grundrisse*, in order for a general category, applicable to all forms of social organizations (in this case, criminals), to be recognized as the central concept of a science, numerous interrelated economic, political, and social developments must occur: "the most abstract categories, despite their validity—precisely because of their abstractness—for all epochs, are nevertheless, in the specific character of this abstraction, themselves likewise a product of historic relations, and possess their full validity only for and within these relations."[1] The following section will outline the various developments establishing the preconditions of emergence of the science of "criminal man." A brief examination of major developments in the legal and penitentiary fields will show the ways in which crime and punishment were redefined at the end of the eighteenth and during the course of the nineteenth century, and relate these changes to economic and political factors. The multifarious functions of criminality within social discourse will then begin to be explored through a first approximation of the web of concepts delineating its extensions in the sociocultural environment: what were the dangers posed by the presence of criminality, where was it located, what could it mean for society?

1 PRECONDITIONS OF EMERGENCE: CRIME AND CRIMINALITY

◆

Crime: its definition and punishment Cesare Bonesana, Marquis of Beccaria, first published his *Dei delitti e delle pene* in 1764 anonymously, for fear of persecution. His book attacked the very foundations of the existing criminal justice systems. It proclaimed the equality of all before the law, denounced the unlimited powers vested in the authorities, demanded the abolition of torture and of the death penalty, called for measures to protect the accused before and during trial, and affirmed the necessity of graduating punishments according to the crime. These revolutionary proposals were to be acclaimed by philosophers and ministers, philanthropists and businessmen, princes and emperors alike. *Dei delitti* was translated and discussed throughout Europe; its author was provided with a chair of political economy at the University of Milan, and appointed councillor of state. What were these revolutionary proposals so obviously acceptable to all enlightened rulers?

Inspired by the writings of Montesquieu, and accepting Rousseau's social contract theory, Beccaria founded the right to punish on the need to protect each individual's rights and freedoms from possible usurpation by others. A set of written laws equally applicable to all members of society allowed them to rise above their state of primitive barbarity and be protected, by the rule of law, from the violent rule of the mightiest. Punishments should be analogous to the crime and administer just a little more pain than the amount of pleasure derived from criminal behavior. Jeremy Bentham, in *An Introduction to the Principles of Morals and Legislation* (1780), developed this principle into an elaborate "felicity calculus": the utilitarian system determined appropriate punishments according to the harm done to society, the fundamental rule being to protect "the greatest happiness of the greatest number" from individual abuse. The classical view of crime, punishment, and society was gradually accepted as the basis for criminal codes throughout Europe, starting in France with the Declaration of the Rights of Man (1789), the Constitution of 1790, and the Codes of 1791 and 1810, and eventually including the Prussian (1851), Danish (1866), Belgian (1867), and Italian (1889) codes, among others. How could the same principles comply to such various political and social organizations?

From the outset it is clear that they could be made to serve the varied interests of the ruling classes. As outlined by Leon Radzinowicz in *Ideology and Crime*, their adoption allowed "enlightened despots" to check the power of both the clergy and the aristocracy (through the selective abolition of certain superstitions and privileges) while enhancing their favor with the people (through the elimination of torture and the softening of penalties).[1] The middle classes equally profited from the abolition of aristocratic privilege, and were further protected from the whims of absolute power (in the forms of torture, *lettres de cachet*, and the like). In fact, the new criminal justice systems gave considerable powers to the middle classes, whose members acted as J.P.s, jurors, and M.P.s able to enact new laws as dictated by (their) changing needs. Thus, different measures could be taken for middle- and working-class crimes. Fines, demotions, or dismissals were judged punishment enough for what has come to be known as white-collar crime, while prison sentences, often qualified with hard labor, were considered necessary for the repression of "ordinary crime" (such as vagrancy, thefts, minor assaults, drunkenness, and disorderly conduct), the infractions of the "lower classes," which were processed without jury in the special circuits of police courts and the summary justice of the Petty Sessions. The Master and Servant Act of 1823, for example, provided different forms of punishment for breach of contract: employers could only be prosecuted in civil law, whereas employees were subject to criminal prosecution.[2]

In theory, however, the criminal justice system was set apart from economic conditions, reified into a set of logical relations between equal individuals: one of the most important functions of the new legal discourse was to erase all class divisions by establishing a blind social *process* in which position and wealth—but also starvation and misery—played no role. In this process, classical principles acquired their universality: they could answer the needs of human nature itself, saving the rights of man from barbarity, only insofar as social organizations were not acknowledged.[3]

The works of the Classical School have traditionally been remembered as the voice of compassion and humanity rising against cruel systems of repression. Some historians, however, have pointed out that their main objective was not so much to punish less but to punish better, more swiftly, and through rational procedures because the old methods were simply not working that well any more. In the face of the death penalty, English juries often refused to find the accused guilty, even when their verdict blatantly contradicted evidence. The chances of being executed when sentenced to death were also constantly diminishing.[4] Reformers like Samuel Romilly wanted to substitute "swift and certain punishment" for this "lottery of justice."[5] The system of "suspended terror" could only work in closely knit societies, where mechanisms of personal benevolence and submission could operate: in large cities like London or Paris the discretionary powers of magistrates to pardon or convict no longer held the same force of example, and imprisonment or release became a game of chance for the accused. Among the most ardent supporters of reform were the members of the middle class involved in manufacturing, commerce, and banking, who were eager to find new and more efficient ways of protecting their property, and sent petitions to Parliament to that effect. The landowners' resistance to reform was eventually overcome; by 1861 capital offenses had been reduced from 200 to 4: murder, treason, piracy, and the destruction of arsenals and dockyards.[6] In France the Revolution reduced the number of capital offenses from 115 to 32.[7]

Although Beccaria and Bentham had proposed a series of punishments analogous to the crime (for theft, restitution and fines, for assault, corporal punishment, and so on), these varied forms were neglected in favor of imprisonment as the universal mode of sanction.[8] However, the establishment of state penitentiary systems was not accomplished without a series of struggles and political upsets. In France prison construction was delayed by debates over the best methods of moral reform. One of the main battles concerned the choice between the solitary confinement system or the Auburn silent system, where the prisoners would sleep in solitary confinement but work together in absolute silence during the day. A Royal Society of Prisons was created in 1819, and various official and private inquiries, reports, and proposals were published with unrelenting regularity from then on, as the issue was a controversial one at the time. It took until 1875 for a compromise to be reached, whereby only prisoners sentenced to one year and one day would be kept in solitary confinement (to prevent their contamination through contact with hardened criminals), while all others would be treated with the Auburn system.[9] In England it was the colonies' refusal to admit convicts, rather than a government policy, that stopped transportation. The temporary cramming of convicts waiting for transportation into warships gave birth to the infamous hulks, which were to be used for eighty years. A national prison system was only achieved in 1877.[10]

From the start, penitentiary scientists and prison officials stood paradoxically in opposition to the legislators and codes which had authorized their emergence. Charles Lucas, recognized as the father of penitentiary science, argued thus:

> Legislators have forgotten the actors and focused on the acts. . . . Such codes are based on false and vicious presumptions. . . . False, because in reality the degree of perversity of a crime changes with each actor since the intentionality is different. . . . Vicious, because reformation is more or less rapid according to this degree of perversity; thus the length of punishment should be proportionate to the actor's perversity and not to his violation as such. . . . Repressive justice should then be focused on agents and not on acts.[11]

Here is a first example of how the status and mandate of a discursive practice determine the limits of its sayable. Legal discourse had to exclude the historic reality of social organizations in order to found the right to punish on the theory of a contract holding within a community of equals. It is only by precluding human beings in concrete circumstances that it could claim to defend the universal rights of man—and be adaptable to various specific social and political systems. It also had to be presented as deriving from enlightened reason in continual progress, to justify the relations of direct domination that it imposed. The limits of its authority could only be recognized in terms of the limits of human nature itself, to allow the socioeconomic conditions of its historical evolution to remain unsaid, and indeed unthinkable, within its established institutional boundaries. The administration of justice, however, required a further specification of the convicted: notions such as "intention to commit a crime," "extenuating or aggravating circumstances," and preoccupations with sentencing and reform began to draw in the notion of the criminal where it had been so efficiently erased by the reformers of the Classical School.[12]

In his treatise entitled *Droit criminel à l'usage des jurés. Science morale, code et vocabulaire du jury* (1854), Gustave Bascle de la Grève thus called upon jurors to pay special attention to the criminal's constitution and educational background before applying the blind rules of justice. Insisting that the moral examination of the accused was especially worthy of attention, he reminded his readers that "undoubtedly, the son of a scoundrel can be a very honest man; but rarely can the son of a man of good standing be a scoundrel." [13] Similarly, the notion of pardonable crimes allowed further social divisions to be drawn. The murder of a husband by his wife or of a wife by her husband were not pardonable, unless the life of the husband or wife committing the crime had been in peril at the moment of the murder. However, in France a husband could be pardoned for killing his wife and her lover if he caught them in flagrante delicto in the conjugal home. [14] The principle of equality before the law was qualified before judges and juries: doxological maxims ("It is unlikely that an honest man's son be a criminal") and rules of behavior according to gender (a husband can excusably kill an adulterous wife—but not the reverse) determined the likeliness or the very existence of guilt, following class and gender divisions. Finally, in the administration of punishment, the criminal's soul—his degree of perversity—constituted the object on which power and authority could be exercised. The possible reformation of the criminal soul through scientific procedures opened new and infinitely expandable fields of knowledge and power, as discussed by Foucault in *Discipline and Punish*:

> It would be wrong to say that the soul is an illusion, or an ideological effect. On the contrary, it exists, it has a reality, it is produced permanently around, on, within the body by the functioning of a power that is exercised on those punished. . . . This real, non-corporal soul is not a substance; it is the element in which are articulated the effects of a certain type of power and the reference of a certain type of knowledge, the machinery by which the power relations give rise to a possible corpus of knowledge, and knowledge extends and reinforces the effects of this power. [15]

Criminality thus became a much wider problem than legal definitions could cover.

How did these new apprehensions of crime and punishment effect the nature and exercise of power? They allowed the middle classes to tend to their economic needs (protect themselves not only from theft, but also from strikes and riots) and gradually increase their power in the political and judicial circles (as makers and administrators of the new criminal justice systems). The power of the central government increased through the establishment of national police and penitentiary systems, and expanded into an elaborate network of surveillance and reform procedures. The form, exercise, and feeling of power were modified in the process. At the turn of the century, power was more of a personal attribute. Magistrates were local men of standing, known to the entire community; jailers or hulk operators were private entrepreneurs, who made their money from their prisoners; watchmen were paid for directly by householders. By the last quarter of the century, all of these operations had been centralized under the control of the state, and power became the attribute of the system rather than of the person who happened to be in a position of authority. This transfer usually marked the entrance of the public as the supposed beneficiary of the new processes of power. For example, prison officials were now paid by the state to reform criminals so that they could be safely returned to the community. Registration and examination procedures, uniform diet and work schedules could be imposed by the system on masses of people throughout the nation, all in the name of science, in the line of duty, and in pursuance of that great cause, public peace. Similarly the watchmen's organizations were replaced by a police force whose mandate was preserving the peace rather than watching the street. When Sir Robert Peel's Police Bill of 1829 introduced an organized police force in England, it was met with considerable suspicion from the upper classes (who feared government spying) and loathing from the working classes, who called them "Peelers" or "Peel's bloody gang." By the end of the century, however, they had become generally accepted as the helpful bobbies, serving the public interest.[16] In fact, the powers they enjoyed were considerable, and allowed close supervision of certain segments of the public: beggars, vagabonds, licensed criminals, strikers, rioters, or anyone who cursed or swore in public could be arrested without warrant.[17] Moreover, the 1869 Habitual Criminals Act allowed magistrates to give twelve-month sentences to anyone arrested for being suspicious and found guilty of that charge. Thus a criminal justice system which systematically imprisoned and punished the "lower classes" derived its legitimacy from the community presupposed by the Classical School.[18]

All of these developments contributed to the emergence of a new science centered on the criminal:

(1) The reduction of the death penalty and the implementation of imprisonment as a general mode of punishment produced a large population of prisoners who needed to be reformed in order to be reintegrated into the community. Concern over the management of these criminals became a social issue which could serve as leverage in numerous and varied power struggles. An urgent *need to know* about criminals would be as strongly advocated by political and economic circles as by purely administrative ones (prison and police officials), thus increasing the issue's proliferation within social discourse.

(2) New fields of knowledge and power were developed from the momentum of administrative bodies: penitentiary science emerged with international associations and congresses to promote its development;[19] police science claimed great advances with the introduction of new methods of identification such as *bertillonnage* (which brought the establishment of anthropometric cabinets), fingerprints, and the beginnings of national criminal files.[20] Considerable overlapping took place between institutions: at the judge's discretion, doctors could be called in to testify in courts, and forensic medicine began as a new specialization. Criminology would cut part of its domain from these interconnected, discursive fields.

◆

Criminality: the sign of broader social maladies   The cities of nineteenth-century England and France suffered from huge management problems, which attained their most acute state in London and Paris. Municipal and state governments had not kept pace with the problems created by unprecedented population growth and increased industrial activity: uncontrolled air and water pollution, contamination of foodstuffs, ever expanding waste dumps and cesspools in slum areas were widely feared as sources of infection. Perhaps more importantly, they were also perceived as symptoms of a physical and moral deterioration of society: images of sewage, filth, prostitution, poverty, vice, and crime blended in contemporary apprehensions of (and for) a sick society.[21] The notion of crime was thus included in a web of concepts where pathology, sociology, and morality interconnected: fields such as "sanitary science," "social hygiene," and "moral and political sciences" covered this hybrid domain.[22]

The "laboring and dangerous classes" were to be the prime targets of these new fields of scientific investigation. For the purposes of clarity, the huge mass of output on their nature and conditions of existence can be ordered into three approaches, each bringing forth new domains of visibility, using different techniques of knowledge production. First, statistical studies of various kinds, originating from penal and government institutions as well as from private societies, afforded a broad view of criminality as a social phenomenon, correlated to such factors as climate, race, sex, and education. Second, empirical studies undertaken by journalists who ventured into the infamous rookeries to then sell their stories to an interested middle-class audience provided knowledge about criminality as the manifestation of degeneration and disease in regions excluded from the purifying influences of civilization. Similar narratives were also produced by those employed by the criminal justice system, either as police officers or as ex-criminals turned informants. Finally, medical studies focused on the bodies of those manifesting the symptoms of criminality, and searched for the physical determinants of their condition. These various analytical grids (from general statistics to first-hand exchanges to the examination of skull formation) eventually delineated the discursive space from which a science of "criminal man" would emerge.

In England statistical societies conducted local inquiries into the moral, physical, and criminal characteristics of the "lower orders"; *The Journal of the Statistical Society of London* published the results of several investigations into slum and average areas.[23] The publication of the first criminal statistics, the *Compte général de l'administration de la justice criminelle en France* (1827), provided the data for the famous works of the French lawyer André-Michel Guerry and the Belgian astronomer and mathematician Lambert-Adolphe-Jacques Quételet, both of whom studied the correlations between such factors as climate, sex, race, age, poverty, education, profession, and crime. Guerry devised a "cartographic method" to represent crime rates by shaded maps which he first presented in his *Essai sur la statistique morale de la France* (1833), and further expanded in *La statistique morale de l'Angleterre comparée avec la France* (1860).[24] Quételet's "social physics" brought him to develop the notion of "propensity to crime," which depended on race, sex, climate, and so on. He discounted poverty as a determining factor per se, but considered that a rapid fall from relative comfort to misery could create conditions leading to crime. Both researchers were astounded to discover regularity in the total number and in the categories of crimes committed per year, as well as in the relative participation of certain groups of the population. From these discoveries

Quételet argued that "society includes within itself the germs of all the crimes committed, and at the same time the necessary facilities for their development. It is the social state, in some measure, which prepares these crimes and the criminal is merely the instrument to execute them."[25]

Such work questioned the foundations of the free will theory of classical jurisprudence which precluded social factors and considered the individual to be solely and entirely responsible for his or her criminal act. However, both Guerry and Quételet hesitated to deny free will entirely, and recognized it as an important factor for the individual and an auxiliary one for society. These studies marked the beginnings of a sociological approach to the understanding of crime, which were empirically pursued by various individuals from the journalistic, police, church, government, and philanthropic circles.

Henry Mayhew, journalist and author of *London Labour and the London Poor. A Cyclopedia of the Conditions and Earnings of Those that Will Work, Those that Cannot Work and Those that Will Not Work* (1851), endeavored to describe the everyday life of criminals and other "wandering tribes" who made their living in the streets. The introduction to Mayhew's four-volume opus began with an anthropological division of human beings in "two distinct and broadly marked races, viz., the wanderers and the settlers—the vagabond and the citizen—the nomadic and the civilized tribes."[26] Recalling the findings of Pritchard and Smith, he differentiated each of these "races" by physical, moral, and intellectual characteristics. The first striking difference rested in the shape of the head: whereas nomadic tribes had highly developed face bones (prognathous jaws and high cheek bones), the civilized tribes were characterized by large skulls, signaling a better development of the brain. As a rule, each civilized tribe of the world had a "wandering horde attached," which would prey on the fruits of its industry. Nomadic tribes were characterized mainly by their "repugnance to regular and continuous labour," their various and violent passions, their lack of provision, religion, and morality toward women, and, perhaps worst of all, by a "looseness" of "notions as to property." All of these traits Mayhew could plainly discern in the "lower classes," the predatory wandering tribes of the English civilization. The criminals among them he further distinguished by a moral defect which caused their determination not to work.[27] Similar views were widely recognized in France, as evidenced in the essay granted first prize by the Academy of Moral and Political Sciences in its 1838 competition. Written by H. A. Frégier, once bureau chief of the Prefecture of the Seine, this treatise, entitled *Des classes dangereuses de la population dans les grandes villes et des moyens de les rendre meilleures*, recognized the laboring and criminal classes as belonging to a single group, the "dangerous classes," and ascribed their physical and economic distress to moral deficiencies.

This blending of crime and vice, disease, depravity, and barbarity authorized the involvement of multiple groups in the social management of crime in general, and the "dangerous classes" in particular. The municipal governments' inquiries were doubled at the state level, where numerous commissions of inquiry were set up during the 1830s and 1840s. Philanthropic associations equally set out to "elevate" the criminal classes, and church organizations marched into the battle.[28] All these efforts were not just aimed at relieving poverty: the main object was to instill the right amount of discipline, the proper values, and the methods of self-help needed to combat pauperism and delinquency, considered as signs of moral weakness rather than economic struggles—the generalization of acceptable behavior remained the principle goal.[29] Such an approach to crime offered the immediate advantage of transferring economic and social problems onto moral and even medical planes which left structures of authority untouched. Edwin Chadwick, former secretary to Bentham, expert in the field of national health, and author of the *Report on the Sanitary Conditions of the Labouring Poor* (1842), could thus propose sanitation as a "universal specific" able to cure all social and political problems.[30]

Medical experts often voiced the fear that uncontrolled "lower classes" would threaten not only the rule of law, but the reign of reason itself. Treatises on subjects as diverse as phrenology, degeneration, physiology, and heredity routinely included criminals as part of their investigations, and usually examined them in relation to insanity. That deviations from the legal or rational scales of acceptable behavior be considered conjointly could be expected, as criminals and lunatics had been locked up together, along with the indigent, vagabond, and unemployed population, since the middle of the seventeenth century. The institutional separation of criminals and the insane, the great revolution of W. Tuke and P. Pinel, dated back to the 1790s—only then did the medical nature of insanity become obvious.[31] However, it also had an immediately recognizable social dimension. Pinel insisted that alienation originated mostly in the "inferior classes of society."[32] The search for links between insanity and social position, criminality and physical constitution would focus on skull structure and brain functions as well as on the effects of heredity.

At a time when human passions and psychic functions were widely associated with the heart and other viscera, François-Joseph Gall proposed a detailed map of the human brain, identifying both animal and specifically human psychic functions to precisely situated brain "organs." Postulating that the skull was molded by the brain, Gall thought that an overly developed faculty would mean larger corresponding cerebral circumvolutions, and cause a perceivable bump on a living human being's head. Gall's "cranioscopy" and "psychophysiology" led to a particular interest in the insane and criminal population: studies of the skulls of criminals condemned to death revealed a greater development of the areas of acquisitiveness or destructiveness situated between the top of the ear and the temple.[33] H. Lauvergne, author of Les forçats considérés sous le rapport physiologique, moral et intellectuel (1841), also examined convicted criminals to verify if they displayed the "murder bump," that "fateful seal," or the general configuration of the "genius of evil," known as the "sugar cone head."[34]

By identifying morality as the function of a specific brain organ, phrenology precluded the social power structures which determine acceptable behavior. From this perspective, deviance could no longer signify protest of any kind, be it political or moral—it became a simple matter of biological damage or malfunction. As far as criminal deviance was concerned, just how much should be blamed on physical organization was a matter of contention. Gall thought that criminal acts could result either from bad physical constitution or bad circumstances. Therefore, he proposed that punishment be determined in accordance with the nature of the criminal and not his act, a solution advocated by penitentiary scientists. Lauvergne hesitated, at times recognizing cerebral constitution as the ultimately determining and inalienable force in certain criminal cases, and at others holding on to a faith in moral reform.

Prosper Lucas, in his great and widely recognized opus on heredity, Traité philosophique et physiologique de l'hérédité naturelle dans les états de santé et de maladie du système nerveux (1850), equally dealt extensively with the question of criminal responsibility, and cut the Gordian knot by arguing that only a propensity to crime was hereditary, and not the act itself: thus, human liberty was preserved, and the spirit of the law maintained. Lucas argued that "a culpable act, even when seeming most spontaneous, is always accomplished under the even more electric light of the soul."[35] To prove the hereditary transmission of a "propensity to crimes against persons" or "against property," Lucas gave a series of short narratives wherein crimes were committed by entire families, which he found in newspaper reports and presented in true popular novel style, complete with exclamations as to the "horrible details" of "hair-raising examples."[36] Lucas thus started a subsection on the hereditary transmission of a propensity to crime quite similar to insanity as follows:

> IV. There are also cases where the heredity of a disposition to shed blood takes on a character which touches naturally on the extreme limits of a passionate state neighboring on madness, without assimilating itself to it.
>
> On May 29 1845, a dreadful crime, unheard of in the annals of the isle of Bourbon, spread stupor among the population of this lovely colony. A small inhabitant of the large woods, Jean Philidor Merlo, taken by a violent passion. . . .[37]

The fascinating feature of this kind of argumentation is that Lucas naturally continued with a discussion of Merlo's trial, giving his legal and medical opinions on the basis of the reports given in the *Gazette des Tribunaux*. Thus the truth of the medical theory of a hereditary propensity to crime was authenticated by its correlations with the law, speaking as "the interior verb of humanity," based on newspaper reports, and produced following the narrative conventions of realist literature. The medical theory itself drew a very fine line between responsibility and irresponsibility—for how "free" could one be if one had inherited a perverse propensity to crime on which education had little effect? The "light of the soul" theory, however, gained its acceptability and high truth value from its position within social discourse. Once recognized and in place, Lucas's work would serve to authenticate other discourse in law, medicine, and literature.[38]

At stake were not only the foundations of the criminal justice system (who was to blame, how should punishments be given?), but the definition of human nature itself: to what extent could people control their thoughts, passions, and actions? Debates over these questions lasted throughout the century, and the discovery and discussion of "moral insanity" played a major role in their direction. This disease was described as a "mania without delirium": its victims would think and reason quite lucidly, but act in a way which offended moral standards. Said J. C. Prichard, the first to coin the immensely successful phrase "moral insanity," "There is scarce any offence against public decorum that has not been frequently the result of mental disease." [39]

At the beginning of the century it was believed that anyone could fall prey to mental derangement: pocket size manuals on how to overcome this condition were published, as Thomas Blackwell's *The Domestic Guide in Cases of Insanity* (1809). Emphasis was given to the power of the will to combat insanity: discipline, moderation, and self-help (that is, "moral management") provided the key to mental health. Once again, certain groups (the "lower classes," and women and children generally) were recognized as needing guidance in this struggle to maintain sanity. However, by the last quarter of the century moral management had lost much of its appeal, and insanity was defined more as a character flaw, largely hereditary, and often incurable. Criminal or otherwise, it became a specific ailment attacking a certain segment of society, rather than an insidious disease threatening anyone who let up on his or her morals.[40] Henry Maudsley brought this point home in his *Responsibility in Mental Disease* (1874):

> All persons who have made criminals their study recognize a distinct criminal class of beings, who herd together in our large cities in a thieves' quarter, giving themselves up to intemperance, rioting in debauchery, without regard to marriage ties or the bars of consanguinity, and propagating a criminal population of degenerate beings. For it is furthermore a matter of observation that this criminal class constitutes a degenerate or morbid variety of mankind, marked by peculiar low physical and mental characteristics.[41]

B. A. Morel had studied the concept of degeneration from a psychiatric perspective in his influential *Traité des dégénérescences physiques, intellectuelles et morales de l'espèce humaine* (1857). He traced the beginnings of human degeneration to original sin: man's efforts to adapt to a difficult environment had caused him to deviate from an ideal primitive type, and these alterations had been transmitted to his children. The noxious influence of climate, insufficient diet, or disease would produce insanity, criminality, or pauperism in the following generations. He identified a set of "stigmata of degeneracy," which included physical and moral characteristics ranging from high-domed palates and distorted ears to innate perversity, and thereby constructed the mental derangement *type*.[42]

Moral insanity tied the knot between crime and mental disease as similar expressions of biological defects: Maudsley stated that "crime is a sort of outlet in which their unsound tendencies are discharged; they would go mad if they were not criminals, and they do not go mad because they are criminals."[43] Both of these ailments were recognized as particularly prominent in the "lower orders," and little hope was now held for reform. Maudsley held that "the criminal *psychosis*, which is the mental side of the *neurosis*, is for the most part an intractable malady, punishment being of no avail to produce permanent reformation. The dog returns to its vomit and the sow to its wallowing in the mire."[44] Rather candidly, he admitted that differentiations between criminality or insanity were of little consequence, as the outcome would be the same—institutionalization.[45]

Both interpretations of moral insanity, as a curable or incurable defect of the moral sense, erased the social structures of power which produced moral standards of behavior by presupposing an organic unity in society: the needs of the social body were somehow transmitted to each individual and inscribed in his or her bio-moral sense—social roles and positions were thus naturalized. In *Self-Help* (1859) Samuel Smiles described character as "human nature in its best form. It is the moral order embodied in the individual."[46] However, by the last quarter of the century, many of the "lower orders" had nowhere to go: degenerates in mind and body, losers in the struggle for life, they seemed only good for institutionalization. Many of those with interests in social matters agreed. General Booth, in his *In Darkest England and the Way Out* (1890), sadly recognized that,

> There are men so incorrigibly lazy that no inducement that you can offer will tempt them to work; so eaten up by vice that virtue is abhorrent to them, and so inveterately dishonest that theft is to them a master passion. When a human being has reached that state, there is only one course that can be rationally pursued. Sorrowfully, but remorselessly, it must be recognised that he has become lunatic, morally demented, incapable of self-government, and that upon him, therefore, must be passed the sentence of permanent seclusion from a world in which he is not fit to be at large.[47]

Penitentiary scientists strongly agreed with this diagnosis. There existed a wide consensus on this point; discourses originating from different institutions (medical, penitentiary, as well as government, private, and "sociological" centers of inquiry) and employing different methods of knowledge production (empirical surveys, statistical compilations, and medical examinations), all agreed to describe a segment of the "dangerous classes," often labeled the "residuum," as lower forms of human life, a race apart suffering from largely incurable physical, intellectual, and moral defects. For the others, the rest of the "lower orders" whose sense of morality could be reformed, measures needed to be taken, in well-defined doses: too much education or indiscriminate charity were recognized as major contributing factors to crime.

Describing criminality as the result of physical *and* moral defects especially prevalent among the "laboring and dangerous classes," nineteenth-century discourse transformed the notion into an effective, multifarious tool of social integration: to be undisciplined or unemployed, unhealthy or drunk, poor or irreligious was in some way to be part of the criminal classes. The concept of criminality transgressed its legal constraints and became entangled in a web of concepts which included morality, rationality, propriety, biology, as well as economic and political standing—an omnibus notion potentially able to authorize all and any means of social control. However, to be fully operational, it needed to be positively "true": the object, audience, mandate, and institutional locus of a new science on "criminal man" had been arranged.

2 CONDITIONS OF EMERGENCE: STAKES AND POSITIONING

◆

Historical outline   Historical accounts of the emergence of criminology as a new human science usually run along the following lines. In 1876 Cesare Lombroso, an Italian psychiatrist and prison doctor, published *L'Uomo delinquente*, in which he described the criminal as an atavistic throwback to prehistoric man. This theory, originally sparked by the discovery of an enlarged middle occipital fossa and an overdeveloped vermis in the skulls of 383 criminals, was elaborated through various means, including batteries of anatomical, physiological, psychological, intellectual, and moral tests, the development of analogical correlations with the vegetable and animal worlds, historical studies of the evolution of crime and punishment, as well as ethnological, linguistic, and social studies measuring certain groups for their relative proneness to criminality. The end result was the production of the *born-criminal type*, characterized by a set of hereditary physical, intellectual, and moral stigmata impervious to any kind of reform: Lombroso believed that the discovery of this type in criminals should lead either to execution or to permanent seclusion from society. Enrico Ferri, a lawyer, editor, professor, and at one time Member of Parliament, and Baron Raffaele Garofalo, whose career would include the functions of lawyer, prosecutor, and magistrate, joined Lombroso and together these prominent figures formed the center of the *nuova scuola*, the Italian School of Criminal Anthropology. In 1880 the school launched its journal, *Archivio di Psichiatra e Antropologia Criminale*; in 1881 Ferri published his world-famous *I nuovi orrizonti del diritto e della procedura penale* (now better known by the title of the third edition, in 1892, *Sociologia criminale*). In 1885 Garofalo published his *Criminologia*, and the First International Congress of Criminal Anthropology was convened in Rome. By then the school had achieved an international reputation and was competing with the juridical and penal communities to influence the elaboration of the new Italian Penal Code. The Third International Penitentiary Congress, held in Rome at the same time, sent observers to the Criminal Anthropology Congress who voiced reservations in the face of the great success enjoyed by the theories of the *nuova scuola*. Alexandre Lacassagne, doctor of forensic medicine teaching at Lyon, sounded the first French rumblings and reminded the audience of the social nature of crime with his soon to be famous aphorism, "societies have the criminals they deserve."

The French opposition rapidly organized: Lacassagne launched the *Archives de l'Anthropologie Criminelle et des Sciences Pénales* in 1886 as the main publishing outlet of the sociological *"Ecole de Lyon."* Gabriel Tarde, a provincial judge, entered the debate with several articles and his *Criminalité comparée* of 1886 in which he introduced his theory of the criminal as a *professional type*, as distinguished by the demands of his or her career (both physically and intellectually) as would be a butcher or lawyer. Henri Joly's *Le crime: Etude sociale* (1888) and *La France criminelle* (1889) made important contributions to the French sociological approach. When the second congress was held in Paris in 1889, the grounds for the battle against the *nuova scuola* had been well prepared. In their devastating attacks, Lacassagne and Tarde were supported not only by judicial and penal authorities, but also by leading anthropologists such as Léonce Manouvrier and Paul Topinard.

Manouvrier criticized Lombroso's theories for "criminalizing" anatomical traits of unknown significance: crime, in his view, was not necessarily contiguous to anatomy.[1] He criticized the documents advanced as proofs of the theory of the born-criminal type (judging their numbers unreliable), and lamented the absence of a control group of honest men (while recognizing the difficulty of defining "honest"). He further argued against the need for a pathological perspective on crime.[2] Describing the born criminal as a "harlequin," he concluded that a born criminal could always find solace by considering that he was honest nevertheless.[3] The Lombrosian type was also criticized by Topinard who stated that some of its defining characteristics were totally normal (such as facial asymmetry or plagiocephaly) while others amounted to simple individual variations from the norm (as in the relative size of the forehead, or differences in the cephalic index), which could not be considered as anomalies; other traits he described as pathological lesions which could be found in any social group, criminal or not.[4] Tarde and Lacassagne insisted on the importance of social factors such as imitation and environment in the determination of a criminal career.

The Italians were not very successful in their replies, arguing generally about their irrefutable "facts" and resorting to ad hominem attacks, accusing their adversaries of contradicting themselves and of displaying great ignorance.[5] They ended the final meeting by demanding that a committee be set up to make a comparative anatomical study of one hundred criminals and one hundred honest men, so that the next congress, to be held in Brussels in 1892, be based on facts and not mere speculations. The committee was formed, but never did the test; the Italian school protested by boycotting the third congress, during which the born-criminal type was generally pronounced dead by the assembly.

In 1901 the Deputy Medical Officer at Parkhurst Prison, Dr. G. B. Griffiths, began the comparative analysis demanded by the Italians. His project received government support and was extended to include the measurement of three thousand convicts from Borstal, Dartmoor, and Portland prisons. Dr. Charles Goring took over the study when he replaced Griffiths at Parkhurst in 1903, and eventually was personally responsible for a large part of the measurements and for the actual compilation and publication of the data, under the auspices of the government, in the 1913 book entitled *The English Convict. A Statistical Study*. This was presented as the final refutation of the Italian theoretical extravaganza. The British had remained rather aloof from the continental criminological debate, often advocating plain common sense as the only valid tool when dealing with crime and its perpetrators.[6] In his introduction Goring expressed the widely prevailing amazement felt by the English: "nothing is more startling than the organised confusion masquerading to-day under the scientific name of criminology."[7] Indeed, Lombroso's serious descriptions were literally a joke for Goring, who could not help adding a few editorial comments when quoting the master, whom he described as "our intrepid explorer borne onward by the flood of enthusiasm."[8]

At first sight, this would seem to provide a clear example of a scientific revolution as described by Thomas Kuhn: a change of explanatory paradigm within a scientific community, which makes communication between competing schools impossible—hence the mirth or violence of the polemics.[9] *The English Convict* is generally recognized as the book which marked the beginning of a truly scientific criminology, and the end of the born-criminal type: did not its author state clearly that "Lombroso's criminology is dead as a science," and that "no evidence has emerged confirming the existence of a physical criminal type, such as Lombroso and his disciples have described"? [10]

◆

History revisited   There are many problems with this history of criminology. The first arises when one considers that Lombroso's *L'Uomo delinquente* presented very little original information: as was shown in chapter one, there was a wide consensus among medical doctors, government, prison, and police officials, sanitation experts, and philanthropists as to the existence of a separate kind of criminal beings, a primitive, degenerate, and immoral race which needed to be controlled and segregated from the rest of the community. Long before Lombroso, penitentiary scientists had promulgated the need to turn from the abstract crime to the criminal individual, and called for the establishment of indeterminate sentences allowing the punishment to fit the criminal's inner perversity rather than his or her actual crimes; early statisticians had correlated crime to such factors as race, sex, and climate, and developed the notion of an innate propensity to crime; medical doctors had studied the hereditary transmission of this propensity, and identified a set of physical stigmata manifesting its presence in individuals and families; all the subgroups involved in the social management of the "lower orders" easily recognized an incorrigible segment among them, which should be isolated permanently from the rest of the community.[11] Lombroso's techniques for proving his theory were also widely used and some were over fifty years old: recourse to skull measurements, criminal statistics, and other testing techniques to quantify the relative importance of heredity or degeneration in criminality were hardly new; the drawing up of hierarchical tables establishing the innate criminal propensity of the "lower orders" or races, or of women and children generally were common preoccupations which arose in all kinds of medical and sociological treatises. Even Lombroso's now rather comical comparisons with the vegetable and animal reigns were not unusual in his time.[12]

In the face of these resemblances in both methods and results between the works of Lombroso and a great number of medical, legal, political, and social treatises, the first question to be raised is why did

L'Uomo delinquente cause such an international commotion? What were the reasons for its function as a discursive *event*, from which a new science would emerge?

Traditional historical outlines of criminology also fail to account for the fact that in spite of violent rhetoric and emotionally charged confrontations, there were very few significant differences between the competing schools of anthropological and sociological criminology. Lombroso only claimed that 40 percent of criminals were *born* with physical constitutions which inevitably led to deviant behavior, and recognized the importance of other factors such as race, climate, sex, and environment in the determination of 60 percent of criminal activity. Ferri insisted on the importance of these factors as well in his *Sociologia criminale*. Conversely, while the French school accentuated social factors, it recognized an innate, incorrigible, and largely hereditary perversity in some criminals, and a personal propensity for evil in most, if not all, of them. Tarde put it quite succinctly: "Stimulations to crimes, from social or other origins, can only be exercised on individuals more or less predisposed to receive them." [13] This confusion of social and biological factors generally originated from a social Darwinist perception of society, whereby social winners were the most physically fit for the struggle for life—and vice versa. Charles Féré could thus recognize the fact that most criminals were indigent, and blame their criminality on inferior physiology and morality, rather than on abject poverty. [14]

Tarde's notion of the criminal as a professional type, as opposed to Lombroso's born type, illustrates the very fine line drawn between biological and social factors by the most combative representative of the French sociological school. Indeed, Tarde contended that every profession—including the criminal one—carried its particular physical type, not only because of the repetitious use of the same muscles, but also because individuals born with the talents required by a specific profession were naturally attracted to it. [15] The class of professional criminals thus consisted of the "naturally" ugly, lazy, perverse, and vicious, who were "born" into the trade—a concept not that far removed from the Lombrosian one. Tarde even recognized the rare existence of innate criminals, who could be neither cured nor reformed. [16]

Joly argued in a similar vein: insisting on the social character of crime, he nevertheless continually described it as the outcome of vicious and perverse *individual* desires. The social milieu was defined in a way that made the "sociological" approach somewhat limited: "The milieu of crime is society, or in other words, it is the set of affections, sympathies, encouragements, and concurrences, but also the rivalries, competitions, jealousies, enmities, and hatreds which constitute the common life of humanity."[17] Not surprisingly, this definition of society led to rather vague suggestions as to the measures which needed to be taken to prevent crime: "The mission of public authorities is then to do everything which, while respecting individual freedom, can bring the propagation of what is good and prevent the propagation of what is bad."[18] Manouvrier followed roughly the same lines as he described criminals as the most unfavored "physio-sociologically" and recognized that they were on the average slightly more imperfect anatomically than the noncriminal or truly honest population. He actually narrowed the definition of social milieu by claiming that no two individuals could be said to belong to the same one; he insisted that a single word, gesture, or look could significantly alter anyone's environment.[19] The sociology of the French opposition was thus so mixed with moral and psychological data as to reduce the antagonism between the two schools to a matter of degree.

Finally, no matter how strongly he ridiculed Lombroso, Goring himself ended up with the same results under slightly different labels:

> The physical and mental constitution of both criminal and law-abiding persons, of the same age, stature, class, and intelligence, are identical. There is no such thing as an anthropological criminal type. But, despite this negation, and upon the evidence of our statistics, it appears to be an equally indisputable fact that there is a physical, mental, and moral type of normal person who tends to be convicted of crime: that is to say, our evidence conclusively shows that, on the average, the criminal of English prisons is markedly differentiated by defective physique—as measured by stature and body weight; by defective mental capacity—as measured by general intelligence; and by an increased possession of wilful anti-social proclivities—as measured apart from intelligence, by length of imprisonment.[20]

Goring, like Lombroso, found a marked association between criminality and "alcoholism, epilepsy, sexual profligacy, ungovernable temper, obstinacy of purpose, and wilful anti-social proclivity—*everyone of these, as well as feeble-mindedness, being heritable qualities.*"[21] He even went further than Lombroso in discounting environmental factors: "relatively to its origin in the constitution of the malefactor, and especially in his mentally defective constitution, crime is only to a trifling extent (if to any) the product of social inequalities, of adverse environment, or of other manifestations of what may be comprehensively termed the force of circumstances."[22] Goring's suggestions for a "crusade against crime" were the conventional ones: education, imprisonment, or sterilization.[23]

These striking similarities between the different schools' evaluations of criminals and the necessary means for their elimination lead to a second question: what were the arguments about? What stakes produced this international discursive event over, what would appear to be, a general consensus?

A third problem posed by historical accounts of the emergence of criminology concerns the identification of Goring's work as the beginnings of a true science. In fact, criminology did not steadily develop from these pioneering texts; its elaboration was marginal and tentative at best, nonexistent in many of the Western countries contributing to its early recognition. This surprising lack of development was documented in the late 1950s, when the University of Cambridge sent Leon Radzinowicz, a renowned authority on criminal matters, on an international investigation of the state of criminological studies, with the intention of rejuvenating their own work in the field. The results of this fact-finding mission were published by Radzinowicz in a book laconically entitled *In Search of Criminology*. Every country the author investigated seemed to offer the same, rather dismal, results: behind a façade of illustrious institutes offering degrees or certifications in criminology were found haphazard programs, with no funds and very little staff, offering incongruous mixtures of practical and theoretical courses to small numbers of students. In Italy, for example, much pomp and circumstance accompanied the official inauguration of the Institute for the Study of Criminal Sciences in the School of Law at the University of Rome on February 18, 1912. Among the honored guests were the "Prime Minister, the Ministers of Justice and Public Education and other members of the government, the President of the Senate, the heads of the judiciary, the Chief Public Prosecutor, the leaders of the bar, the Mayor of Rome and many other personalities prominent in the cultural and political life of the capital."[24] The event was internationally recognized as a major breakthrough for criminological studies. And yet, apart from space in the law faculty and a library, the institute received no funds for research or the appointment of senior staff; its four months' courses provided students (law students, police and prison officers, and indeed anyone who met the director's criteria) with certification if they attended class, and a diploma if they passed an oral exam. In 1961 Radzinowicz described the institute as "at present in a state of disintegration," and affirmed that "the fate of the school at Rome is symptomatic of the condition of criminological studies in Italy generally."[25] France presented a similar tableau, in that its eleven institutes of criminology established within faculties of law across the country were "all in a grave predicament," not only as far as funds were concerned, but also in regard to their theoretical and practical orientation.[26] Radzinowicz summed up the situation as follows: "The path to the recognition of criminology as an academic science is still rugged and thorny. . . . What parades under the name of criminology is no more than a cursory survey of elementary information about the treatment of offenders, tacked on to the instruction of law proper."[27]

Why did the development and consolidation of the field of criminology prove to be such an arduous, if not impossible task? What were the stakes involved in its sudden emergence and subsequent failure on an international scene? If no new or especially revolutionary knowledge was being produced, what factors accounted for the fierce competition between schools, the scramblings of the penitentiary scientists, and the interest of the press? Why were criminological institutes established with great ceremony and then left stranded with no money and no staff?

◆

Strategic positioning   The Italian School of Criminal Anthropology never considered its main goal to be purely theoretical: from the start it affirmed in a combative tone that the scientific facts it uncovered about criminals demanded a reevaluation of the entire judicial and penal systems. Denying any reality to the concept of free will, they repudiated penitentiary reform procedures; they asserted the need to broaden the legal minds of magistrates with the scientific advances of medicine, psychiatry, and sociology; they called for the abolition of the jury, who could not be expected to have the necessary expertise to determine whether or not a criminal was of the incurable born-criminal type. All of these proposals threatened established judicial and penal organizations which did not welcome this apparent takeover move by newly self-proclaimed criminologists.

Unlike their Italian adversaries, members of the French school were careful not to tread on the territory of penal and judicial authorities: their milder version of determinism, which recognized environmental factors as well as individual moral perversion, did not attack the theoretical grounds for either the right to punish or the value of reform procedures. Such a compromise offered the distinct advantage of not attacking the position of the *juge d'instruction*, whose work depended largely on the presumption of free will and reasoned behavior in the accused. Moreover, the doctors of forensic medicine involved in the French attack (Lacassagne being the most prominent) had special reasons to nurture good relations with the judicial community, as careers in their field depended entirely on the judge's discretionary power to allow professional testimony in his court: Robert Nye makes these points and insists that any serious rift with the judicial community could jeopardize "income and professional status."[28] Finally, the French appreciated the importance of their credibility with the juries, and hesitated to use radical theories which could alienate them from public opinion: Magnan thus argued during the second congress (1889) that the born-criminal type was useless, and that only the individual examination of suspects by doctors of forensic medicine could be of value to presiding magistrates.[29]

Penal authorities were equally unwilling to accept the notion that physical constitution could determine criminal behavior, as this idea attacked their mandate of education and reform. During the second congress, Herbette, the French director of penitentiary administration, spoke of the necessity of tact and discretion in the rendering of this public service. Arguing against biological determinism, he advocated the need for criminologists to adopt psychological explanations for deviance, which would preserve the notions of human conscience and liberty, and encourage both prison officials and inmates to persevere in reform.[30] The French school of criminology would heed these warnings.

Finally, the zeal with which anthropologists of the stature of Manouvrier and Topinard joined in the attack against the *nuova scuola* is at least partially explained by Nye as a measure to protect the integrity of their science: they opposed applying the word "anthropology" to Lombroso's project, and Topinard asked the assembly of the second congress to use Garofalo's term, "criminology," rather than criminal anthropology.[31] Manouvrier, surely the most active critic of the congress, attacking representatives of both the Italian and the French schools, particularly resented attempts to annex parts of the anthropological field, and argued that the criminological venture could only make sense as a subsection of anthropology.[32]

The convergence of these different interests thus explains why judicial and penal authorities, doctors of forensic medicine, and anthropologists alike could rally in a common opposition to Lombrosian doctrines. The debate over criminal anthropology illustrates how a subgroup could attempt and fail to gain power through the determination of a new field of specialized knowledge. The Italian Code of 1889 repudiated the positivist doctrines and did not even recognize limited degrees of criminal responsibility; the freedom enjoyed by penal authorities in the determination of the proper means of administering punishment continued to increase; law students, magistrates, and judges were not retrained in criminological science. However, power struggles among subgroups involved in the administration of the criminal justice system do not fully explain the violence of the opposition to the Italian school. There seemed to be a general consensus in social discourse, not just in scientific circles and in penal administration but also in the press, to reject the Lombrosian definition of criminal man. The reasons for this rejection will only become apparent through further textual analyses, but before undertaking this task, the role of the state in the emergence of criminology needs to be considered a little more closely.

As a rule, the institutionalization of a science requires the backing of the state in one form or another, yet it seemed of particular importance in the case of criminology.[33] State governments actively promoted the development of criminology and the personal advancement of its proponents. Delving into criminological matters brought considerable personal reward and public recognition. Tarde was a rather obscure provincial *juge d'instruction* for over twenty years until his works in criminology became known internationally: he then was appointed director of criminal statistics in the Ministry of Justice in 1894; in 1900 the assembly of professors at the Collège de France elected him for the Chair of Modern Philosophy, a vote ratified by the minister.[34] Both he and Lombroso received ranks in the *Légion d'Honneur* (Tarde was made a *Chevalier* in 1895, Lombroso a *Commandeur* in 1906). Apart from giving awards, state governments usually sponsored criminal anthropology congresses, and moreover sent delegates to them—a level of support which was always gratefully acknowledged.[35] Even when the Italian school boycotted the 1892 congress, representatives of the Italian government did attend.

As previously noted, however, this celebratory backing for congresses and awards was paradoxically not followed by adequate financial provisions for day-to-day pedagogy and research, at least not until conditions were more favorable. In 1961 Radzinowicz could still complain of the unwillingness of governments to fund criminology, citing the U.S. Congress as a prime example of this reticence.[36] This situation, however, radically changed in the mid-1960s, when a much publicized crime wave prompted the president of the United States to declare a war on crime in a speech to the House of Representatives. The Omnibus Crime Control and Safe Streets Acts was passed by Congress, and from then on formidable funds were made available, and schools and institutes, government committees and official inquiries proliferated once more. All the major original criminological texts were reprinted, and once again, the need to know became a critical issue. The President's Commission on Law Enforcement and Administration of Justice stated in 1967: "The Commission has found and discussed many needs of law enforcement and the administration of criminal justice. But what it has found to be the greatest need is the need to know. . . . There is virtually no subject connected with crime or criminal justice into which further research is unnecessary."[37] Somewhat predictably, a new science emerged: "victimology" made its official debut at an international symposium held in Jerusalem in 1973. The new field of knowledge was divided just as criminology had been roughly a hundred years earlier. Its main concerns were "the definition of the concept of the victim," "the locus of victimology in the realm of the social sciences," "victim definition and classification, and their impact on empirical research," and, of course, research into the means of providing "the restoration of the social equilibrium in all its aspects, individual and collective, following the disturbance by the criminal act," and the discussion of "problems related to the treatment of the victim at the hands of the criminal justice system."[38]

The similarities between the modern resurgence of criminology and its emergence at the end of the nineteenth century are amazingly numerous and far-reaching. All the old theories are being revived, from the simple recognition of innate individual evil ("Wicked people exist. Nothing avails except to set them apart from innocent people,") to the utilitarian, professional view of criminal activity ("A person commits an offense if the expected utility to him exceeds the utility he could get by using his time and resources at other activities,") and its accompanying deterrence theory of punishment.[39] Once again, the boundaries between criminal and deviant behavior are becoming blurred, while attempts are made to expand state processes of social control. Richard Quinney illustrates this expansionary movement in his *Class, State and Crime* by discussing the recommendations given in the 1975 report of the National Advisory Commission on Criminal Justice Standards and Goals, which include a suggestion that alternative agencies be established to handle deviant behavior:

> The Commission advises, in particular, alternatives to legal processing outside of the criminal justice system. Cases are to be diverted from the courts, and new agencies ("non-criminal-justice institutions") are to deal with cases formerly handled by the police and the courts. This leaves the criminal justice system free to deal with serious offenses against the state and the economy and at the same time makes a wide range of social behavior subject to surveillance and control by the state. Criminal justice is expanding.[40]

Thus criminology has a history of emerging—or at least of becoming a social issue of enough importance to be publicized and promoted—when the state lets it. The intertextual circulation of criminological discourse has coincided with periods marked by civil unrest: during the great depression of the end of the nineteenth century, when movements fighting for the rights of the working classes in general or women in particular were increasing their momentum, and toward the end of the twentieth century, during the 1960s and 1970s, when civil rights movements, ban-the-bomb marches, feminist organizations, and even consumer groups were actively protesting established structures of authority. It is as though organized opposition to power-knowledge relations triggered the proliferation of discourse and research on criminals—as though criminology's first function was to generate discourse capable of widening the definition of deviance and of authorizing tighter control procedures. As other discourses dealing with crime were already in place (penitentiary and police sciences, legal definitions of crime and punishment), it seems possible to assume that the concept of "criminal man" (or the current "dangerous offender") must present specific ideological advantages warranting the emergence of criminology, the science of "criminal man," when authority structures are threatened. An analysis of the textual modes of production of scientific knowledge on the criminal at the end of the nineteenth century will clarify this issue.

3 Textual Construction: The Production of Scientific Proofs

♦

Intertextual science Whether they identified biological or social factors as the main determinants of criminal behavior, criminologists were united by a common postulate, that of the existence of a continuum between the physical, psychological, moral, and social dimensions of the criminal. It was this postulate that established criminology as a sciential discourse, in contradistinction to the metaphysical treatises of the Classical School. The new criminologists claimed to be interested in measurable facts, rather than abstract considerations on human nature and social contracts. This postulate logically brought them to apply virtually the whole of contemporary knowledge to their object: medicine, physiology and psychiatry, anthropology, zoology and botany, linguistics and philosophy all contributed to the elaboration of criminological discourse. Thus, criminology was constructed as an intertextual *bricolage*, which received its elements of content and theoretical models from the natural and human sciences, to produce its own objects.

Most often, these bits of prefabricated knowledge were annexed by criminological texts through the simple means of analogy and induction. For example, in a passage dealing with the effects of climate on criminal behavior, Lombroso started by reporting the effects of intense heat on the leaves of the *Drosera Rotundifolia* (paralysis of the tentacles at 130°F); he continued his demonstration by studying the effects of cold on the Esquimaux, rendered so meek as to not even have a word for quarrel in their vocabulary; he finally concluded that "the influence which is most apt to produce a disposition toward rebellion and crime is that of a relatively moderate degree of heat," which "explains why, not only despotic Russia, but also the Liberal

Scandinavian countries, have rarely experienced revolutions."[1] Thus it is by drawing a series of analogies between botanical, ethnological, linguistic, and political knowledge that Lombroso induced a criminological thesis on the effects of climate on crime. What epistemological configuration allowed such statements to make sense?

Whereas deductive reasoning proceeds from a stated general rule to draw conclusions about a specific case by means of an intermediate class connected to both, inductive reasoning draws general rules from the observation of numerous individual cases which are related through analogies. Inductions operate within the realm of the "obvious": facts are brought to light so that the receiver of the message may be convinced of their meaning by simple recognition rather than by abstract reasoning—the underlying thesis authorizing the establishment of analogical correlations is never stated in inductions, and their truth value is largely determined by their correspondence to the receiver's expectations. Lombroso's juxtaposition of diverse statements mentioned above is thus made possible by the presupposition of two correlated theses: (1) truth is absolute and cumulative (as no theoretical framework is needed to qualify its content or extension—what is true in botany is found in linguistics and also applies to political and criminal behavior); and (2) reality is a given (the object of scientific investigation can be immediately grasped and measured, and need not be specified first through a theoretical model). These two correlated theses establish the epistemological foundations for the production of criminology as what Bachelard would call prescientific knowledge, that is, one that considers its object as a given, measures it precisely with instruments of unknown sensitivity, and interprets this data with unverified theories.[2]

The presupposition of these epistemological theses and their effect on the determination of criminological knowledge are perhaps best exemplified in Lombroso's often quoted narration of his initial discovery of an enlarged occipital fossa and vermis in 383 skulls of criminals. This observation would determine the orientation of all his research. Although he would enlarge his theory of atavism to include moral insanity and epilepsy, Lombroso never strayed from this original inspiration:

> This was not merely an idea, but a revelation. At the sight of that skull, I seemed to see all of a sudden, lighted up as a vast plain under a flaming sky, the problem of the nature of the crimi-

nal—an atavistic being who reproduces in his person the ferocious instincts of primitive humanity and the inferior animals.
Thus were explained anatomically the enormous jaws, high cheek-
bones, prominent supercilliary arches, solitary lines in the palms,
extreme size of the orbits, handle-shaped or sessile ears found in
criminals, savages, and apes, insensibility to pain, extremely acute
sight, tattooing, excessive idleness, love of orgies, and the irre-
sistible craving for evil for its own sake, the desires not only to
extinguish life in the victim, but to mutilate the corpse, tear its
flesh, and drink its blood.[3]

This famous passage vividly demonstrates that the reality described by
criminology does not correspond to exterior objects in the world (to
a primary empirical reality) but rather to objects as they are known.
The referential illusion activated by these texts, consisting of a de-
nial of the conditions of knowledge production, that is, of the relay of
theoretical models between subject and object, settled them from the
outset in ideological discourse. Indeed, by taking an enlarged occipital
fossa as a material index of barbarity, without formulating the necessary theoretical relations between anthropological concepts of primitivism, moral descriptions of barbarity, social distributions of habits,
and medical definitions of "normal" anatomical traits, Lombroso used
it as a textual index, a *shifter* connecting the text to intertextual descriptions of crime: he could then "read" the skulls with all and any
ideological maxim on vice, immorality, antisocial activity, and so on.[4]
"Criminal man" as an object of scientific investigation would thus consist of an amalgam of ideological maxims on deviance, the norm being
the upper- and middle-class white male—the social group of the producers of criminology.

   This process of ideological construction is most apparent in the measurement techniques used to "test" the criminality of criminals. For example, amyl nitrite was administered to measure the criminal's blush-
ing capability: deficiencies in this respect were registered as proof of
a low level of morality. Similarly, female prisoners would be questioned about their crimes, and then about their menstrual cycle: the
relative shame induced by these questions would determine the extent
of their remorse and morality.[5] Such tests were entirely determined
by ideological maxims on correct behavior: moral people blush when
reminded of their wrongdoing, decent women will not discuss certain
subjects. Sphygmographic tests to measure changes in the criminal's

pulse in relation to different thoughts would be conducted as follows: the experimenter would show the criminal a glass of wine, a cigar, a picture of a naked woman, or of a frog, or snake, and measure the response.[6] The choice of each of these objects presupposes an ideological maxim on typical criminal behavior: they like to drink, indulge in orgies, but are cowards at heart. The classifications themselves very often consisted of a series of value judgments: comparing his results to Corre's, Lombroso could state that "the physiognomies of 105 portraits of military criminals studied by Corre are divided by him in the following manner: insignificant, 22, gentle, 17, disagreeable, asymmetrical or brutal, 66. . . . This is almost the proportion that I myself found for the criminal type."[7] The knowledge so produced was totally unfalsifiable: when a physiognomy did not fit the preconceived categories, it was simply labeled "insignificant."

Thus, the textual production of "criminal man" as an object of scientific knowledge was entirely determined by intertextual ideological maxims on race, sex, class, and morality. This explains why the analogical relations drawn by criminologists, and the general rules they inductively discovered about criminals, are not just untrue but largely unthinkable for modern readers whose intertext is widely different. As the theoretical framework was presupposed, criminologists being more preoccupied with the amounts of tests and the standardization of records than with the accuracy of testing procedures or indeed the definition of the object to be measured, the value of criminological knowledge—its acceptability and truth value—depended on the bricoleur's inventiveness: how well he chose his facts, how cleverly he assembled them, how useful were his results. The strength of argumentation was all important for the production of criminology.

◆

Argumentative strategies   If reality is a given and truth is absolute and cumulative, the scientist's role is to assemble and clarify immediately perceptible "facts." This explains why many of the arguments utilized by criminological texts to produce their scientific knowledge were drawn directly from common knowledge, proverbs, and works of art: the scientist's goal was to explain the causes of effects quite obvious to all. Referring to the characteristic ugliness of criminals, Tarde argued: "The merit of anthropology is to have sought to specify the causes of the impression that everyone feels more or less at the sight of certain faces, and to have clarified that diagnosis."[8] To show that a scientific theory was generally recognized by public opinion (the *doxa*) was to prove its authenticity. Describing the criminal, Tarde specified: "he is very hairy and not very bearded.—Beware of the beardless, says an Italian proverb."[9] The reader's common sense was at times directly invoked as the ultimate judge of the validity of a thesis. After listing a great quantity of cranial anomalies in criminals, Lombroso asked his reader: "Is it possible that individuals struck by such a great number of alterations could have the same degree of intelligence and the same feelings as men with completely normal skulls?"[10]

Scientific criminology was thus elaborated from the grounds of the verisimilar, the commonly acceptable, and its truth value was a coefficient of its relevance to its audience's needs and expectations. The intended receivers of criminological discourse were a relatively restricted group. Criminals were totally excluded from this discourse which dehumanized them: considered as underlings on the evolutionary scale, as a result of either atavism or degeneration, their words literally made no sense unless they were interpreted by criminologists. Said Lombroso: "They speak differently than we do, because they do not feel the same way; they speak like savages, because they are veritable savages in the midst of the brilliant European civilization."[11] The dialogical community for the elaboration of criminology, this "we," was never specified in detail, but a series of textual interpellations to "any learned man," "enlightened moralist," "head of state," identifies some of the necessary qualifications for membership. Class, race, and gender distinctions also served to exclude potential participants; the following remarkable passage in J. Dallemagne's *Les théories de la criminalité* (1896) thus condenses ideological maxims on non-Western industrialized nations, children, and the working class in a single sentence describing how "moral atavism" can be discovered:

> L'atavisme moral, au contraire, se déduit de la comparaison entre les sauvages encore existants et les criminels civilisés, de l'analogie entre les criminels et les enfants, reproduction passagère du passé moral de nos ancêtres, et des traits communs entre les criminels et les gens du peuple, retardataires de la civilisation.
> [Moral atavism, on the contrary, is deduced from the comparison between the still existing savages and the civilized criminals, from the analogy between criminals and children, the passing reproduction of the moral past of our ancestors, and from the common

traits between criminals and common people, the latecomers to civilization.][12]

By identifying the "lower" classes and races and children as objects of criminological studies, this passage excludes them as participating subjects in the dialogical community of criminology—which, through a series of such operations, is effectively reduced to white male middle- and upper-class members, with few exceptions. A brief analysis of this sentence will begin to show more specifically how intertextual ideological constructs could be assembled into "scientific" knowledge.

Whereas an indefinite article would have presented the noun phrase "moral atavism" as a *possible* concept, the definite article "*l'*" presupposes the existence of this phenomenon (as would a demonstrative article) and thereby allows the author to bypass the difficult task of defining the theoretical foundations of a scientific search for "moral atavism."[13] The same analysis applies to the definite article preceding "savages." Familiarity with criminological texts of the period makes the identification of the referent quite simple: native Africans, Australians, and the nonwhite races in general. The use of the definite article presupposes their savageness, which is thereby presented as a fact of life which need not be theoretically justified, but simply assumed by the text. The juxtaposition of the explanatory clauses following the noun phrases "the children," and "the common people" signals that the theories justifying the postulation of an innate immorality (or low morality) in children and an inferior evolutionary development in the "lower classes" were not considered as obvious as the initial racist statement by Dallemagne. The ellipsis of the definite pronouns and verbs of these clauses ("*les enfants [qui sont la] reproduction passagère*"; "*les gens du peuple [qui sont les] retardataires*"—"children [who are the] passing reproduction"; "common people [who are the] latecomers") transforms them from defining statements into descriptive ones. This syntactic construction thus allows adjectival clauses to presuppose what defining ones would have posed explicitly: Haeckel's biogenetic principle of recapitulation and the vague social Darwinist preconstructs founding these ideological characterizations are presupposed and therefore rendered indisputable by the text. Finally, the statement that moral atavism is deduced (the proper term should be induced) by a comparison of these groups presupposes the epistemological configuration previously analyzed, establishing reality as a given and truth as absolute and cumulative: without these epistemological presuppositions the entire exercise would make no sense—it could not produce knowledge recognized as scientific.

Several levels of presuppositions are thus involved in the production of scientific criminological knowledge. Logico-semantic presuppositions carried by the use of definite articles and pronouns (in ellipsis) allow the author to bypass both the definition of his object (moral atavism) and the presentation of the theories justifying his choice of test population groups. Ideological maxims on the moral savageness of certain races and the "lower classes" and the social Darwinist preconstructs generating them are equally presupposed, thereby avoiding the need to establish theoretical relations between physical constitution and morality, evolution and morality, social evolution and physical evolution, and class position and evolution. Finally, the dogmatic presentation of the entire scientific exercise presupposes its epistemological foundations. Through these argumentative strategies, the grounds for the production of scientific discourse are laid.

On these grounds all and any divergence from the white male bourgeois norm could serve to clarify criminality. Not surprisingly, the authors of these texts continuously described their findings as self-evident or easily observable. Lombroso concluded a series of descriptions of young criminals and their acts by noting that "from the physical point of view, these types are absolutely dissimilar; but when examining them with care, *it is easy to read on their faces* that from the moral point of view, the ideas, the low and common sentiments are identical, and that these are what brands them with a common stamp."[14] Joly always found criminological matters rather straightforward. His book *Le crime: Etude sociale* is strewn with expressions like: "there is no need to reflect profoundly to answer these questions," "one can guess these without trouble," "it is superfluous to prove," and "prior to any examination one cannot prevent oneself from doubting."[15]

Arguments of authority were equally widespread. Lombroso could confirm the accuracy of his descriptions by pointing out a series of famous paintings portraying criminals in like manner: the damned in Michael Angelo's *Last Judgment*, the executioners in Giotto's *Massacre of Innocents*, Titian's *Martyr of Saint-Laurent*, and others plainly bore the mark of the born criminal.[16] Works of literature proved to be useful authorities on the subject: "But perhaps the strongest argument in its favor [of criminal anthropology] is that our conclusions are adopted, almost unknowingly, by men of genius such as Zola, Daudet, Tolstoi, Dostoiewsky, whose preoccupations and literary task have nothing to do with our science."[17] Joly's claim that prostitution was the source of a multitude of crimes was backed up with a biblical quote: "Yes, with prostitution we are on grounds where all kinds of crimes grow with prodigious speed. As the Bible says 'the courtesan sets her ambushes on the road like a thief, and she increases iniquity among men.'"[18] Joly equally made frequent references to newspaper reports on criminal activity to authenticate his work.[19]

In inductive reasoning the aim is less to prove the truth of the argument than to stage it: to represent its validity by an illuminating example which will strike the receiver as so obvious that it will provoke an immediate recognition rather than a reasoned acceptance. Metaphors are crucial in this context, and criminologists used them extensively, not just to illustrate, but to produce knowledge. Consider the following argument by Tarde:

> Les délits sont en quelque sorte les éruptions cutanées du corps social; indices parfois d'une maladie grave, ils révèlent l'introduction, par le contact avec les voisins, d'idées et de besoins étrangers en contradiction partielle avec les idées et les besoins nationaux. [Offenses are in a way the cutaneous eruptions of the social body; at times indices of a serious illness, they reveal the introduction, through contact with neighbors, of foreign ideas and needs in partial contradiction of national ideas and needs].[20]

This complex sentence consists of three clauses. In the first clause the use of the definite article "*du*" presupposes the existence of such a thing as a "social body," which in turn presupposes an ideological maxim postulating an organic unity within social organizations, whereby interests "naturally" converge for the promotion of the common good: class conflicts and power struggles are therefore elided by the syntagm. This ideological presupposition provides the semantic grounds for the metaphorical reference to crimes as skin blemishes. The identification of crime as a symptom of disease presupposes a pathological nature to criminal acts—crimes are thus presented as abnormal occurrences in the social body functions, and not as functions of social, economic, and political structures themselves. The reference to "cutaneous eruptions" could imply a rather superficial problem. This implication is specifically denied by the second clause "*indices parfois d'une maladie grave*" [at times indices of a serious illness]. The ellipsis of the noun and verb phrase ("*les délits sont les*" [offenses are the]) establishes the second clause as a subordinate adjectival clause, which need not be elaborated: the need to justify the presupposed medical/political theory is thereby avoided, and its acceptability is increased by the use of the restrictive "at times," which, like the adverb "in a way" endows the whole argument with the prudence required by scientific observation. The final clause drops the metaphorical mode, speaking of "ideas and needs" rather than germs: it would seem that the stated political message on the "noxious influence" of foreigners required more precision than the presupposed one—once a national unity had been presupposed, "national ideas and needs" could be stated explicitly in a context which made sense. The whole of the sentence, therefore, allows a subtle passage from well-known and easily accepted medical knowledge (skin rashes are symptoms of a disease) to ideological knowledge (society functions as an organic whole, defined by national boundaries) to the political identification of foreign needs and ideas as threats to the nation. This final point neatly attributes the origin of crime to foreign sources, delivering the "social body" from the possibility of inherent constitutional deficiencies.

The reception and circulation given to Lacassagne's most famous aphorisms are also instructive of the crucial role played by argumentative strategies in the elaboration of criminology:

> Le milieu social est le bouillon de culture de la criminalité; le microbe, c'est le criminel, un élément qui n'a d'importance que le jour où il trouve le bouillon qui le fait fermenter.

> Les sociétés ont les criminels qu'elles méritent.
> [The social milieu is the culture fluid of criminality; the microbe is the criminal, an element which only acquires importance the day it finds the fluid which makes it ferment.

> Societies have the criminals they deserve].[21]

Although said separately during the first congress in 1885, these two statements would be continuously quoted and discussed in criminological texts. During the second congress they even became an object of discussion in themselves, each scientist explaining why he agreed or disagreed with the *image*. The conciliatory Ferri ended his presentation by recalling Lacassagne's words to remind his audience that if society was indeed the culture fluid of criminality, it could have no effect without the criminal microbe, and that "therefore microbe and fluid, the biological and social sides, are the two fundamental aspects of criminality and make up . . . the essential data of criminal anthro-

pology."[22] Bajenoff defended the Italian school against attacks deriving from the "famous comparison of the criminal to a microbe in a
culture fluid," by pointing to its limitations: the microbe's morphology
needed to be studied, and it was "the great glory of Mr. Lombroso and
the new Italian School to have opened this course to other investiga-
tors."[23] In spite of Lombroso's annoyance with the whole debate, the
image was to survive with great tenacity and demonstrate a remarkable versatility.[24] In his introduction to Paul Aubry's *La contagion du
meurtre* (1896), A. Corre could thus use it in an inversed form with
equal success, making the fluid stand for the individual and the germ
stand for the idea of crime.[25] The long life of the Pasteurian analogy,
surviving more than a decade as an object of controversy, and its capacity to generate various perceptions of crime and criminals signal a
particularly successful piece of discursive bricolage, which warrants a
closer look.

Lacassagne's analogy establishes a similarity of relationships between disparate sets of phenomena:

Criminal : Society : : Germ : Culture Fluid

As the content of the vehicle is one of the most well known in medicine, the whole of the argument acquires an air of simplicity and ob-
viousness: the value of the medical argument (germs will proliferate
under certain environmental conditions) is immediately recognized,
and the assertion of the criminological thesis (criminals abound in certain social conditions) is thus rendered highly acceptable. The metaphorical assemblage of the two assertions produces an easily identified
and highly probable meaning—it makes sense. The second sentence,
often quoted as added proof of society's responsibility toward its criminals, is a variation on the proverb "*Qui sème le vent récolte la tempête*" or
"You reap what you sow." This annexation of a doxological maxim to
a scientific principle serves to increase the acceptability of the criminological thesis. However, the most important part of the argument
remains unsaid: by stating a correlation between the germ and the
criminal, the first clause presupposes that the criminal is, by nature, an
agent of evil. The condemnation of society is thus attenuated, as guilt
is distributed evenly between the individual and society. Furthermore,
by associating society to a culture fluid, the analogy presupposes an
organic social organization, which precludes the existence of inherent
structural conflicts. This kind of strategy would be constantly resorted
to by representatives of the sociological school. Manouvrier's formu-

lation presented the criminal as a violin and society as a musician: the same instrument would produce good or bad music, depending on the musician and the quality of the instrument.[26] Through this form of argumentation, the sociological school of criminology successfully positioned itself within established discursive practices: it could *state* the importance of social factors while *presupposing* just enough individual responsibility to allow legislators to maintain penal codes, judges to convict individual offenders, and prison administrators to reform them through education and discipline.

The fact that Lacassagne's metaphor could become in itself an object of contention in criminology reveals a second epistemological presupposition establishing that language is transparent, and can directly "express" reality, "as it is." Criminologists recognized no mediation between discourse and reference to an objective external reality: to argue about words *was* to argue about empirical entities. This was explicitly acknowledged in criminological texts. Dallemagne started his description of Lombrosian theories on the born criminal by saying "We will follow the Italian master's exposition and let him speak as often as possible, because, after all, the debate more often rests on words, formulas, and turns of phrases than on ideas or observations."[27] As if to confirm this assessment, Joly earnestly argued for the substitution of the word "accident" for the word "occasion" in Ferri's category of "occasional criminals," to get at the truth of the matter.[28] The same epistemological presupposition allowed Lombroso to use etymological arguments to prove criminological theses. He could thus demonstrate that crime among the "savages" was the general behavioral rule, and that criminal and noncriminal actions were originally indistinguishable by arguing as follows: "According to Pictet, our *crimen* derives from the sanskrit *karman* . . . which is equivalent to action, *kri*, to do. . . . In any case there is the word *apaz*, which in sanskrit means *sin*, and which seems to correspond to *apaz*, work, *opus*; the latin word *facinus* derives from facere, and *culpa* would derive, according to Pictet and Pott, from *kalp, klrp*, in sanskrit to do, to execute."[29]

This presupposed transparency of discourse is never as obvious as when a criminological thesis is elaborated through narration. Criminologists would not hesitate to use all the trappings of realist or naturalist novels to elaborate knowledge about "criminal man." Joly thus presented the category of the master swindler ("*l'escroc de haute marque*") in his *Le crime: Etude sociale* by telling this story:

Let us suppose a lucid and sufficiently strong intelligence: it lights the way to good and to evil equally. . . . But if the attention of the individual were to bear with a certain complacency towards evil . . . here are the dangers which he will have prepared or aggravated for himself.

First the consciousness of a certain intellectual superiority flatters the pride or encourages the sensuality of the delinquent, . . . it excites him to more refined pleasures. . . . One finds that his clients are decidedly "too stupid" and that it is impossible to resist the temptation to rob them: "they're only getting what they deserve."

He gets used to the idea of evil: the subtlety and agility of his conceptions then bring him to invent plans which seduce him. . . .

He reaches execution: his intellectual skill ensures the impunity of his first offenses which in turn will give him a false security and bury him deeper in evil. So it is that man reaches little by little those prodigies of audacity, cynicism and depravation whose stories will fill the columns of our newspapers. *In a footnote*: Example: the swindler Allmayer—at the moment when I am transcribing these lines.[30]

It is difficult to differentiate this passage of a scientific treatise from the outline of a novel which could have been written by the Goncourt brothers or Rosny. The opening sentences establish the premises of the world to be explored, one in which good and evil are clearly distinguished and quite obvious to the sensual hero of superior intellect. Direct quotations reveal his thoughts to the reader, and give him the appearance of a real-life individual. The final sentences describe the inevitable destiny of such types, who reach the darkest depths of depravation, to see their wrongdoing splashed all over the newspapers. Just as in popular novels of the time, the author can directly step in and footnote a proof of the truth of his tale: the case of Allmayer, the swindler so famous that the simple mention of his name suffices to invoke a similar tale. Allmayer was indeed well known, and his capture and trial in the fall of 1888 attracted international attention. The press coverage given to this case will be analyzed in chapter six, but it is possible to note from the outset that a widely romanticized press story could be presented as proof of a criminological thesis on a criminal type, which was itself elaborated through a narrative on master swindlers, constructed according to the rules of a popular literary genre. This kind of knowledge production through narration could only occur within an epistemological configuration which postulates that reality is a given, truth is absolute and cumulative, and discourse is transparent—otherwise, stories would be stories, and not criminological science.

Narratives did not represent passing aberrations in otherwise rigorously scientific texts. Their role was crucial, for they intervened whenever dogmatic or enthymematical discourse could no longer reason what had to be demonstrated: at that moment, short stories would take over and function as the *direct manifestation of reality*. For example, the postulate of a continuum between the biological, psychological, moral, and social dimensions of life made it necessary for criminal anthropologists to find criminal behavior in vegetables and in animals—and they did. If statistical evidence for such theories was not readily available, vast reserves of documented stories were. To prove that theft existed among animals, Lombroso presented this remarkable anecdote, which he had obtained from the works of Rousse:

> A big dog in Rennes was suspected of stealing and eating sheep; its master denied it, as he had never found it without its muzzle. One time he watched his dog carefully and saw that at nightfall it unfastened its muzzle by itself and after having devoured its prey, washed its snout in water, put back its muzzle and quickly returned to the kennel.
>
> This would constitute an example of premeditated theft in opposition to the now hereditary results of education in this domesticated species.[31]

These passages vividly demonstrate the invincible strength of criminology: virtually unfalsifiable, its scientific knowledge was infinitely expandable. Erasing their presence as texts, denying the constraints of discourse or scientific method, criminological texts could grasp whatever "immediately perceptible fact" suited the production of knowledge on "criminal man."

Although there were variations between schools, there was a general consensus as to the existence of a criminal *type*, whether he was called "born" or "incorrigible," a product of atavism or degeneration. This type was basically characterized through his lacks: lack of intelligence, sensitivity, morality, forbearance, sense of propriety, and respect of property and authority. Everyone agreed that he was ugly and often plagued with anomalies of the skull, brain, viscera and bone structure, to name but a few. Physiologically the criminal was distinguished by a general insensitivity (the senses being less developed, although his eyesight was considered acute) and a marked "disvulnerability": he was capable of enduring the worst treatment without suffering. Very often left-handed, he blushed with difficulty, and had an above average temperature and pulse. His physical insensitivity was doubled by a moral one: "the moral sense, in most of them, is absolutely lacking."[32] The criminal knew neither love, nor courage, nor remorse; he was frivolous, vain (liking jewelry and clothing), lazy, dirty, mean, vengeful, and ferocious; he loved orgies. Socially, criminals preferred to stay with their own race; they assembled in small hordes, used a particular slang language and had specific habits, such as tattooing: criminals also practiced primitive forms of art and literature, and had evolved a crude religion reminiscent of the one shared by savages and madmen. All of these characteristics naturally led the criminal type to commit illegal acts. Other influential factors were climate, race, prison, alcoholism, money, education, religion, age, sex, heredity, city life, and country life. Criminologists arrived at impressive quantifications of criminal activity. Ferri developed a "law of criminal saturation": "As a given volume of water at a definite temperature will dissolve a fixed quantity of chemical substance and not an atom more or less; so in a given social environment with definite individual and physical conditions, a fixed number of offenses, no more and no less, can be committed."[33]

What function did the notion of the criminal *type* play in the elaboration of criminology? A Bachelardian perspective would identify it as a verbal epistemological obstacle for criminology, which held it at a prescientific stage of development. Indeed, this notion did allow criminology to accomplish, in Bachelard's words, "this strange reversal which purports to develop thought by analyzing a concept, instead of implicating a particular concept in a rational thesis."[34] As the criminal type was considered real, but rarely found in actual criminals (even Lombroso could only spot it in four out of ten cases), it constituted what the author calls a *denkmittel*, an object both concrete and ideal, halfway between empiricism and scientific abstraction. Discourse analysis would reject this view of the type as a barrier preventing criminological knowledge from progressing to the discovery of scientific truth. The theoretical premises of this study would rather identify the criminal type as the end result of a general objectification process which authorized the establishment of new power relations based on criminological knowledge. A closer analysis of the extensions and implications of the criminal type will demonstrate that it was intended to transform the relations of power exercised in the judicial system; it made possible the preclusion of social and economic factors in the determination of crime; finally, it favored the development of totalitarian relations of power by allowing knowledge of the criminal to be transferred to other kinds of deviance.

◆

Knowledge and power By denying the notion of free will and posing that illegal acts were biosocially determined, criminology changed the rules for the administration of justice. The Classical school had defined it as an exercise in logic: justice would pass from the sovereign to the people through the person of the judge, whose function was restricted to the determination of guilt and the application of laws. With the new criminologists, the judge's role would be expanded considerably, for once the offender had been identified, the judge would then have to assess his or her degree of perversity, in order to select appropriate punishment. The syllogism of justice would be followed by examination procedures, with all the mechanisms of objectification and domination they entail.[35] The right to punish and the type of punishment to be administered would no longer be a matter of legal definitions based on a social contract between equals. The judge would base his verdict and sentence on his knowledge of "man," which authorized him to determine whether or not the convicted individual could be "cured" of his criminality. The powers of the judge thus derived from his knowledge—not from the community. "The essential branch which must enter in the course of juridical sciences is knowledge of man, of his soul, of his actions and dealings, normal or abnormal; moreover the instruction of jurists must include the lessons of psychology, anthropology, criminal psychology and psychopathology."[36] Criminologists called for the abolition of the jury, who could not possibly possess the expertise required for a diagnosis of the *temibilità* (the dangerousness) of the accused, or his or her correspondence to the criminal type. Only a small circle of men knowledgeable in criminological matters would determine the fate of the convicted criminals. The introduction of scientific knowledge about "criminal man" and the production of the born-criminal type thus transformed the theoretical grounds for repression, further restricted the circle of those empowered to dominate (because of their special knowledge), and virtually destroyed any limits to this power—once a person had entered the criminal justice system, the only way out would be to demonstrate to the expert administrators of social justice that he or she had been "cured."

If criminologists continually described their enterprise as a valiant attempt to uncover the truth,[37] Lombroso pointed to the practical advantages of scientific knowledge of the criminal type when he presented it as the best justification for the death penalty or life imprisonment.[38] The discoveries of criminological science identified death, transportation, life imprisonment, and sterilization as the only solutions for born criminals or "incorrigible" ones; Lombroso logically maintained that social defense required that born-criminal children also be institutionalized.[39] For all other criminals, whether by accident, occasion, or passion, sets of corrective and preventive measures were proposed. Among the former, perhaps the most important was the call for indeterminate sentences, whereby a criminal would be released from prison at the administration's discretion, when proper behavioral norms had been attained.

This will to normalize and standardize behavior extended to the sociocultural environment as a whole in emerging criminology. Tarde insisted that diversity in thought, ideals, or government in a nation necessarily increased its criminality: "The morality of a people is so narrowly linked to the fixity of its manners and customs, as in general that of an individual to the regularity of his habits, that we cannot be surprised to see periods troubled by great crises, nations stirred by long struggles between two religions, two civilizations, two parties, two armies, signal themselves by their exceptional criminality.[40] Ferri proposed "imprisonment for an indeterminate period" for any adult or minor engaging in "rebellion, revolt [or] resistance to authority."[41] Tarde went further and extended the field of criminality to include *any* deviation from the norm:

> Is it not true that, really to feel the importance of criminality, it is necessary to go behind the crimes and offenses registered in statistics to glimpse and guess at the half-crimes, the half-offenses, the infractions against usage and the violations unpunished by law, which swarm in fermenting nations. The *embryology of crime*, which rightly concerns the positivist school, must be studied in this manner in my opinion, that is *from the first and slightest individual dissidence in an until then rigidly conformist environment.*[42]

All of these theories and practical measures presented "occasional" crime as the outcome of administrative failures rather than inherent social conflicts. This is perhaps best illustrated by the series of pro-posed crime prevention measures, or "penal substitutes" as Ferri pre-ferred to name them, which usually took the form of direct antidotes to specific crimes: forgery should be eliminated by the use of metallic currency, which is harder to duplicate; larger numbers of toxicologists would prevent poisonings; better registration procedures would stop bigamy, while wider, illuminated streets, and the widespread use of alarm systems, safes, and security chains would prevent theft, as would the suppression of ghettos.[43]

Socialists such as Filippo Turati and Achille Loria criticized crimi-nal anthropology for its preclusion of political and economic factors. Loria accused Lombroso and his followers of refusing to recognize that the physical characteristics identified as signs of criminality were "simply the last detritus and external indications of a long erosive pro-cess worked out by economic conditions, mercilessly operating upon human life."[44] Describing crime as "a morbid emanation of capital-ist conditions," Loria also pointed to the class differences entrenched in the law: "The Italian code, likewise, inflicts very severe penalties upon theft and proceeds with vigour against strikers; while it treats with manifest indulgence a large number of crimes especially char-acteristic of the richer classes."[45] Loria identified morality, law, and politics as some of the most important "connective institutions," which made the oppressed class accept an economic order working against its interests.[46] Such Marxist criticisms of both criminal anthropology and the founding principles of the criminal justice system were relatively isolated and virtually ignored, finding no resonance in recognized forums of knowledge production or in governmental and administra-tive circles.

Criminologists were not totally blind to the economic dimension of certain forms of criminality. For example, Lombroso suggested: "since the great country estates, by perpetuating the wealth of the few, per-petuate also the illness and poverty of the many, why should they not be expropriated to the state? and why should not more prejudi-cial agrarian contracts be modified, and the peasants receive a larger share in the profits?"[47] Similarly, Ferri presented his penal substitutes as "the point of departure in passing to a social order . . . adopting the collective ownership of the means of production and labor, and . . . thus assuring really human conditions of life."[48] However, Ferri recog-nized that even these ultimate transformations would not prevent "a minimum of natural and atavistic criminality due to anthropological factors," which would have to be repressed.[49] Other criminal activity would be avoided in the future social order by an extremely efficient manipulation of individual desires and actions, made possible by scientific knowledge:

> To propose these equivalents for penalty amounts to saying this: It is necessary, in legislative dispositions (political, economic, civil, administrative, and penal), from the great institution down to the slightest details of its existence, to give the social organism an orientation such that human activity,—instead of being uselessly threatened with repression shall be constantly guided in an indirect manner into non-criminal ways, and such that a free overflow shall be offered to the energies and needs of the individual whose natural tendencies will be hurt as little as possible and who will be spared as much as possible the temptations and occasions of crime. This fundamental idea of the equivalents for penalties shows how necessary to the sociologist and to the legislator is the preparation in biological and psychological knowledge on which Spencer rightly insisted.[50]

Criminological discourse thus oscillated between extreme left- and right-wing theories of power: collective ownership of the means of production on the one hand, and, on the other, the execution of criminal types, the imprisonment for indeterminate periods of those who resisted authority, and institutional control over the "slightest details of existence" of the general population. This kind of discourse conflating left and right extremes has been analyzed by Zeev Sternhell, Jean-Pierre Faye, and others as typical of prefascism and fascism.[51] And indeed, Ferri, who had professed his socialism on May Day in 1894, and served as editor of the socialist newspaper *Avanti*, would follow Benito Mussolini (who had also been editor of *Avanti*) into fascism, and there know more acceptance for his theories than ever before.[52]

The particular value of the notion of the criminal type was that, in its abstraction, it could be applied to other social groups and justify their repression on scientific grounds. Criminologists were quick to recognize the working classes in general and women of all classes as physically, intellectually, and morally close to the criminal type. Their failure to reach the higher evolutionary stage of the cultured male elite was ascribed partly to physical constitution and partly to hereditary influences—and their attempts to acquire economic or political rights were identified as obvious manifestations of a latent criminality which, left unchecked, would bring the end of civilization. Tarde thus recognized agitation among workers as a major reason for the increase in crime rates, while Lombroso held a similar view toward women's rights movements:

> Concerning the public opinion which favors an increase in femi-
> nine political leagues and other feminine organizations of aggres-
> sive character, it is an error which will result in the lowering of
> the nature of women. . . .
>
> At home, and in elementary schools, there are enough occupa-
> tions of elevated character to retain women; their work is there far
> better than men's; and it is because housework and school work is
> presently improperly executed, that our civilization has fallen in
> physical degeneration, pauperism, and crime.[53]

Children were also described in relation to the criminal type. Like born criminals, children were lazy and improvident, cruel and vain; they indulged in games and alcohol, and used a particular slang. Said Lombroso, "The germs of moral insanity and of crime are found, not exceptionally but normally, in the first years of man . . . so much so that the child would represent a man deprived of moral sense, what alienists call a moral lunatic, and we [call] a born criminal."[54] Without proper training from authorities, children would *naturally* become ha-bitual criminals.[55] Criminological findings on children justified the im-position of correct behavior patterns in educational institutions—and the "slightest details of existence" would thus gradually be enmeshed in the domination processes authorized by criminology.

Crowds were perhaps the most successful application for crimino-logical apprehensions, for their description allowed a combination of the characteristics of primitivism, feminine emotionality, and childlike enthusiasm, which could then be generalized to the "lower orders," or indeed to the people as a whole. While the origins of this kind of description can be traced to Hippolyte Taine and his *Origines de la France contemporaine* (1868), it was Tarde who first raised the spe-cific relation between criminality and crowd psychology in his 1890 *Les lois de l'imitation*. He also presented papers on the question during the 1892 Congress in Brussels. Scipio Sighele expanded the subject with his *Psychologie des sectes* in 1894, and Gustave Le Bon's *Psychologie des foules* in 1895 marked the most widely recognized and acclaimed formulation of the theory. Le Bon's work was used by Freud, and its success continues to our time.[56] The following passage illustrates the amalgam of ideological maxims produced by descriptions of crowds; it also illustrates the desires of those who wrote such texts, and wished that workers and all women (whatever their class) would only keep their proper place, and fulfill their natural roles:

> The crowd holds within its unconscious hands the definitive fate of the world. Its share is immense; but it is a passive share. It is—in regard to the product which is civilization—the woman whose love arouses work and reward. It is for her that the hero works, as man works for woman; but just as a woman she cannot produce on her own. . . . And so should she have as unique function to love and serve the men of the elite, as a woman loves and serves her husband, but, on the contrary, the crowd is neither mother nor wife, she is only woman, and most often her gratitude consists in crucifying the saviors. . . .
>
> Barbarians—who were the great crowds of antiquity, as workers are the great crowds of our day—would assuredly not have built the edifice of Roman civilization; but when the edifice wavered, the Barbarians ran up to ruin it and render possible the construction of a new civilization with the remainders of the old colossus.[57]

The unconscious, impulsive, and powerful being produced by this text through a series of analogies represents the major social groups threatening the male bourgeois order. Crowds, workers, and women generally are described first and foremost through their dependent relation to the male elite. When a woman (or a crowd) is "neither a mother nor a wife," when she is "only a woman" (that is, unconnected to a male), she crucifies her saviors. When crowds of workers no longer observe their unique function of "loving and serving the men of the elite like a woman loves and serves her husband," they become hordes of invading barbarians, working to destroy the social and economic order.

While finding its most politically powerful extension in crowd psychology, the criminal type served numerous other functions. Lombroso used it to describe anarchists and men of genius, naturalist novelists to depict the "lower orders" in their inner-city dens, and Max Nordau to explain the extreme decadence of naturalist writers and impressionist painters, who equally bore the well-known stamp of degeneration characteristic of the criminal type.[58] This discursive reiteration of the type, its repeated discovery in various fields, endowed it with a high truth value. To invoke the criminal type could suffice to understand, classify, and solve practically any economic, political, social, or cultural threat to the established order—even when this threat lay in an inner evil haunting every reasonable man. Indeed, criminologists recognized a criminal essence existing independently of crime, which could be traced in many an honest man: "It is thus that individuals with latent criminal instincts pass for honest men all their lives: the moment has never arrived at which crime would be more useful to them."[59] In a fascinating paradox, this inner evil of the individual was associated with the unconscious crowd, acting on impulsive desires, primitive and childish, emotional and sexual.[60] Sighele illustrated this identification when he stated that all crimes were *collective*: "Is not the individual, even when acting alone, propelled, unbeknown to him and to ourselves, by an invisible and innumerable crowd, that of his ancestors, of his compatriots, of those who raised him, whose diverse influences combined and imagined in his brain, all of a sudden awaken together at certain moments, as a true interior multitude which swarms and ferments in a skull?"[61]

The criminal type thus indicates both the limits and the origins of the power exercised by a knowledgeable white male bourgeois elite. It marked the limits of the elite's power in that it represented all the forces which threatened insurrection at home, at work, and on the streets. Women and children or crowds of the "lower orders," even unconscious desires, were all virtual manifestations of the criminal type, which, if left uncontrolled, would rise up to destroy the elite and bring the end of civilization. The criminal type simultaneously served to generate power for the elite, for its production as an object of scientific knowledge allowed the elite to impose and justify its privileges.

With these broad powers authorized by criminological knowledge in view, it is now easier to understand why Lombroso's theory of atavism was so vehemently attacked not only by French and English criminologists, but also by several of the subgroups in positions of power. Both the sociological and anthropological schools of criminology accepted social Darwinist elaborations of the theory of evolution, whereby certain social or racial groups would either slide down or stay down the ladder of perfection. The French sociological school attributed criminality in civilized nations to the effects of degeneration, itself a product of heredity and milieu. The Italian school of criminal anthropology, while not denying these effects, added *atavism* as an important factor in the generation of criminals.

The difference between the schools was slight, but all important in its implications. Indeed, degeneration was considered as a slow process which could be halted and even reversed with proper management. Lower-class victims of degeneration could be nurtured back to health, elevated into civilization, while the criminals among them could be restored and reformed, through moral management, education, punishment, and discipline. Such a view opened infinitely expandable fields of power not only for prison officers but also for government agencies and philanthropic and church organizations. The French were conscious of the need to allow a locus and an object for the exercise of power. During the second congress both Herbette and Bertillon clearly stated that the theory of the born criminal could not be accepted by penitentiary administrators as it would relieve them of their efforts at rehabilitation and care of criminals.[62]

More importantly, pronouncing certain criminals incurable attacked the foundations of the elite's dominant position: if degeneration and devolution were considered common in the "lower orders," evolution and progressive refinement were conversely regarded as natural in the "higher" ones—the elite was born to lead, as the masses were to be led. Similarly, evolutionary processes called for the domination of the colored races by the white ones. Said Kovalevsky: "But there is again something other than the quantity of nervous elements; it is their quality. In this connection it is doubtful that the importance of heredity can be denied. We can state positively, in all safety, that the elements of a European, thanks to their secular culture, are more perfect than those of the Mongol, the Negro, etc."[63]

Charles Létourneau devised an effective scientific account of this natural superiority in his theory of the parallelogram of forces, outlined in his treatise entitled *Physiologie des passions* (1868). Like Lombroso, Létourneau rejected the notion of free will, and asserted that physical constitution determined moral and intellectual faculties: "*To each clear moral imprint corresponds an equally clear physical imprint.*"[64] However, Létourneau maintained that secular evolutionary processes had determined different levels of moral and mental development according to race, sex, and social position. On the basis of scores of measurements, he arrived at a rather predictable scale of relative development. The most perfect form of human evolution corresponded to the white middle-class male, followed by his lower-class counterpart: "On average, the brain is less developed in common people than in the more or less literate middle classes . . . and it is enormous in the men of truly superior intelligence."[65] The white female, approximately equal to the black African male (himself superior to the Australian), then followed; white European children were judged roughly equivalent to black adult males. Response to environmental stimuli was determined mechanically by the parallelogram of forces: "Any being, just as any body, while suffering multiple attractions of variable intensity, obeys to their resultant, the meaning of which is principally determined by the predominant force."[66] Whereas in the inferior sex, races, and classes, the predominant force was animal instinct, the white male elite was directed by its strongly developed intellectual and moral senses.[67] The theory of the parallelogram of forces thus offered all the advantages of biological explanations of racial and social class conflicts, while preserving the intellectual and moral superiority of the elite.

Lombroso's theory of atavism introduced elements of chance and fatality in hereditary influences, which dangerously restricted the power base of the established authorities. By doing so, he added a trait to the concept of "criminal man" which was not pertinent, indeed which was unacceptable, for his class's praxis and position. As argued by Luis Prieto, "in the construction of a concept . . . the characteristics of the object are kept or set aside depending on whether or not they 'count' for the practice necessarily underlying the concept. . . . The practice which is implied by any knowledge is of course not imposed by the object, but rather always emanates from the subject. However the subject is necessarily a social subject, in that his survival is organized within a group, and that consequently he must respect a certain legitimacy in force within the group."[68] Subgroups in positions of domination rallied together in violent opposition to Lombroso's theory of the born criminal as an *atavistic* throwback to prehistoric man, because the added trait of atavism threatened the legitimate basis for the exercise and justification of power in democratic capitalist countries such as France and England.

The difficulties which marked the institutionalization of criminology also become more readily understandable, in that this emerging discursive practice eventually proved to be a science with no object and no mandate of its own. Several other discourses (legal, penitentiary, police, and medical) had already produced a concept of criminality according to their institutional praxis, and the men employed by these institutions were not willing to give up their field for others to exploit. Moreover, crime and criminals are not usually a politically profitable subject: times are rarely good enough for politicians to run for office on a platform of heavy expenditures in the criminal justice system.[69] However, during times of political protest, the emergence of a scientific discourse centered on "criminal man" offers the promise of scientific solutions to political strife, by allowing criminal deviance to include organized opposition to established norms, through the notion of the criminal type. It would seem, therefore, that criminology's first function is to produce discourse on deviance, which helps to reaffirm existing relations of power—and that once this role has been carried through, it "naturally" (that is, politically) loses both academic and state support, and becomes an obsolete form of discourse.

The example of British penal reform in the early 1900s would tend to support this view. Indeed, if the British generally kept out of the official confrontations between the sociological and anthropological schools of criminology, they nevertheless monitored these developments very closely and incorporated all findings useful to their proclaimed pragmatic and common-sense approach to the "social question" in general, and crime in particular.[70] Throughout the century, various proposals were advanced to deal with the dangerous classes, and these usually included close supervision, the instigation of discipline, and, for the "residuum," outright seclusion. As argued by Jones, the goal was to distinguish between the deserving and undeserving poor, in order to integrate the former and exclude the latter; the many model dwellings projects and the settlement projects were emblematic of such efforts, and their mitigated success demonstrated the difficulty of extending disciplinary processes into the homes of the "million." Moreover, in spite of the backing of such noteworthy advocates as the economist Alfred Marshall, Reverend Barnett, and General Booth of the Salvation Army, the long held hope of permanently secluding the "residuum" proved to be politically unviable, when conceived in terms of class distinctions.[71]

However, a series of acts of Parliament in the early 1900s realized many of the proposals advanced by philanthropists and economists, and supported by criminological science. The 1908 Prevention of Crime Act, for example, instituted a semideterminate period of preventive detention of five to ten years for habitual criminals, that is, those convicted of at least three criminal offenses since the age of sixteen. This sentence would be added to the term of penal servitude given for the actual offense; release from preventive detention depended on administrative decisions, and was followed by a period of supervision for five years. The 1907 Probation of Offenders Act

Figure 2   Criminology Grid

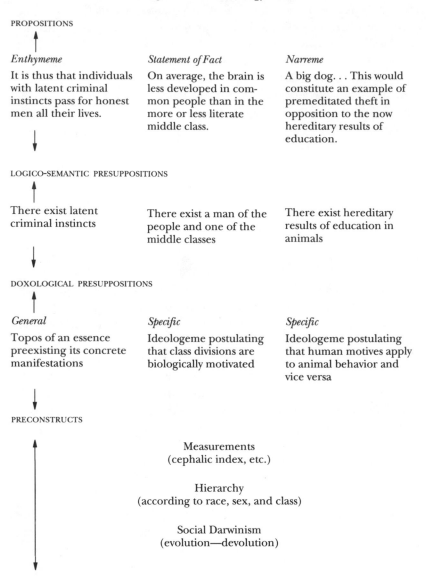

PROPOSITIONS
↑

Enthymeme	*Statement of Fact*	*Narreme*
It is thus that individuals with latent criminal instincts pass for honest men all their lives.	On average, the brain is less developed in common people than in the more or less literate middle class.	A big dog. . . This would constitute an example of premeditated theft in opposition to the now hereditary results of education.

↓

LOGICO-SEMANTIC PRESUPPOSITIONS
↑

There exist latent criminal instincts	There exist a man of the people and one of the middle classes	There exist hereditary results of education in animals

↓

DOXOLOGICAL PRESUPPOSITIONS
↑

General	*Specific*	*Specific*
Topos of an essence preexisting its concrete manifestations	Ideologeme postulating that class divisions are biologically motivated	Ideologeme postulating that human motives apply to animal behavior and vice versa

↓

PRECONSTRUCTS

Measurements
(cephalic index, etc.)

Hierarchy
(according to race, sex, and class)

Social Darwinism
(evolution—devolution)

EPISTEMOLOGICAL PRESUPPOSITIONS

Reality is a given—truth is absolute and cumulative; language is transparent

---

Most important object of knowledge produced: the criminal type, applicable to any group under domination, and authorizing vast powers of repression.

began a national professional network of supervision which ensured that released prisoners led an industrial and quiet life, that they lived in acceptable areas, did not mix with unacceptable characters, and, after its extension in 1914, refrained from consuming alcoholic beverages. Other measures worked to intensify procedures of regulation and control: the 1898 Inebriates Act allowed their detention for up to three years, depending on their character and antecedents, and this sentence could be imposed above the one given for their criminal offense; the 1913 Mental Deficiency Act allowed "moral imbeciles," that is, those who could not be trained to behave properly in other educational or penal institutions, to be detained (it also provided for the detention of any woman "in receipt of poor relief at the time of giving birth to an illegitimate child or when pregnant of such child").[72] These multiple measures allowed admission into the homes and families of large numbers of the "lower orders." Such measures, politically unacceptable when applied to a social class, became possible because of the new categories of deviance: no one, not even labor or socialist groups, could successfully defend "habitual criminals" or "moral imbeciles"— it had become, and largely still remains, rhetorically ineffective to be *for criminals*.[73]

Current research dealing with crime often has difficulty explaining the silence surrounding repressive measures targeted toward the "lower orders." David Garland, for example, notes this lack of protest by working-class organizations in *Punishment and Welfare*, and concludes that "this lack of resistance . . . would seem to raise some fundamental questions about the nature of the Labour movement in Britain and its relation to the classes it claims to represent."[74] The following chapters of this study will try to account for this situation by further exploring the mediating functions of criminality in social discourse. These analyses will outline how the fight against crime was critical to the redistribution of knowledge taking place in the nineteenth century (with the spread of literacy and the emergence of a mass-produced press), and fundamental to the establishment of new relations of power: the exclusion of the criminal served not only to contain certain segments of the population, but also, and more importantly, to discern the limits of a consensual "we," identified with "the people of the nation," or to that well-known character, "the public."

II THE PRESS

Where did "the public" first appear? The most succinct answer to that question would be: in the columns of the penny dailies. A slightly broader perspective would consider that the gradual development of the technologies of power made possible by the discovery of "the population" toward the end of the eighteenth century resulted in the recognition of the public as a major figure in the exercise of power during the last third of the nineteenth century: the public then started (and continues) to act as silent backer or as justification for diverse administrative and political strategies, and the press was (and continues to be) recognized as the most obvious locus for the manifestation of its will.[1] Nothing, however, could have seemed more difficult or unlikely at the beginning of the nineteenth century.

At that time, the prospect of literate masses—let alone literate masses with ready access to a free press—provoked concern, and occasionally outright panic, among political, economic, and religious men of authority. It was feared that should "the million" be able to read, the natural order of society would be irremediably upset, existing economic and political systems would collapse, and civilization itself would be threatened. More pragmatically, conservatives worried that the "lower orders" would learn to be discontented with their lot in life. Well into the nineteenth century the notion of "teaching their heads to reason rather than their hands to work" was denounced as a certainly dangerous, and possibly seditious tendency.[2] Nevertheless, a politically "free," mass-produced, and cheap press, bringing "all the facts" to the people, was eventually developed in both England and France, under the approving eye of the established order. It could then be taken for granted that universal literacy and a free press meant progress, economic prosperity, and political stability—the pernicious tool of sedition had officially become the first safeguard of freedom and democracy. The following chapters will begin to investigate the many factors which allowed this remarkable reversal to take place, and examine more specifically the vital role played by discourse on crime and criminals in the process.

Throughout this long debate, those for and against widespread literacy argued their cases in relation to law and order: criminality would surely surge, or virtually disappear, with a literate people with access to a free, mass-produced press. The necessary correlations between knowledge and power were an acknowledged, and indeed quite obvious fact of life for those living at the beginning of the Age of Education. Scientific, artistic, economic, political, and religious attainments had always been the privilege of the dominant classes, while folklore, a largely oral tradition, consisted of different kinds of understandings appropriate for the social position of its holders. The people themselves saw little use for book learning. Sending their children to school brought them no apparent advantage in life, while it did deprive the family of much needed assistance in its daily fight against misery.[3]

With demographic expansion, industrialization, and urbanization, together with the French revolution and its aftermath in England, existing social structures were radically transformed, and the power relations which had kept different kinds of knowledge separate no longer held. The French revolutionary government recognized the natural right of every man to acquire and communicate knowledge freely (article eleven of the Declaration of the Rights of Man). In England the "Wilkes and Liberty" episode of the 1760s served as catalyst in the freedom of knowledge question. In the first issue of his paper the *North Briton* (1762), Wilkes strongly asserted the right of the people to full knowledge of the workings of government, through the medium of a free press: "The liberty of the Press is the birthright of a Briton, and is justly esteemed the firmest bulwark of the liberties of this country."[4] Years of agitation, riots, and persecutions eventually led to Wilkes's "greatest victory." Although it remained a criminal breach of privilege, Parliament made no effort to stop the publication of its proceedings after 1771, and the people's right to know had been acquired in practice.

These landmark occurrences, however, did not signal the beginnings of carefully planned programs for the spread of literacy or the establishment of a free press. As a rule, major advances in popular education were prompted by the competition taking place between subgroups scrambling to inform the people correctly (or propagandize them effectively, depending on one's perspective), in order to reinforce their position of dominance, and, perhaps more importantly, prevent other interest groups from increasing their own. Similarly, relaxations in government controls over the press were usually the result of struggles between political groups, the outcome of lobbying by economic interests, or the consequence of strategic positioning on the part of particular publications, rather than the achievement of policy decisions on freedom of speech.

These various confrontations made possible the delimitation of a new discursive practice, with a distinct status, a specific mandate, and its own object: the mass-produced press, as fourth estate, would express the voice of "the People of the Nation," and further democracy, by disseminating "objective information." Resulting from numerous economic, political, and social developments, the emergence of this discursive practice effected a general redistribution of the relations of knowledge and power in social discourse, and allowed the public to assume the prominent place of a consensual "we," forged largely, as further analyses will show, through its opposition to crime (economic, political, moral) and its perpetrators. The next chapters, therefore, will move away from "criminal man" as an object of knowledge to analyze further the mediating functions of criminality in the establishment of norms. The study of the preconditions of emergence will focus on the battle for the education of the "lower orders," and its two main fronts: the production of proper knowledge and reading material for the adult population, and the development of a national education system for their children. The analysis of the conditions of emergence of the mass-produced press will focus on the economic and political factors which determined the limits of its sayable; how did the "new journalism" come to be identified as necessarily "featherbrained," and nevertheless indispensable to the economic and political strength of the nation? The final chapter of part two will examine the textual construction of crime reports and investigate their role in the apprehension of "criminal man," and the determination of his collective, national opposite.

4 PRECONDITIONS OF EMERGENCE: RISING MASS LITERACY

◆

The case for literacy: elementary education against crime At the beginning of the age of "March of Mind," popular education was viewed as part of a greater problem, that of the development of efficient social management policies to maintain the established order, safeguard property, and ensure economic prosperity. Opponents argued that "a little knowledge is a dangerous thing." Universal elementary education would only breed social unrest and criminal activity, for it would raise the expectations of the poor beyond their natural station in life. A letter to the *Gentleman's Magazine* thus warned in 1797 that "There are, perhaps, more criminals among the class of men who have had a superficial education than among those who have never been taught either to write or read. The laborious occupations of life must be performed by those who have been born in the lowest stations; but no one will be willing to undertake the most servile employment, or the meanest drudgery, if his mind is opened, and his abilities increased, by any tolerable share of scholastic improvement."[1] Advocates insisted that sound learning in proper principles would actually fight criminality, pauperism, drunkenness, and immorality. In *A New and Appropriate System of Education for the Labouring People* (1806), Patrick Colquhoun stated that "the importance of giving a right bias to the minds of the rising generation is an object of the very first importance, since it is but too evident that the great increase of criminal offenses, as well as habits of idleness, and the corruption of morals among the inferior classes of society, . . . can be attributed only to a general inattention to the religious education and moral habits of the children of the lower classes of the people."[2]

Similar arguments would be repeated throughout the century. During the 1840s the London Statistical Society presented tabulations proving a direct inverse relation between education and crime. As late as 1881 W. Stanley Jevons insisted that the initial cost of the spread of knowledge through public libraries was "likely, after the lapse of years, to come back fully in the reduction of poor-rates and Government expenditure on crime."[3] The sheer longevity of such arguments signals their high profitableness in social discourse. Indeed, identifying strikes, riots, rick burning, and pauperism as crimes due to immorality or ignorance allowed those in positions of authority to be officially concerned with the "social question," and wholeheartedly engaged in its resolution, while never dealing with its economic or political dimensions. For example, Place told the Select Committee on Drunkenness in 1834 that if the stamp duties had been abolished three years earlier, thereby affording cheap knowledge to the people, he had "not the smallest doubt there would not have been a single trades' union either in England or Scotland."[4] Such reasoning not only implied that trade unions resulted from a mistaken understanding of economic problems, but that their unfortunate existence could be prevented with proper communication within the established economic system. The double argument presenting social protest as a crime, and education (through cheap schools and newspapers) as its remedy thus reaffirmed the value of the established order as absolute—that is, not related to social, economic or political factors, but rather correlated to "man's" progress toward truth or enlightenment.

As the century progressed, the links between capitalist, philanthropist, and educationalist became clearer: an all inclusive program for the distribution of proper knowledge at school, in the factories, and in the homes of the "lower orders" would impede criminal behavior, reinforce established institutions, bolster the economy through improved workers, and open new channels through which growing state bureaucracies could reach, discipline, and supervise the people. However, major disagreements arose when it came to defining the nature and amount of knowledge suitable for the "lower orders." Landowning interests, judging that the laboring poor should only learn deference and discipline, were often opposed to church-run schools teaching them how to read the Scriptures. Rival church organizations established competing school networks in England in order to win the greatest amount of followers.[5] In France similar battles were fought between the state and the Catholic Church, in their race to propagate respect for proper values, that is, either civic virtue or Christian morality.[6]

In spite of these internal struggles, all concerned recognized the teaching of morality as the proper foundation of any educational system, as immorality was thought to be the cause of crime and pauperism. An indispensable prerequisite for entry into the teaching profession was moral certification, by the Anglican Church in England, and by the state in France, where under the 1793 law a certificate of civic virtue was compulsory.[7] Political imperatives were never far behind moral goals. When the Minister of Public Instruction François Guizot introduced his 1833 law which obliged every village to maintain an elementary school, he made his ultimate objective quite clear to his prefects: "We have tried to create in every commune a moral force which the government can use at will."[8]

In both countries political and economic principles favorable to the maintenance of the established order were transmitted in the name of morality. In *Easy Lessons on Money Matters*, written by Richard Whateley, Archbishop of Dublin and one of the Irish commissioners of national education, poor elementary school pupils learned the proper response to class discrepancies: "When you see a rich man who is proud and selfish, perhaps you are tempted to think how much better a use you would make of wealth if you were as rich as he. I hope you would: but the best *proof* that you can give that you would behave well if you were in *another's* place, is by behaving well *in your own*. God has appointed to each his own trials, and his own duties."[9] In France the government's need to legitimate the new social order and its will to drive out the Catholic Church's influence in education (and elsewhere) prompted the production of a secular version of morality, "civil instruction," to be disseminated throughout the nation in school textbooks. In his *La première année d'instruction civique* (1880), Ernest Lavisse thus explained: "*Society* (Summary): (1) French society is ruled by just laws, because it is a democratic society. (2) All the French are equal in their rights; but there are inequalities among us that stem from nature or from wealth. (3) These inequalities cannot disappear. (4) Man works to become rich; if he lacked this hope, work would cease and France would decline. It is therefore necessary that each of us should be able to keep the money he has earned."[10] Both versions of moral training absorbed individual aspirations in a broader and better whole: God's will, or the good of the nation. Patriotism was strongly advocated; the French revolutionary government renamed its schoolmasters *instituteurs*, because their primary function was to institute the nation—to generate a population which would speak French, count metric, and be enlightened by the principles of republicanism.[11] Military service and war were presented as sacred duties toward the nation. Social inequalities were thus simultaneously acknowledged and demeaned—or rather integrated in a moral framework which cut off avenues to social transformations.[12]

Developments in key economic sectors (agriculture, the steel and textile industries) lessened the demand for child labor and created a need for skilled workmen: by the 1860s disproportionate numbers of children were out of work and out of school, and the need to meet the new requirements of the workplace made their education a vital concern.[13] Expanding business and government organizations required clerical and administrative staff, as did large financial and banking institutions engaging in international transactions. Following international exhibitions bringing home the threat of foreign competition, and in the wake of the Franco-Prussian War, a national education system came to be recognized as a worthwhile investment for social stability and prosperity.

Costs, however, were kept to a minimum. Indeed, in spite of the grand designs of government and religious authorities involved in education, the actual praxis of instructing the "lower orders" was perhaps best described by a dame schoolteacher who said "It's little they pay us, and it's little we teaches (*sic*) them."[14] Conditions in elementary schools in both England and France have been described by historians as appalling, and producing very meager results, well into the nineteenth century. As late as 1863, only 59 percent of French school buildings (or rooms) were considered barely adequate.[15] As a rule, the teaching profession attracted social misfits who could not find other employment, and were willing to work in overcrowded, ill-ventilated rooms, teaching vast numbers of children for little money and less prestige.[16]

Teachers and students of the "lower orders" were meant to acquire minimal skills, appropriate for their natural station in society. This attitude was institutionalized in England with the implementation of the recommendations of the Newcastle Commission of 1858–61, which had been set up to find appropriate measures "for the extension of sound and cheap elementary instructions to all classes of the people."[17] The system of payments by results which ensued from its recommendations had radical repercussions. As government grants were made dependent on test results of children examined by inspectors on the three Rs, most teaching was limited to drilling pupils to perform well on the exam. This system was denounced vehemently by Matthew Arnold, who served as school inspector. He lamented the fact that tests were made on a few prescribed texts: "The circle of the children's reading has thus been narrowed and impoverished all the year for the sake of a *result* at the end of it, and the *result* is an illusion."[18]

However from another perspective, the system was perfect, for it cut costs considerably, and limited learning in directly proportionate measures. The "antiknowledge" fostered in children who were drilled until they were able to read texts without understanding their meaning was well suited for their intended social station. The ultimate aim of the payments by results plan was clearly expressed by its inventor, Robert Lowe: "The lower classes ought to be educated to discharge the duties cast upon them. They should also be educated that they may appreciate and defer to a higher cultivation when they meet it."[19] The people were not meant to be enlightened, but rather equipped with the ability to read the Bible or penny newspapers, and there find all the intellectual nourishment they needed. The very thought of education allowing widespread social mobility was completely unacceptable for those in power during the Third Republic, as it had been throughout the entire century. *Déclassement* was feared as a major social problem, causing a variety of ills ranging from criminality to revolution.[20]

Thus, the many struggles between various subgroups attempting to solidify their position of dominance and to prevent crime in the "lower orders" through education, the practical experience of establishing and teaching a curriculum where morality and patriotism were prominent, and the ever present will to cut costs eventually resulted in the development of methods of teaching which were known to be profitable to the state and the economy—education acts could then be passed without difficulty, in the name of morality, and for the good of the nation.

◆

Making them know better; "giving the right bias"   The beliefs and behavior of the adult population of the "lower orders" were of even greater concern to government and religious authorities who disseminated their policies or doctrines through tracts and leaflet campaigns. Religious tracts were produced and distributed in untold millions by numerous agencies.[21] Religious periodicals of every description, from *The Methodist Magazine* (1807), to *The Record* (Anglican, 1818), and *The Latter-Day Saints' Millennial Star* (1840), propagated their didactic message along with entertaining tales of heart-moving conversions, strange animals, and horrible deaths, to ensure wider audiences. Governments adopted similar procedures of broad distribution in order to incite mass appeal for their leaders or policies.[22]

Numerous philanthropic agencies entered the fray for the minds of the adult population. Hannah More's Cheap Repository Tract movement (1795–98) served as model for many of their ventures. The principles directing this group of enterprising Evangelicals were rather straightforward. Circulation figures of radical pamphlets proved that the people *were* reading, however hesitant the ruling classes remained as to whether or not they should read. The main objective then was to counterbalance irreligious and seditious writings by appropriate ones. Poems, ballads, and stories containing a rather blatant message of social subservience were published in the form of the material they were meant to drive out of the country, as tracts and broadsheets illustrated with woodcuts, and sold cheaply by hawkers along with their usual ware. Although sales figures broke every record of the publishing industry, their success in convincing the "lower orders" that their lives hid a "beauteous upper side" to be known in the "world of light" is not easily determined.[23] Radical opponents of the movement were quick to suggest domestic uses of a basic kind for the paper tracts, which they denounced as attempts to justify oppressive political and economic measures.[24] Perhaps the most important point of the entire campaign was that industrial and political circles began to realize (as the Church had known all along) the importance of designing the "right" kind of knowledge for the people, and to gain first-hand experience on how to produce and market the religious, political, and economic beliefs considered indispensable for the maintenance of social order.[25] These lessons would prove vital for the development of a mass-produced press.

Almost every decade brought forth a new strategy to produce the right bias in the common people through the introduction of cheap and wholesome reading matter in their homes. Family periodicals such as *The Family Herald* (1843) or *Eliza Cook's Journal* (1849) could divert thought from politics to the niceties of life: a smattering on marvelous technical developments, a little about foreign countries and customs, some thoughts on home management and cooking, a note on etiquette, and gradually all minds in the nation would be elevated into innocuousness. Other ventures into the minds of the masses included campaigns for cheap books and public libraries (offering strictly controlled and limited selections of suitable works), the various activities of the Society for the Diffusion of Pure Literature among the People, and those of its reverse, police agency, the Society for the Suppression of Vice, as well as the establishment of adult education organizations, such as the Mechanics' Institutes or Working Men's Colleges.[26] In France the Société de Saint-Vincent-de-Paul, a Catholic philanthropic organization, operated along similar lines, publishing 125,000 monthly copies of its *Petites Lectures Illustrées*, in an attempt to limit the circulation of crime stories and pornographic material. Protestant groups were equally involved in such work.[27]

Radical working-class organizations shared the belief that knowledge was power; Richard Carlisle exhorted the readers of his *Republican* (October 4, 1820) to "endeavour to progress in knowledge, since knowledge is demonstrably proved to be power." From the radical press of 1816–19, to the "War of the Unstamped Press" of 1831–36, to the Chartist agitation and the organization of trade unions, from Carlisle and Cobbett to Hetherington and Lovett, a single slogan was constantly used in the fight for a free press and radical reform: knowledge is power. "Moral-force" Chartists, led by William Lovett, demanded education as a human right, and recognized it as an indispensable component for the spread of justice and happiness.[28] Skilled Parisian artisans started to demand education as a right as important as the right to strike or to earn fair wages by mid-century—some hoped that with the spread of knowledge would come the fusion of classes.[29] Leaders of working-class political associations, mutual improvement clubs, corresponding societies, and trade unions worked not only to inform, but also to mobilize their class and make it use the power of knowledge to change society. For example, Hetherington's writing activities with the *Poor Man's Guardian* (1831) were doubled with involvement with the National Union of the Working Classes.[30]

Such developments worried political elites who were painfully aware that their power rested on the delicate balance achieved when private opinions could be expressed in public, while public opinion remained solidly on the side of established governments. Numerous attempts were made to "write down" the publications (a strategy made famous by religious and philanthropic agencies): Cobbett's twopenny *Register* (1816), for example, was countered by a governmental *Anti-Cobbett, or, Weekly Patriotic Register* (1817). When such methods failed, more direct ones were applied. In England the government's main weapons against critical papers were rising stamp duties and advertisement taxes, and prosecutions for libel and seditious writings; all of these were increasingly used throughout the century.[31] However, after hundreds of prosecutions had been met with increased sales of unstamped newspapers (to the point where in 1836 their circulation exceeded that of the stamped press), commercial publishing interests and certain members of the political sphere began to view the taxes as an exacerbating factor of—and not the solution to—the problem of a radical popular press.[32] Philanthropic and religious organizations shared this view, as their ventures into the minds of the million were constantly slowed by financial pressures resulting from taxation. Knight's *Penny Cyclopaedia*, published in weekly instalments from 1833 to 1844, ended with a loss of £30,788, with £42,000 spent on content (text and illustrations) and £16,500 spent on paper duty. Knight, who financed the venture himself, was a prominent campaigner for the repeal of the taxes on knowledge.[33]

In 1851, under the direction of Milner-Gibson, a House of Commons Select Committee on the Newspaper Stamp was established. Richard Cobden conducted most of the questioning and friendly witnesses, middle-class liberals involved in education and reform, clergymen, and respectable leaders of the publishing industry testified that, in their view, cheap publications would reduce crime, pauperism, and drunkenness, while bringing general enlightenment, social order, and progress.[34] Reverend Thomas Spencer (Herbert Spencer's uncle) brought the argument full circle when he stated that it was God's will that the people read cheap newspapers.[35] Several attempts were necessary for the Parliament to abolish the duties (which had been reduced in 1833 and 1836): the Advertisement Tax in 1853, the Newspaper Stamp in 1855, and the Paper Duty in 1861. What the 1836 act had not achieved was finally made possible: a cheap daily press soon emerged, with the *Daily Telegraph* taking the lead.

In France the inalienable human right to freedom of knowledge and speech was substantially qualified by the workings of government. Between 1789 and 1870 some 140 legislative measures were taken regarding the press; each new government as a rule started its term by liberating the press to some degree, and then quickly reimposed measures to limit the extent of free speech. The extremes to which both the press and the government were willing to go were demonstrated in the July Revolution. In the face of turmoil, political leaders identified the press as the first enemy to be stopped: in his report to Charles X, the Minister of Justice Chantelauze affirmed that the press was "by nature" the main, if not the exclusive, cause of social unrest, and was responsible for turning public opinion against the monarch and the ministry.[36] The Ordinance of July 26 suspending the liberty of the press was met with protests by journalists and calls for rebellion. The revolution that followed confirmed the fears regarding the strength that could be mustered through press channels. In England as well, agitation for universal male suffrage during the thirties and forties kept warning the political elite of the need to educate properly the constantly rising "lower orders." The Reform Act of 1867 made the education of the masses a question of political survival.[37] And more than anything—more than schools, libraries, or cheap encyclopedias—the press was considered as the most promising channel through which to capture—enlighten, direct, inform, whatever—the minds of the people.

◆

Finding the mean: shilling shockers, police gazettes, and penny dailies   While the fear of crime in all its forms, from immorality to revolution, propelled political, religious, and philanthropic organizations in their efforts to give the right bias to the minds of the masses, business interests were busy making a profit from the love of crime, or more precisely of crime stories. The development of this taste into a large industry was eventually a factor of primary importance in the preparation of the grounds for a commercially based mass press.

Tracts, broadsheets, and ballads, *canards* and *occasionnels* were the cheapest and most common reading material available to the people. Dating back to the fifteenth century, these single sheets, illustrated with woodcuts and sold cheaply on the streets, circulated most widely during the first half of the nineteenth century. Apart from news of crimes and punishments, these tracts brought tidings of great discoveries, royal births and deaths, natural catastrophes and miracles, vicious attacks by wild or rabid animals, as well as scandalous stories of illicit romances, household hints, and calendars.[38] When no actual event could provide the necessary subject matter for such copy, fictional ones ("cocks") were used with equal success. James Catnach broke existing publishing records with execution papers, broadsheets, and ballads of the most electrifying kind, based on fact and fiction, and churned out by hack writers paid by the line. Thus, fictional and factual stories were written in the same style, on the same themes, very often by the same authors: popular novelists were generally successful journalists, and vice versa.[39] A single publication could offer both kinds of stories without crossing any distinct categorical barriers, as illustrated by titles such as *Bell's Penny Dispatch, Sporting and Police Gazette, and Newspaper of Romance, and Penny Sunday Chronicle.*

Crime novels were immensely popular, and deep concern was constantly voiced for the people's passion for the publications of the *Bibliothèque bleue* or for the sixpenny leaflets packing all the murders, thrills, and adventures typical of the works of Clara Reeve, Ann Radcliffe, or Matthew Gregory Lewis in thirty-six pages. The hole-in-the-wall publication houses of Salisbury Square also published novels in serial parts in the 1820s (a practice taken up in the 1850s in France), to make the poor able to afford their love for tales of murder, rape, incest, sadism, and torture, all in the thrilling decors of ruined castles in German forests, isolated convents, damp cellars, and gloomy underground passageways. In the 1830s and 1840s, although gothic novels continued to be ever popular, "social realism" invaded popular fiction, and dark German dungeons were exchanged for dark English or French criminal ghettoes, making murder a truly national pastime. "Factual reports" of criminal activity had increased in the 1820s, with various police gazettes, the *Gazette des Tribunaux* (1825), and the publication of the part fact, part fiction memoirs of Vidocq (1828–29), the ex-criminal turned police informer and then investigative agent for the *Sûreté*; such publications often served as inspiration for fictional urban crime stories.

Sunday newspapers provided their popular audience with a mixture of crime reports, crime stories, sports news, and general information. After the radical press had been quashed in England by the Six Acts in 1819, they were also the principal medium for the expression of radical political thought. However, as noted by Altick, it is difficult to ascertain whether Sunday newspapers owed their radical tone to political or economic motives, as scandalous details of state misbehavior were sure circulation boosters.[40] Whatever motives guided their development, Sunday newspapers allowed the empirical discovery of an immensely profitable content (a political, crime, sports, and general news mixture) to be refined. A truly mass market could not be far away.

In France, where as a rule all forms of publishing were tightly controlled, the government and the press were eventually caught in a dilemma unprofitable to both: subsidized papers lauding the government had few readers, while the development of a press industry with a national readership was impeded by legal and financial pressures which limited profits and kept the price of newspapers high. Two major developments originating from the press provided a way out of this stalemate situation. The first was the development of a stronger commercial basis for the press, through increased advertisements, as pioneered by Emile Girardin in *La Presse* (1836). The second was the development of a new product, "objective information" (as opposed to political opinion) which could simultaneously satisfy the demands of a mass market and the exigencies of constituted authorities. The launching of Moise Polydore Millaud's *Le Petit Journal* (1863) marked the beginning of this development. In both occurrences the public's love of (and the government's tolerance for) crime stories proved to be indispensable.

Girardin sold his paper at half the usual rate in order to transform the newspaper from an expensive and restricted product into an ordinary commodity, to be consumed daily by large segments of the population; lost revenue was recuperated through increased advertisements. The concept was simple enough, and was exploited by papers in England (most notably by *The Times*) and in the United States (with Benjamin Day's *New York Sun* in 1833). Girardin's huge financial success derived from his talent for pleasing both readers (with prestigious smatterings of "*culture générale*") and advertisers (with large circulation figures), while ensuring his paper's political survival (with a consistent middle of the road policy).[41] Efforts to broaden the reading public brought innovations in press content; one of the major weapons in this competition for middle- and lower middle-class readers was the publication of *romans-feuilletons*, and certainly one of the most famous was Eugène Sue's *Les mystères de Paris*. The events surrounding this novel's publication deserve description, as they illustrate most clearly how various political and economic interests could be made to converge and thus gradually delimit the grounds for building a consensual "we," through the discovery of profitable ways to process crime, misery, and injustice in the press.

Like many authors of popular novels, Sue came from a prominent middle-class family, and at first resorted to writing for financial considerations. Under pressure from creditors he started *Les mystères de Paris* without any overall plan, as a novel on the dangerous classes. It was published, primarily for circulation purposes, by the conservative and legitimist newspaper *Le Journal des Débats*, and ran for a year and a half (1842–43). To the great astonishment of all concerned, *Les mystères de Paris* was read by all classes: the highbrow readers of *Le Journal des Débats* shared their fascination for prince Rodolphe and Fleur de Marie with the "lower orders" themselves, who recognized in Sue the first author to describe their misery. Hailed by socialists as the "writer of the people," Sue gradually became convinced of his mission, and integrated socialistic theories promoting cooperative movements, banks for the poor, and other such plans in his fiction. Bitterly denounced by moralists and conservatives as a degenerate poison sickening the soul of the nation, the novel was nevertheless devoured by members of all classes, bringing fame and fortune to the author, and high profits to the *Journal*.

From the outset, the apparent paradox of such a wide appeal can be partially resolved by the assumption of varying reading practices. As noted by Angenot in his analysis of *Les mystères*, working-class readers who embraced the story as a true representation of their lives and unabashedly wrote the author to suggest ideas for future episodes experienced a different kind of reading than did the closet middle- and upper-class readers who relished the action packed stories as a slightly caddish and yet agreeable pastime.[42] More importantly, the narrative itself allowed for different readings to be ideologically satisfactory all around. Now characterized as typically bourgeois paternalistic or utopian reformist, Sue's writings blamed most social injustice and misery on corrupt upper-class individuals and legislative shortcomings.[43] Thus, working-class readers could derive some satisfaction from seeing urban misery exposed in an elitist newspaper such as *Le Journal des Débats*, while upper-class readers could find their basic belief in progress justified, as patchwork reforms were presented as viable solutions to social problems shown as temporary aberrations.

Nevertheless, Sue's novels preoccupied established authorities. His writings and their effect on the working class were blamed for the 1848 revolution; in 1850 the Riancey law imposed a stamp on any newspaper publishing *feuilletons*; Sue's entire opus was placed on the *Index* in 1852. However it was obvious that the novelist had hit upon something golden with his tale. By watering down the descriptions of urban slums and deleting socialistic theories of reform, a product could be achieved which would satisfy a wide market, bring high profits to newspaper owners, leave political circles virtually untouched, and, most importantly, provide a form of entertainment which cut across class distinctions. The works of authors such as Alexandre Dumas and Paul Féval, G. W. M. Reynolds, and James Malcom Rymer, which perfectly met these requirements, quickly developed a mass market without any persecution. Thus, the emergence of social realism in newspaper crime novels in the 1830s and 1840s shows how various economic, political, ideological, and narrative pressures gradually determined an acceptable model for profitable and entertaining discourse on crime, which had the effect of producing a transclass consensus. At this stage the interdependence between popular press and fiction, and their mutual reliance on crime stories to attract readers, were paramount. However, stamp duties prevented a truly cheap daily press from emerging in France until the publication of Millaud's *Le Petit Journal* in 1863.

It was by publishing news only, objective information rather than partisan views, that Millaud was able to avoid the stamp duty, lower the price of his newspaper, and thereby push Girardin's principle of selling more by selling cheaply to unprecedented levels. The paper adopted all the time-tested formulas of popular literature to translate its official program of news coverage into a modern broadsheet format.[44] *Le Petit Journal* thrived on crime reports: its coverage of the famous Tropmann murders boosted sales from 357,000 when the first body was found (September 23, 1869), to an unprecedented 467,000 when the seventh victim was discovered.[45] Crime novels equally helped its popularity, with favorite authors like Alexis Ponson du Terrail (of "Rocambole" fame) and René du Pont-Jest. One of its main assets was the columnist Timothée Trimm (a pseudonym for Napoléon Lespès), known throughout the capital by posters highlighting his long red hair and thick mustache, his round hat, and huge gold chain. With his daily column taking the whole front page, Trimm became a national celebrity: a brand of champagne and a polka were named after him, buttons were stamped with his effigy, and a pipe was molded after his features.[46] The marketing abilities necessary to produce this national cultural figure were matched by unsurpassed business and organization skills, which effectively eliminated the paper's main rivals.[47] The only possible competition came from the governmental *Moniteur*, which stole Trimm by doubling his salary.

It was only logical that competition should come from the government, for *Le Petit Journal*'s nonpolitical stance in fact served the established order well, if only by distracting masses of readers from politics, providing them with a shared cultural experience, and feeding them stories of terrible murders and scandalous romances as objective information. When the Third Republic officially freed the press with its 1881 law, experience had shown that the best way to neutralize the press was to allow it to develop as a commercial enterprise. When the Press Charter was finally tabled in the Chamber, it was passed by 448 votes to 4. Although some items were eventually debated, the major problem at times was to get the Chamber's attention—by then, the issue of a free press no longer posed any problem.[48]

Thus, by the last quarter of the nineteenth century, knowledge and truth were officially free in England and France. In both countries the state provided universal education and a free press was allowed to emerge, unhampered by political controls, and produced at a price which eventually would make it accessible to the nation as a whole. With these developments, the production and dissemination of knowledge ceased to be considered as essentially political activities. The old fighting mottos of "knowledge is power" were replaced by phrases presenting the pursuit of knowledge as an essentially pure endeavor, separated from immediate social and political concerns—*Lux et Veritas Floreant* could adorn school buildings. A national educational system and press allowed the concept of a national community of interests to make more sense. Newspapers could present editorials or report political speeches on the needs of the nation, even though that part of the English nation educated in state elementary schools and reading illustrated police gazettes had very little in common with those educated at Oxbridge and reading *The Times*. Yet these divisions were made insignificant: because knowledge was free, the choices people made—whatever their social origins—could be seen as reflective of their individual penchant, not of class differences. Free schools and a free press acted as a buffer zone between those in positions of authority and the people, who now had only themselves to blame for their ignorance: if the lower orders systematically turned to trashy novels and papers rather than the classics and *The Times*, their lack of power was only natural.

5 CONDITIONS OF EMERGENCE: RUNNING THE SHOW

◆

Economic and political determinants of the press business   The golden age of the press in England and France was one of unprecedented expansion. Newspaper sales rose dramatically: there was a fivefold increase in the circulation of Parisian dailies (and a tenfold increase of provincial dailies) between 1875 and 1914, while sales in England multiplied by at least 600 percent after 1856.[1] Unprecedented profits were reaped in this ever expanding market. With the price per issue and the French franc remaining stable, the gross profits made by *Le Petit Parisien* increased 55 times between 1880 and 1914, going from 85,000 to almost 5 million francs.[2] Before the harder times caused by the split over Home Rule, the *Daily News* gave dividends of 133 percent.[3] From a sideline occupation of printing establishments, the newspaper business was transformed into a full-fledged industry requiring large amounts of capital for its operations; its organizational structure evolved from small family firms and partnerships to joint-stock companies in the 1860s, corporations and syndicates in the 1880s, and to the beginnings of the amalgamated press at the turn of the century.[4] Ownership was concentrated to the point where in London in 1910, as noted by A. J. Lee, "two-thirds of the morning and four-fifths of the Sunday circulation was shared by only four proprietors."[5] In Paris in 1914 four large dailies together sold 4.5 million copies a day, or 75 percent of the capital's newspaper circulation and 40 percent of the total circulation of all French dailies.[6] The end result was the creation of a few large, vertically integrated enterprises, owning their own paper and printing plants, office buildings, distribution networks, and, at times, advertising agencies.[7]

The emergence of mass-produced dailies and their rapid growth have often been correlated to the expansion of the middle and lower middle classes, and to various transformations occurring in the market-place which made mass advertising an integral part of business development. In *The Long Revolution*, Raymond Williams argues that whereas most products were sold without elaborate advertisement at the beginning of the factory system, during the second half of the nineteenth century product branding (especially in new patent foods) and attempts to organize and control the market made large-scale advertisement, mainly through the medium of the press, absolutely indispensable.[8] A mass-produced press drawing most of its revenue from advertising thus allowed big name products to be successfully launched on the market (Meunier chocolate, *Eau de Lubin*, and the like), and new department stores (*le Bon Marché, le Louvre*) to attract sufficient numbers of consumers to sell cheaply by selling more.[9]

Financial circles, both foreign and domestic, engaged in intricate exchanges to secure their interests through the press. Foreign embassies routinely bought the services of politicians and journalists to promote investment in their countries, as shown in the vast orchestration of favorable articles which took place immediately before and during the 1904–05 revolution, in order to secure Russian funds.[10] The handling of such funds became a normal part of political, financial, and journalistic operations.[11] Domestic financial manipulations (epitomized in the Panama Canal scandal), usually involved the farming-out of stock market reports and financial bulletins in newspapers. As favorable reports needed to be unanimous to be effective, specialized firms were established to act as intermediaries between advertisers and newspapers; such firms were often connected with commercial advertising agencies. Monopolistic trends were soon noticeable in these practices, and denounced by parties as diverse as the police *préfecture* (which warned of the dangers inherent in this situation in an anonymous report in 1914) and Jaurès, who lamented the organization of a trust of financial reports leading "all of public opinion like a herd along the same path" in a speech to the Chamber of Deputies on April 6, 1911.[12]

The effectiveness of such criticisms, however, was limited by the close relations between the press and government which accompanied these economic developments. At the beginning of the nineteenth century, printers and publishers involved in newspaper production were denied access to government and judiciary positions, as it was feared that journalists on the local council or bench would be dangerously susceptible to bribery and political manipulation. Even in the

1880s it was considered difficult for a journalist to assume the function of Justice of the Peace; by the end of the century, however, such reservations were considered obsolete.[13] Journalism had acquired the status of a profession, and the positions of academic, lawyer, journalist, M.P., or J.P. were often considered as interchangeable in a successful career path.[14] Ministers often used honors to secure friendships among journalists; theirs was the most decorated profession in France, while famous English journalists were often ennobled.[15] These individual links were redoubled at the institutional level. In spite of its loudly proclaimed freedom, the press continued to receive political subsidies; governments also used monopolistic news agencies to filter foreign news according to their priorities.[16]

Thus during the last quarter of the nineteenth century and up until the First World War, political, economic, and press interests converged to the point where orchestrated manipulations of information (foreign or financial news, and political coverage) could take place routinely, with large sums of money being involved. Governments could filter foreign news and direct financial reports through the collaboration of news agencies and individual newspapers and journalists; these in turn were given privileged information, titles, and money for their services.[17] Financial groups could also use the press to obtain access to French savings and to counteract social developments considered harmful to business development, such as the rise of socialism before the war.[18]

These developments were bitterly denounced by some contemporaries. L. T. Hobhouse wrote in 1909: "the Press, more and more the monopoly of a few rich men, from being the organ of democracy has become rather the sounding-board for whatever ideas command themselves to the great material interests." [19] Such criticisms were countered with affirmations that the press had obviously never been as free, as strong, and as widespread in its readership; anyone with a halfpenny could have access to the news of the world; there had never been a greater popular educator.

◆

The implications of a mass market   When the economic survival of newspapers depended on political subsidization, their target market was necessarily a small group of readers sharing the same political beliefs and enjoying an elevated economic status. In an article entitled *"La presse parisienne,"* Emile Zola described the relationship between the newspapers of the first half of the nineteenth century and their readers in terms of a family where each member had respect for and faith in the paper received at home, read thoroughly from title to advertisements, and collected with pride over many years. Papers were not sold on the street and did not fall into the hands of passersby: each copy was addressed to a specific subscriber.[20] The primary product of such a press was opinion, or "influence" sharing: a newspaper's viability depended on how well it answered the political and economic aspirations of both its backers and its audience. This applied even to *The Times* which, although it proclaimed its independence from political subsidization in the 1830s, owed its success mainly to its ability to crystallize the economic and political expectations of its middle-class readers. Made famous by its thundering for reform ("The Bill, the whole Bill, and nothing but the Bill"), the paper always knew how to pick a winning cause, and stand "ever strong upon the stronger side."[21]

The economic survival of emerging mass newspapers depended on circulation. This new basis for newspaper production, which still applies today, radically transformed the end product of the press, as outlined by Roger Martin in the Canadian newspaper *The Globe and Mail* (July 28, 1983):

> In studying the structure of an industry it is necessary to define the product and its market. The definition of the product of a modern newspaper is important to the analysis. At first blush, the answer appears to be news information, but in actuality the product is not information that is sold to readers; it is readers who are "sold" to advertisers. Fully 80 per cent of newspaper revenue comes from this source. . . . The reader is part of the production process; to sell its product, the newspaper must "produce" readers. If it cannot produce readers it has no product to sell.

The target market thus necessarily became the mass, or the broadest possible cross-section of the reading public. The methods used to attract and maintain mass readership radically transformed press content and selling procedures.

From the outset, marketing techniques were geared to capture street consumers through their curiosity, senses, and emotions. Mass journalism started with a bang: vendors cried out sensational titles, shoved free first issues of the latest serial in the hands of pedestrians, and ran behind buses offering their papers at the end of a pole to the passengers; bands followed by carriages or bicycles proclaiming a new title roamed the streets, which were often painted over with ads; buildings were covered by posters; sandwich men worked the sidewalks and squares—city streets were overtaken by a sudden flow of more information, for more people, for less money than ever before. Tubes filled with gold sovereigns were buried in the streets of London and Paris, and readers searched for clues in the newspapers and for treasure in the streets. Ties of friendship and solidarity between readers and "their" newspaper were carefully fostered to promote sales: insurance against railway accidents was offered by Newnes' *Tit-Bits*, and sales shot up to 700,000; to help readers of *Pearson's Weekly* through an influenza epidemic, the paper was sprayed with eucalyptus.[22] Newspapers "took care" of their readers, not only by providing information, but also by giving them a chance in life: to get a prize, find financial security, become a winner.

This family spirit, however, had to be broadened to produce enough readers, and national events were sponsored by the new penny dailies. The *Daily Telegraph*, famous for its appeal to save the elephant Jumbo in 1882, organized the presence of 30,000 children in Hyde Park for the 1887 Jubilee.[23] Sports activities were also backed by major papers, with *Le Petit Journal*, for example, sponsoring the first bicycle race between Paris and Brest in 1891, and the first automobile race between Paris and Rouen in 1894.[24] As good corporate citizens, newspapers also championed charitable and patriotic ventures. National subscriptions organized by the Parisian press provided the French naval forces with a submarine in 1899 (thanks to *Le Matin*'s campaign), and the same method was used to offer the war minister, Alexandre Millerand, the first military air force in the world.[25] Despite appearances to the contrary, newspapers were essentially accomplishing the same task when they were fighting to save an elephant or to establish a military air force: their prime concern was to mobilize a mass market for their product. In the process, penny dailies gained a higher status as they participated in the moral, civil, and military life of the nation. In spite of their dubious taste for trivia and their frivolous ad campaigns, the noblemen in charge of the cheap press after all did run charities and participate in government and military operations.

Competition was fierce between large newspapers, and the name of the game to increase circulation was to flatter the most while offending the least. Even witch hunting required tact; during the Dreyfus affair, *Le Petit Journal* lost 600,000 readers to *Le Petit Parisien*, for having talked too much about the matter. The last editorial, which tried to close the subject long after the readers had gone, started with "What if we talked about something else."[26] From the precarious position of filling page after page with the least (the least economic, political, social, or religious issues) to acquire the most (a national readership covering as many classes as possible) came many of the characteristics of new journalism: the accent on the human interest story, the interview, the endless columns of *faits divers*, more sports, less politics, and so on. These were the traits that made many describe the cheap papers as "feather-brained," and blame the mass for their existence. Matthew Arnold, the man credited for coining the phrase "new journalism" described the situation as follows: "it [new journalism] is full of ability, novelty, variety, sensation, sympathy, generous instincts; its one great fault is that it is *feather-brained*. . . . Well the democracy, with abundance of life, movement, sympathy, good instincts, is disposed to be, like this journalism, *feather-brained*."[27]

However comforting this argument might seem, the readers of the mass-produced newspapers were not yet the "million." Apart from statistical evidence demonstrating that not everyone bought a newspaper, it is hard to imagine people living in slums going without food to read the latest news. The cheap papers found their readers in the middle and lower middle classes, the new army of clerks, shopkeepers, and skilled artisans. Moreover, it was becoming apparent even at the time that all newspapers, including the prestigious ones, were adopting at least part of the new journalistic formula. Finally, it is not inconceivable that the serious readers of *Le Temps*, for example, who enjoyed its melodramatic serial crime novels, could also indulge in *Le Petit Parisien*.[28]

The theoretical premises of the present study suggest that the economic and political basis of the commercial dailies narrowed the range of their allowable content until it became feather-brained: the new press could only champion conservative political, economic, and artistic interests. Conversely, to build up circulation and win a larger share of the reading market, it had to promote winning causes, issues considered safe and simple: nationalism and its adjuncts, militarism and imperialism, *Revanche*, spy mania, and, most prominently, crime stories. This double process of narrowing the range of sayable, acceptable truth while promoting specific discursive exchange has been described by Roland Barthes as the most powerful form of censorship: "Real censorship, however, deep censorship, does not consist in prohibiting (in cutting, excising, starving), but in overfeeding, in maintaining, retaining, choking and ensnaring in stereotypes (intellectual, romantic, erotic), in giving as all nourishment the consecrated speech of others, the repeated material of current opinion. The true instrument of censorship is not the police, it is the *endoxa*."[29] If this content appeared superficial at best, manipulative at worst, it certainly was not trivial—too much money and political power were involved for the press to be so dismissed.

6 TEXTUAL CONSTRUCTION: PRODUCING INFORMATION

◆

The naturalization of cognitive processes Objective information—
up-to-the-minute, full, worldwide, and above all true—was not just a
new commodity thrown on the market by mass journalism, but its most
central concept, its proclaimed raison d'être. In its first issue (February 26, 1884), *Le Matin*, which had for its motto "*Le Matin* sees all,
knows all, says all," expressed its program as follows: "*Le Matin* will be a
newspaper which will not have any political opinions, which will not be
enfeoffed to any bank, which will not sell its patronage to any business;
it will be a newspaper giving news information, telegraphic, universal
and true." [1] The information sold by penny dailies was officially intended for the nation as a whole, from hamlet to palace. When J. M.
Levy took over the *Daily Telegraph* and reduced its price to one penny,
on September 17, 1855, he stated in his first editorial that "If artisan
and Peer alike can peruse daily the same wholesome literary matter,
produced by first-class writers, the general tone of society must bene-
fit." [2] The highly successful Harmsworth held a more practical view
of his immediate market share, which he outlined to Max Pemberton
in 1883: "The Board Schools are turning out hundreds of thousands
of boys and girls annually who are anxious to read. They do not care
for the ordinary newspaper. They have no interest in society, but they
will read anything which is simple and is sufficiently interesting. The
man who has produced this *Tit-Bits* . . . is only at the beginning of a
development which is going to change the whole face of journalism." [3]
    Such marketing strategies had a profound effect on content. If
Hébrard of *Le Temps* is said to have instructed his editors to be pom-
pous and boring, Millaud described the secret of success in new journalism as "One must have the courage to be stupid." [4] Kennedy Jones,

editor for Harmsworth's *Evening News* favored the dictum "Don't forget that you are writing for the meanest intelligence."[5] The time-tested popularity of the broadsheet format, with its predilection for stories of crimes, fires, and floods mixed in with political and religious scandals, made it stand out as the preferred content for a mass-produced press.[6] Sales revenues determined the value of such items as information: "The only thing that will sell a newspaper in large numbers is news," said Harmsworth, "and news is anything out of the ordinary."[7]

However, because of their institutional status and mandate (to inform the electorate, guard democracy, and express the voice of the nation), emerging mass newspapers could not afford to seem frivolous: headlines were used to catch the reader's attention, more space was allowed between articles, but on the whole their appearance was generally reserved. The press had to negotiate a difficult position in social discourse: while economic and political imperatives favored the circulation of information reinforcing social norms and values, the press's mandate to inform the people necessarily involved the coverage of thorny economic and political issues.[8] Even the ever popular crime reports were not problem free, as their conspicuous presence could eventually signal social dysfunction. Argumentative strategies therefore were all-important, as they were the best means available to erase the contradictions between the economic and political determinants of the press and the issues its mandate was to cover. The following sections will first analyze the concept of objective information and outline the rhetorical means which were used to achieve its production in journalistic texts, to then outline its implications for praxis. Although these analyses will concentrate on crime reports, other kinds of stories will also be examined to establish their textual surroundings.

Luis Prieto's probing semiological work can help to analyze objective information as an ideological construct. Prieto opposes "class" to "concept": a concept is determined by its coextension with a number of classes, themselves constituted by sets of objects, equivalent as regards practice, which make the concept true.[9] Thus the meaning of the concept of objective information is determined by its coextension with classes such as "neutrality," "impartiality," and "exhaustiveness"; these classes are constituted respectively by objects such as (1) "letting the facts speak for themselves," "plain and simple facts"; (2) reporting "both sides of a story," reporting news "from nobody's point of view"; and (3) giving "full coverage" of "all the facts." These objects

Figure 3   Objective Information as an Ideological Concept

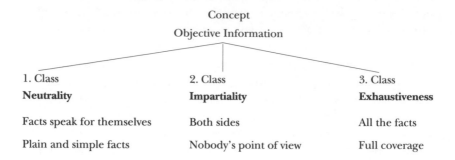

Concept
Objective Information

1. Class	2. Class	3. Class
Neutrality	**Impartiality**	**Exhaustiveness**
Facts speak for themselves	Both sides	All the facts
Plain and simple facts	Nobody's point of view	Full coverage

are established by various textual and technical devices which make argumentation seem neutral, impartial, and exhaustive—which make the information objective and true (figure 3).

The concept of objective information was widely acceptable during the age of positivism, when fact gathering was practiced in fields as diverse as the social and moral sciences and naturalistic literature. In most of its applications it operated the same denegation of the conditions of knowledge production. Whereas *information theory* provides the following model for the transmission of information (simplified here for the purposes of the argument)

Emitter ⟶ Receiver
Message

"letting the facts speak for themselves," "presenting all the facts" from "both sides," or *objective information as an ideological construct* performs the following transformations:

Facts ⟶ Receiver
Message

By erasing the emitter, this model erases the economic and political factors, the sociocultural praxis, which produce facts, and turn them into news—and this is a typical form of ideological knowledge. Indeed, Prieto has shown that reality becomes an object, that is, is conceived, only when it is recognized as a member of a class by a social subject. To erase the emitter (the social subject engaged in the production of knowledge), is to naturalize cognitive processes, to claim that knowledge somehow derives naturally from the essence of reality. Prieto and others have demonstrated that knowledge which is said to derive naturally from the order of things is ideological.[10] Thus, like criminological texts, newspapers worked to erase their presence as texts, and act as neutral conduits between the world and the reader. This was especially clear in the textual strategies used for crime reporting.

As a rule, emerging mass newspaper avoided the discussion of crime per se, and concentrated on the reporting of *criminal cases*, as part of the disconnected events of the day—the ideological construct of objective information authorized a presentation of criminal occurrences as simple facts of life, to be registered like any other by the press. When the subject of crime seemed to impose itself, as on the occasion of an international conference of criminologists, or the publication of reports (the Annual Returns of Judicial Statistics, the Reports of the Police Commissioner, or of the Prison Visiting Committee), it was dealt with in terms of its *institutional processing*, and described as in constant progress: prisons were better kept, punishment was more humane, prisoners had higher standards of morality, crime rates were down, police were better organized and less corrupt, and, at any rate, things were better at home than abroad. One such editorial in *The Times*, discussing international ways of treating people who resisted the police when in the performance of their duties, commented that: "The Italian penal code would be particularly trying for an Irish agitator to live under," and ended by stating that the report "ought to lead professional breakers of the peace to be grateful—grateful that their sphere of enterprise is neither Germany, nor Italy, nor Galicia, but the United Kingdom." [11]

The selection of the *kinds* of criminal occurrences to be reported and of the *format* for their presentation allowed newspapers consistently to align these events with recognized social norms. Three main formats were used for the reporting of criminal activity, and each produced a different notion of criminal man. Police columns and reports of criminal court proceedings were used to cover the common crimes of the "lower orders," at the moment of their handling by the criminal justice system; short narratives standing alone or in the *Faits divers* columns served to describe daring crimes and successful swindles shortly after the time of their occurrence; finally, the full range of newspaper reporting techniques was used to tell the stories of extraordinary crimes (reports of police investigations and coroners' inquests, editorials, eyewitness descriptions, and letters to the editor).

There was a certain preference in French newspapers to report

petty thefts and assaults when their perpetrators were being arrested
—there being no common criminal like a caught one. English newspapers carried a daily police column in which their fate was reported
in a series of short paragraphs. Daily coverage legitimized the judiciary
institution, as its proceedings were considered worthy of registration
and dissemination to the public. It also gave the constant message that
social order was maintained, that criminals were taken care of, caught,
processed, and sentenced.[12] A terse style prevailed throughout, and
each case usually followed the same pattern: the names of the court,
the judge, the defendant, his/her age, address, and occupation, followed by the charges, the statements of the arresting police officer,
witnesses if any, and ruling. Once named, all persons involved would
be referred to by their legal status ("prosecutrix stated"), thus favor-
ing their apprehension as various impersonal moments of a process.
The meaning of actual events was often dissolved by these exercises
in upholding the law. *The Times* reported the following case of a man
charged with indecently assaulting a nine-year-old girl:

> After all the evidence had been taken, the learned Judge asked
> the jury whether they wished to hear more of the case. Several
> members of the jury said they did not, and it was understood that
> the jury had found the prisoner *Not guilty*. He was accordingly dis-
> charged. As soon as he had left the dock one of the jurymen got
> up and intimated that they had misunderstood his Lordship, and
> that they had not agreed to a verdict. The learned Judge, however,
> said it was too late to remedy the error [*The Times*, December 20].

Paradoxically, as has been noted by Douglas Hay, the submission of
the administration of justice to the formalism of the law contributed
to its strength as ideology:

> The punctilious attention to forms . . . argued that those admin-
> istering and using the laws submitted to its rules. The law thereby
> became something more than the creature of a ruling class—it
> became a power with its own claims, higher than those of prosecu-
> tor, lawyers, and even the great scarlet-robed assize judge himself.
> To them, too, of course, the law was the Law. The fact that they
> reified it, that they shut their eyes to its daily enactment in Par-
> liament by men of their own class, heightened the illusion. When
> the ruling class acquitted men on technicalities they helped instil
> a belief in the disembodied justice of the law in the minds of all

who watched. In short, its very inefficiency, its absurd formalism, was part of its strength as ideology.[13]

The constricted style used to describe these proceedings had the double advantage of producing an illusion of objectivity and precluding comments or objections to the proceedings. However, comments by court officials or journalists could appear in the otherwise neutral reports, usually to reinforce either the law or other institutions. One *Times* report, quoting the judge's sentencing address verbatim, presented such warnings as: "the law cannot be broken with impunity, and the law is far too strong for you or they to strike against. The law will overcome you"; and "whenever you have a wrong the law will provide you with a remedy, but you must never take the law into your own hand" (October 12). A judge's backing of the system of free enterprise could equally be worthy of report:

> Testimonials to the good character borne by the prisoner were produced. The prisoner pleaded "Guilty" and explained that he had committed the offence [theft] in consequence of his getting into debts, as the wages he was receiving—10s per week— were quite insufficient to provide him with food and clothes. Sir Andrew Lusk remarked that if an employer wanted a man to keep honest he should pay him fair wages. The wages were very low; but as the prisoner agreed to accept them, he could not find fault with them. He sentenced the prisoner to two months' imprisonment with hard labour [*The Times*, September 8].

Amid these several daily columns of objective reporting, occasional descriptions were strewn. Some of them simply redoubled the proceedings' legitimacy: prisoners accused of being disorderly were regularly described as "dissipated-looking" or "rough-looking." Others expressed a certain surprise at finding respectable appearances or good families involved in such proceedings: "At Lambeth, a young man named Arthur Klason, with no fixed abode, but stated to belong to a respectable family, was charged" (*The Times*, September 18). "At Croydon Borough Police-court, Ryder Rhodes, of 16, Great Coram-street, St-Pancras, whose family is highly respected in Croydon, was charged" (*The Times*, September 10). These occasional comments act as markers; they point to a disparity, the appearance of the unexpected in otherwise predictable proceedings. More importantly, their presence implies what is considered ordinary and insignificant: that homeless laborers constantly appear before magistrates for stealing, drunkenness, and assault, and receive imprisonment with hard labor as retribution. Considered normal, these occurrences required no comment—and the problem of relating crime to social conditions, at a time when in England "about a third of the people lived in a state 'incompatible with physical health and industrial efficiency'" was thereby avoided.[14] An analysis of the press coverage given to the Ripper murders, which happened in one of the poorest districts in London, will uncover these unsaid assumptions. However, just how well this kind of reporting worked as a practice of social integration can already be illustrated by John Tooling's story, as told in *The Times* police column of December 10, 1888:

> At BOW-STREET, on Saturday, John Tooling, 68, was charged with begging from foot passengers in Cockspur-street. The prisoner was seen begging from persons who crossed the road at the bottom of the Haymarket, under the pretence that he had swept the crossing. He did not sweep the crossing, although he had a broom in his hand. He had been several times convicted of begging. Mr. Bridge said that under the Local Management Act, 18 and 19 Vic., cap. 120, sec. 118, the vestries had power to appoint crossing-sweepers. If this were done and they were given armlets to wear there would be fewer facilities given to impostors of the prisoner's class. He sentenced him to three months' imprisonment.

By reporting this story in a police column, the need to address the question of the criminality of begging was bypassed: the ideological construct of objective information authorized John Tooling's prosecution to be treated as any criminal case, and registered as a fact of life by the press. Indeed no voice of protest was registered in the paper; the economic and political context of this case was so obviously accepted that it need not be mentioned or justified. The reasonable solution to begging for survival in old age had become better civil administration, closer supervision, and larger prisons—and the personal and class suffering of John Tooling could be made insignificant, demeaned by the well-known truths about such cases, and displaced behind prison bars.[15]

The terse style used to report ordinary crimes was used throughout the penny dailies, to ensure their neutrality. One of the most important and efficient textual devices for the production of neutral information was the use of the *dispatch* as format for news transmission. As is clear from the *Matin* program (quoted above), telegraphic news was considered the epitome of new journalism. Its extensive use and tremendous appeal probably derived from the fact that it satisfied political, economic, as well as symbolic needs: the rise of imperialism made information about remote parts of the world imperative, and the telegraph, by making this information instantly available, answered these needs and functioned as material proof of the validity of the age's faith in progress.[16] The telegraph simultaneously shrank the world and increased power and knowledge.

The transmission of news in a series of disconnected, short paragraphs, each headed by the place, date, and often the time of emission, erased the work done by newspaper editors, and transformed the press into a transparent medium. The telegraphic style, which crams the maximum of information into a minimum of words, strengthened this illusion by producing an *effet de réel* by which the importance of language faded in the face of facts. The choice of news items, the ordering of their presentation and the absence of commentary need not be justified in such columns; and the fact that the movement of political stars and royalty usually filled them could thus be taken for granted.[17] *The Times* column of "Foreign and Colonial News" could present this sequence of items on September 21, 1888:

The Miners' Strike in France

> St Etienne, September 20.

The men on strike have succeeded in inducing nearly all the miners to join them. The strike is now almost universal in the St Etienne coal basin.

Football in New Zealand

> Christchurch, New Zealand, Sept. 20.

The English football team to-day played a fifteen of Canterbury, and won the match by one goal and five tries, the Colonial team failing to make any points.

By giving a miners' strike in France the same space as a (victorious) football match in New Zealand, *The Times* report has the triple advantage of reducing the importance of a threat to social order, avoiding commentary on a sensitive issue, and giving the readers the lovely feeling of belonging to a solid, stable, winning nation. This kind of reporting can be taken for granted, indeed can only *make sense* within the ideological construct of objective information, which lets the facts speak for themselves, and merely presents things the way they are. The social, political, and economic structures which determine the meaning of these items are presupposed in the process and therefore remain unsaid, and, more importantly, unquestionable.

The *telegraphic style* was used throughout the papers because of these advantages. For example, the Opportunists' line as regarded *revanche* was, in Gambetta's words, to "think of it always, speak of it never," in the hope of stabilizing the Republic and achieving a peaceful foreign policy.[18] *Le Temps*, a staunch supporter of the regime whose readership was drawn mainly from the upper classes, rarely spoke of *revanche*. However, with unfailing regularity, its *"Bulletin de l'Etranger"* column had a paragraph on Alsace-Lorraine, in which—almost invariably— stories of Germans treating loyal Alsatians and Frenchmen as criminals were reported:

Items from Abroad.
(Havas dispatches and private intelligence)
Alsace-Lorraine
The civil tribunal of Metz, during its session of September 8, condemned to one month in jail and a fine of 20 marks a certain Mathieu Kirsch, worker, native of Schrasig (Grand Duchy of Luxemburg), residing at Saint-Julien-les-Metz, who had cried "Vive la France!" in a local drinking establishment [September 12].

Such reports made sense as news only within the presupposed problem of *revanche*, and the Opportunist way of dealing, or rather bypassing the issue, while never letting it die.

Le Petit Parisien, on the other hand, had a larger popular audience, and its anti-German attitude was more aggressive and melodramatic, appealing to the indignation of its readers in anything but a telegraphic style. A front-page article on October 9, entitled "BARBARIANS YOURSELVES!" thus gave the soul-stirring story of a Frenchman whose request for a passport to visit Alsace had been refused by the German embassy in Paris. The article ended with "A better idea of the cruelty of this refusal [to grant a passport] will be gained when we will have said that the petitioner wanted to kiss his [dying] mother one last time before his departure for the Isle of Bourbon: barbarians yourselves, Messrs Teutons!"[19] *Le Petit Parisien*, however, made extensive use of the telegraphic style to present the endless lists of *faits divers* which made most of its copy. By using headings like "Paris" or "*Les Départements*," and then giving a series of disconnected reports of such events, the newspaper avoided the rather difficult problem of explaining why crimes, fires, and floods were about the only newsworthy happenings in the country.

This comparison of the different uses made of the telegraphic style in prestige and popular newspapers shows that it constitutes the zero degree of newspaper writing, the crossroad at which reader expectations are met closely enough by the information being transmitted that any contextualization becomes redundant.[20] The choice of items to be presented in this style gives indications of the economic and political interests of the emitters and receivers of such messages—paradoxically, one of the most neutral presentations of objective information is therefore the most revealing of the newspaper's position in social discourse. This also applies to verbatim reports, ostensibly the ultimate form of objective journalism: *The Times*, the *Daily Telegraph*, and *Le Temps* all transcribed speeches by illustrious politicians or business tycoons with the introduction, "X said." This simple syntagmatic construction was useful in that it presupposed the importance of the event, thus eliminating the need to justify the choice of speeches to be reported. The fact that Ferdinand de Lesseps's campaigns for funds for the Panama Canal venture received more and better coverage than socialist meetings did not become an issue, and the social structures determining the relative value of these events were reinforced at the presuppositional level of discourse.[21]

These syntagmatic textual mechanisms allowing newspaper reports to appear neutral are based on the same epistemological presuppositions as those encountered in criminological texts—reality is a given, truth is absolute and cumulative, and language is transparent. Indeed, by denying the social and political structures which determine "facts," verbatim reports and columns of telegraphic messages presuppose that reality is a given. The simple juxtaposition of news items in columns presupposes that truth is absolute and cumulative, as the choice of items and the ordering of their presentation is considered insignificant: truth is to be shown wherever it lies, and simply stated in a cumulative list. Strikes and football matches can be given the same space and style of presentation, for language is transparent and serves only to present things the way they are.

Impartiality was purportedly achieved by always giving both sides of the story. This, however, often meant that an imaginary compromise was devised so that the paper could promote a conservative perspective on thorny issues. During a carpenters' strike in 1877, *Le Petit Parisien* insisted that the situation was deplorable and that it was high time that the legislators attend to it: "a very simple, very clear, very plain law giving once and for all legal life to trade associations is, in our opinion, the only practical way of protecting the rights of the workers while safeguarding the interests of the employers." As the strike continued for several months and became a press issue, *Le Petit Parisien* eventually declared that it did not want to intervene in the debate which involved "purely personal questions," and that it would wait until better information was available to publish further on the matter.[22] Although proceeding with less candor, the prestigious press operated along the same lines: to attack an occasional black sheep, but not social structures; to depoliticize any peaceful workers' movement, and criminalize any violent one. *Le Temps* (December 5) finished a report on the British Trade Union Congress with these words: "On the whole, and without making a tactical or political judgment, it is impossible to deny the virility of their attitude, their positivism, their spirit of enquiry and their admirable faculties of resistance."

The economic and political interests vested in newspapers thus provided the impetus for the production of a kind of antiknowledge (related to that produced in elementary schools): to reduce events to their human, individual size; to present European political relations to the rhythm of royal trips and imperial hunting expeditions, to depict political and economic relations as interpersonal struggles, and describe strikes as misunderstandings within the family of employers and workers. Moreover, such information was constantly marketed as full, complete, comprehensive coverage of worldwide events; the exhaustiveness class implied (and continues to imply in today's broadcasting) that what had not been reported was insignificant, thereby bolstering the truth value of the sayable of the press. The end products of new journalism were more entertaining than the "leaden" articles of before, sold more papers, and therefore seemed to answer (some of) the readers' needs. The people involved in the business of mass journalism could not lose: the information that sold the best was that which helped to strengthen the social order from which their power derived—and even went as far as to make them the champions of truth, as communicators of objective information.

Perhaps one of the most successful methods for producing impartial reports while avoiding an uncomfortable middle-of-the-road policy was to angle a story and avert the problem of presenting both sides.[23] The previously quoted *Le Temps* article on the British Trade Union

Congress ended with words of praise apparently giving a balanced view; however, the closing virility angle, with its traditional sexist association of rationality and strength, in effect allowed the paper to avoid taking an overtly political stand by displacing the problem from labor relations to manhood and positivism—values which a conservative upper-class paper could (still) safely promote to its readers.

Certainly the most popular angle to cover crime stories was to present them as daring exploits of master criminals. The master swindler was particularly prized, and although carried as objective reports, articles describing his criminal achievements assuredly held a high entertainment value. These usually took the form of short narratives propped up with well-known catch phrases to spark the reader's interest: "daring burglary" was the preferred title for such reports in *The Times*, which often assured the reader that "no stone will be left unturned in the endeavours to discover the offender or offenders." French newspapers, when reporting the activities of swindlers, used clichés like "choice sharper," "hardy swindler," "audacious swindler," "hardy scoundrel," "skilful swindler," and so on. The narrators of the tales of their exploits always expressed their appreciation for an "original" method of swindling, a "new, rather ingenious procedure," a "skill which would not have disavowed a prestidigitator," in a swindler "gifted with a true talent."[24] Whenever possible, swindlers were described as handsome, impeccably dressed, and well mannered:

> Allmayer is setting a fashion: like him, every swindler wishes to own a carriage and operate with the manners of a lord and master. The police are presently looking for a swindler of this kind who, under the name of Adler, has made many dupes among the tradesmen of the elegant quarters of Paris. Adler, like his predecessor Allmayer, is a gentleman of attractive appearance, a tall, thin, handsome boy, blond mustache, light auburn hair; most elegantly dressed, with a perfectly cut black morning-coat, pale trousers, dazzling patent ankle-boots, grey top hat, having in his entire person a very British air of dignity which lets him be taken for some Lord passing in Paris [*Le Temps*, "*Faits Divers*" column].

When not described as ambitious, young, and individualistic men, they were said to be part of business organizations with names such as "the band of Catusse, Lacaille, and Co." (*Le Temps*, September 9), and running along the same principle as any growing enterprise, with specialization of trade and personnel, division of labor, and so on:

"The Security service has just discovered an association of swindlers of Austrian nationality which specialized in burglarizing the numerous Italian emigrants which come through Paris on their way to some other country. The association is fully staffed; labor is divided very intelligently, each one having his own clear-cut employment" (*Le Temps*, September 12). Finally, whereas the swindler was described as either a successful, rugged individualist or a member of a well-organized business, the victim was invariably presented as a dupe or a woman— somehow always associated in these learned articles. The model of the press swindle story thus ran:

"Master Swindler ⟶ Performs Daring Operation ⟶ On
Dupe ⟶ Gets (or Will Get) Caught."

This model provides a neat message of social integration. The label master swindler, whether applied to a watch stealer or a bungling embezzler, erases the offender's social class and presents him as the exception which proves the well-known rule that criminals are stupid and vicious. The act is presented as one of a kind, and its field of application limited to dupes—a nonthreatening category, in that it usually excludes the immediate reader. And in spite of all this intelligence and determination, the forces of the law prevail—implying a high rate of success in their dealings with the more common criminals. The story thus leaves its reader, and the established order, untouched by criminal activity. Finally, the exclamatory, excessive style used in these narratives transformed the criminal into a larger than life hero, much closer to fiction than to fact—so much so that real-life swindlers were regularly compared to fictional ones. Jean Frollo's editorial of September 11, entitled "*Les malfaiteurs élégants*" (*Le Petit Parisien*), spoke of the then famous Allmayer as a kind of reincarnation of Rocambole:

Perhaps you remember the time when the novelist Ponson du Terrail would exclaim: "Rocambole is not dead!" Sure enough, he always resuscitated, this type of eminent thief and, just at the moment when we believed him dead, we saw him reappear all of a sudden as a man of the world, luxuriously dressed, elegant and mocking. Well no, Rocambole is not dead: from time to time he lives again in the person of one of these adventurers whose daring confounds us, and who, multiplying their misdeeds, laugh at the police and live the life of a Russian prince.

Such is the case of Altmayer [*sic*] who was arrested only after many long years. He already has his legend, that hardy rogue, with his escapes, his transformations, his prodigalities, his gallant-ries.

During his trial, Allmayer was again described as the perfect example of the swindler type:

> Eugène Altmayer [*sic*] seems to have received from nature all the attributes which constitute the master swindler: invention, a pro-digious range of mind, the gift for persuading simpletons, care for setting the stage and attention to details, the genius of disguise, infinite precaution. . . .
> He is the woman's man whose qualities analysts of contempo-rary literature have in vain tried to describe, who pleases because he pleases, from the start, by a marvellous hypnotism whose secret old, ill-tempered scientists would be the last to discover.

Allmayer's every feature had been made to fit the fictional type so well, that he would eventually walk right into a novel. Roughly twenty years later the lawyer/journalist Gaston Leroux published the first locked-room mystery, *Le mystère de la chambre jaune* (1907), in which one of the characters, Frédéric Larsan, is discovered in the end to be Ballmeyer, the famous swindler:

> Is it necessary for me to recall here Ballmeyer's exploits? For twenty years, they were in police columns and in the news. . . . Ballmeyer was the very type of the high-class swindler; there was not a gentleman more gentlemanly than he; there was no presti-digitator more light-fingered than he; there was no "apache," as they say, more audacious and more terrible than he. Received in the best society, welcomed in the most exclusive circles, he had stolen the honor of families and the money of the great with a masterly skill that was never surpassed.[25]

Through this intricate system of intertextual authentication, the master-swindler type was produced—an incomprehensible but ever so well-known exception to the rules of social organization, provid-ing entertainment for all, and serving different functions in each dis-cursive practice presently under study. Joly's criminological treatise footnoted press reports of the Allmayer case to authenticate its own narrative establishment of the master-swindler type as a scientific fact (see chapter three). The reference to a newspaper report worked as an index to "objective reality," everyday facts that anyone could read and recognize as true. This demonstrates just how well the press' claims of providing objective information had been accepted in social discourse (including scientific discourse). It also manifests intertextual modes of knowledge production. Criminological texts abandoned enthymematic argumentation for narrative presentation when they were unable to prove by argument or measurement what needed to be demonstrated as true; such narratives required corroboration in newspapers and other discursive practices, in order to ensure a solid truth value. Newspaper reports used fictional references to "angle" the Allmayer story into the nether zone of fanciful fact or factual fancy: Rocambole reincarnated. This allowed the fictionalization of objective reports, which in turn increased their circulation value by rendering them highly entertaining. References to fictional versions of the master-swindler type also served to increase the value of the newspaper narratives, which never tired of pointing out that truth (their domain) was unquestionably stranger (and more interesting to buy and read) than fiction. Finally, press reports were used in Leroux's work to point once again to reality, and increase the novel's verisimilitude and market value.

The fictionalization of the swindler in the press contributed to distance such crimes from social realities, and allowed them to be considered entertaining, and treated accordingly. Papers announced court sessions much like theater seasons, with comments on the relative interest of each case, the presence of star lawyers, the choice of witnesses, and so on: "the detectives have arrested twelve swindlers in the South of France who belonged to the Catusse, and probably to the Allmayer, band. Among them is a woman named Flora, who was well known to the gamblers of Monte Carlo. Parisians will therefore have a number of attractions in the shape of sensational trials during the ensuing month" (*Daily Telegraph*, "Paris" column, October 29). The internationally famous Prado trial (Fall 1888) was billed by *The Times* as "a trial . . . which promises to be one of the most extraordinary of our times" (November 6). Spectators and readers were told to expect their share of the excitement: "Undoubtedly, Prado will try to intrigue his audience with sphinx-like attitudes" (*Le Petit Parisien*, November 4). After listing the accomplices who would be tried along with Prado, the *Daily Telegraph* added: "All this strong 'cast' will figure in the truly dramatic representation which will begin on Monday in the Assize

Court of the Seine" (November 3). When the big day finally came, the *Daily Telegraph* described the audience as follows: "Among those on the first row were M. Daubray, the comic actor of the *Palais-Royal*, and several well-known members of that portion of the *Tout-Paris* which goes everywhere, from a première at the *Français* to a dernière at *La Roquette*" (November 6). A week later, the paper commented: "Prado looked 'fitter' than ever to-day for this conflict with the Judge, and the relâche of Sunday had given him ample time to meditate over his case" (November 13). *Le Petit Parisien* also characterized the accomplices as various incarnations of theatrical types: Eugénie Forestier, "the very type of the demi-mondaine, of the fashionable courtesan," Mathilde Dault, "representing the legendary type of the grisette of Paris, with her modest dress and her unpretentious hair-style," Garcia, "the degenerate Moor," and finally Lorenzo Ybanès, who "represents no less than Spanish pride" (November 7). The individuals involved in this textbook case all but disappeared behind such easily recognizable types, which made their processing through the criminal justice system that much easier.

The extensive use of theatrical metaphors to describe the court proceedings allowed the press reports to present them as a form of light entertainment. The strength of the tactic was that the resemblances between the trial and a play were established at the presuppositional level of the text, where they need not be justified or even discussed. Indeed, the use of the theatrical term "cast" to refer to the defendants (in the first metaphor quoted above) rests on a semantic operation by which the limited number of shared semes between the terms "trial" and "play" are presented as though they applied to their coextension.[26] This process can be described as follows:

(1) A trial and a play share certain formal characteristics, as both entail the acting out of roles (in a trial those of judge, witness, defendant; in a play those of hero, ingénue, villain), in front of an audience:

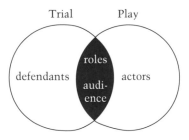

(2) The use of the term "cast" to refer to the defendants is based on this—unsaid—intersection of formal resemblances between different entities.

(3) However, the metaphor presents these shared characteristics as though they extended to the entirety of the terms: unlike a comparison which keeps the elements of the correlation as distinct units, a metaphor presents a relation as though it were coextensive:

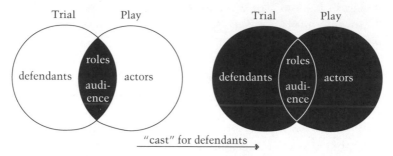

These metaphors thus erase the differences between a play and a trial and constitute rhetorical "pseudo-propositions," statements that are at once true and false: defendants are members of a cast, yet they are not. Rhetorical statements "do not have a logical meaning, but they nevertheless express diverse meanings without requiring that one be selected, even prohibiting that one be selected. If a choice were possible, verification would also be possible."[27] In journalistic texts such statements reify language and transform accounts of a trial where a man's life is at stake into light-hearted texts consumed for personal enjoyment.

◆

Knowledge and praxis: what could "we" want to do?   What kind of practice could be generated by the objective information produced and circulated in the press? What could the press public want to do, in view of what it could know? The previous sections have shown how economic and political developments both prepared the grounds for the emergence of a mass-produced press and determined the limits of its sayable in social discourse; how did the press influence praxis in its turn? Beginning with a general description of the organization of press information, the following section will then examine this question from the limited perspective of crime stories—and the Ripper murders in particular—in order to trace the methods by which a consensual position supporting hegemonic truths was forged out of the discursive apprehension of a series of events potentially threatening to the established order.[28]

Worldwide coverage of the day's events organizes information along spatial rather than temporal vectors: the developments leading to the day's happenings are as a rule either totally neglected or summarily reported. The reader of mass journalism is fed with more and more information about places and events over which he or she has little or no control, and about as much understanding, since the usual absence of follow-up and detailed analysis of events makes them hard to comprehend.[29] Moreover, the preferred techniques of new journalism— looking for the human interest story, working from interviews, and so on—neglect the structures that determine the meaning of an event in order to concentrate on a single, grabbing facet. The spatialized world of up-to-the-minute information, therefore, tends to devaluate events, by making them appear either as unforeseeable happenings in an uprooted present or as helpful confirmations of hegemonic ideological constructs. Thus, a strike is typically described as the unpredictable outbreak of violence or irrationality rather than the outcome of specific conflicts developing over time. Newspaper reports which focus on marches, picket lines, and violent clashes between police and strikers do not equip readers with information enabling them either to understand the reason for the strike or to decide whether or not to support it. Faced with such reports, turning to the next story is not an unusual reaction—nor is it an unwelcome one.

As it devaluates and demeans the events of the "outside world" by an aggressive marketing of the latest, quite disconnected occurrences, the press tends to valorize itself as an institution and its reader as a participant. In the midst of political and natural upheavals, the production and consumption of newspapers are made to appear as two of the very few steadfast and continuous activities, in a way associated with individual stability, if not survival. The customary year-end summary of *Le Temps* in 1888 expresses this quite clearly:

> I have just gone through for you the collections of illustrated journals. Some black, some white.—The same procession as every year: as many dead, as many new great men, as many triumphant entrances of kings, presidents, ministers, under arches of flowers,—as many hostilities from things, floods, earthquakes, explosions, shipwrecks, mine collapses, train derailments,—as many perversities in men, strikes, street riots, scandals, revolutions,

interviews of sovereigns, alliances, misalliances and battles, as many bronze and marble statues erected to the memory of heroes, as many infamous heads thrown in the bran basket. . . .

There is not one year at the end of which each one of us cannot repeat to himself the words of Sieyès who was asked what he had done during the Terror: "I lived."

We have lived, my dear friends, while iron, fire, microbes, anguish and pain lay so many others beneath the grass [December 27].

The article then proceeds to list, black on white, the deaths of illustrious people, the plays presented in famous theaters, the most acclaimed works of fiction, the various "*potins européens*" of political games, the most notable *faits divers* and remarkable crimes and trials, ending with a note on the progress of the construction of the Eiffel Tower, which is described as a "surprising act of faith." This remarkable feat, of first denying the importance of events and their publication and then proceeding to list them in a newspaper article, illustrates the subtle transference of value operated by newspaper reporting: in a complex and largely unchangeable world, lying just beyond reach, the important thing is to record events faithfully, to know about them and share them with a nation of readers. In the incomprehensible mix-up of national and international developments, continuity and coherence can be found in the ordering of the news in an unchanging sequence in each paper, the categorization of events in specific columns ("*Faits Divers*" for the relatively unimportant, "News of the Day" or "From Day to Day" for the more consequential in *Le Temps*), the discussion of important issues in three leader articles (always found at the same place in each paper), and the constant reporting of other institutional discourses (government, courts, and scientific congresses).

Moreover, in this endless series of conflicts between workers and employers, between and within nations and families (as divorce courts were also covered), community can be found in the gradual development of a close relation between the writers and readers of newspapers. Penny dailies such as *Le Petit Parisien* had constant recourse to narration in a popular tone, sometimes melodramatic and sometimes indignant, to present both news and editorials, and blend their copy of *faits divers* into a kind of street-corner conversation, taken up each day, as between old friends. Many articles cultivated this closer, more personal relation with the readers, through other methods. Typically, it was *Le Petit Parisien* which carried this the farthest: a column entitled "Small Correspondence" would answer unpublished letters in a cryptic style, understandable only to the reader who wrote in a question, increasing the one-to-one ties between paper and reader. The correspondents of the prestige press sent in reports which read like letters a very erudite or distinguished friend might write. Columns on the arts or sciences, or on life in London or Paris generally adopted a friendly, narrative style, revealing the inside secrets of a profession or city, over a period of time, in a series of articles.[30] Finally, numerous letters to the editor gave the readers a sense of direct participation in the composition of the paper and, through this medium, of affecting "society."

These various textual strategies made the press into a user-friendly medium between the "outside world" and the readers. As previously outlined, popular papers carried this role of intermediary to extremes, by actively participating in the moral, civil, and even military life of the nation. If the objective information provided by the newspapers generated a kind of nonunderstanding of the world, making attempts to transform it hard to conceive, the stable presentation of the press, its daily presence at the breakfast and dinner table, its loudly proclaimed freedom, and its role as guardian of truth in a democratic society made participation in it (knowing it all, partaking in the debates and current scandals) become a kind of vicarious quasi-political activity or substitute for activity. Contemporary critics strongly denounced this effect (without necessarily explaining its causes): "As for the public, each morning, the newspaper is its true *café au lait*. The public's passions find an obvious satisfaction in the attacks against men and things it hates and despises. The public then stands up and attends to its business or pleasure, satisfied. It has paid its contribution to social defense."[31] Mass journalism thus brought truth for all, as the police offered law and order for all, and the judiciary system meted out justice blindly between social equals: with mass journalism the press had attained its rightful place in the institutional gateway system neutralizing access to positions of authority.

The question of whether or not newspapers provided the truth to their readers is thus readily answered: newspaper knowledge was indeed true, in that it actively sustained and participated in the discursive production of knowledge and power, which generated the "truth" of the time. It did not matter, then, that the owners and writers of mass journalism hardly believed that the "white peril," as it was called, could provide knowledge or power to the people. Nor did it matter very much whether the readers believed the information, or simply accepted it as a form of light entertainment, as proclaimed in this song of the 1880s: "Me I don't like the big papers / That talk about politics / What do I care if the Esquimaux / Have ravaged Africa / What I need is the *Petit Journal* / The gazette, my mother's cross / The more drowned there are in the canal / The more it's my business."[32] What mattered was that the press had joined other discursive practices in the promotion and maintenance of order.

The coverage given to the Ripper murders clearly illustrates how the press could use crime reports to produce a consensual position supportive of established power relations, while increasing circulation and taking on the role of champion of truth, and of the just cause. Sadistically inflicted on prostitutes working among the "perishing and dangerous" classes of the Whitechapel slums, these crimes made the living conditions of the "lower orders" become a press issue for several weeks. However, this debate only served to confirm the accepted truths about the victims and their surroundings; not only did it justify existing systems of control, but it also led to calls for better and more extensive means of disciplinary supervision.

The Ripper murders offered all the elements which made contemporary gothic novels so popular: violence, sadism, torture, and sex, all happening in modern city ruins, the East End slums.[33] Shockingly gruesome, the murders left most readers feeling safe: after all, the vast majority of them were not prostitutes in Whitechapel. The crimes were also a great social leveler, as everyone agreed that they were atrocious, *even* the criminals, according to a *Times* report: "Sergeant Thicke, who has had much experience of the thieves and their haunts in this portion of the metropolis, has, since he has been engaged in the present inquiry, been repeatedly assured by some of the most well-known characters of their abhorrence of the fiendishness of the crime, and they have further stated that if they could only lay their hands on the murderer they would hand him over to justice" (September 11).

The press coverage they received varied greatly between the French and English papers. *Le Petit Parisien* used them mostly for their sensational value: articles with titles like "The London Killer" dwelled on the horror of the mutilations. They also served as a useful introductory angle for other frightful discussions. An editorial entitled "Macabre Industries" (October 11) started with a description of the

Ripper murders and then continued to explain in great detail the process of manufacturing skeletons: how these were picked clean, then
boiled, then dried and reassembled, how their prices varied depending on size and condition, and other such useful information. Life
in the slums where the murders occurred provided the grounds for
naturalistic tales comparable to J. H. Rosny's later descriptions of the
"lower orders":

> A few meters from the Strand, the meeting place of the most
> correct clubbists, who never go out at night without a gardenia
> in their buttonhole, sprawl tortuous streets, dreadfully miserable
> courtyards, inhabited by a fantastic population.
>
> Beggars—the likes of which cannot be seen in the most under-
> privileged quarters of Paris—without shirts, without clothing and
> fleshless like skeletons, live in humid caves, among rats, wood lice,
> and spiders [September 14].

The ultimate message to French readers came through quite clearly:
such violence, such poverty, and such degeneration could never even
be imagined at home.

Le Temps's handling of the murders was more low key: its reports
were hidden in the "Courrier de Londres," hardly an eye-grabbing
title. Only at the very end did they warrant an understated subtitle
of their own, "The New London Crime." Poverty or prostitution were
hardly mentioned. The Ripper murders were mostly used to criticize
the police, not generally as a social institution, but specifically, as an
English one, totally incapable of handling the particularly devastating problem of *English* crime. *Le Temps*'s correspondent did not think
it was possible to establish, "for any other country in the world, a
more considerable sanguinary balance-sheet" (September 28). All descriptions of the events were invariably qualified as English, relating
the crimes and their mishandling by the police to ethnic rather than
social or economic factors: "English swindler," "English mysteries,"
"English police," "English assassinations," and "English legislation."
Everyone involved was criticized as particularly English, from simple
eyewitnesses to the system of coroners' inquests:

> I have often indicated how useless these inquests are; one ex-
> ample, dating from yesterday, will allow me to prove once more
> that they are generally so poorly conducted that they hinder
> rather than help the pursuit of justice [September 25].

He [a witness] noticed that the client was carrying a black leather bag. In all English assassinations, the black leather bag is a must; unfortunately such clues are vague, and are nevertheless used to publish the portraits of assassins [October 9].

The general image thus produced, of John Bull, nose to the ground, muddling through as best he can—that is, very badly indeed—undoubtedly implied a superior French system. More importantly, it literally took the place of other possible issues (of social organizations of repression and control, of poverty, prostitution, or madness) and transformed the entire series of events into further proof of the peculiar shortsightedness of the English neighbors.

The same story thus received different coverage, each one corresponding to reader expectations and the individual newspaper's economic and political position. Both versions were constructed through spatialization (such things can only happen in England) and identification (such things are representative of Englishness), proven techniques of new journalism which held the distinct advantage of leaving the social order intact.[34] Had the events been apprehended dialectically as part of broader social, economic, and political conflicts taking place in industrial societies, French readers could have been implicated in, rather than diverted by, the crimes. The newspaper texts however were designed to produce knowledge mainly pertinent for one kind of praxis—the repetitive consumption of press stories for personal interest and pleasure.

In England the crimes took on the proportions of a national crisis, and received extensive daily coverage: the press was filled with reports of the murders, speculations on the murderer and the best way to catch him, reports of coroners' inquests, debates in the House of Commons, editorials and innumerable letters to the editor discussing every possible aspect of the crimes, their causes, and the place of their occurrence, the inhabitants of the East End, Western civilization, and the list goes on. As stories of murders, wife and child battering resulting in death, or death from starvation were reported on a daily basis without ever provoking any major reaction, the first problem to be investigated is why the Ripper murders caused such a flow of discourse.[35]

The sheer repetition of the same vicious attack was probably an important factor: the murders kept on happening, without hindrance, over a period of four months. This provoked discussions of institutions normally taken for granted, such as the police force. Criticisms were made against the organization of the force, doubts were expressed as to the intelligence of the officers, and Sir Charles Warren and Mr. Matthews were criticized for their handling of their respective jobs of chief commissioner of the Metropolitan Police, and secretary of state for the Home Department (Warren eventually resigned). Throughout these criticisms, *The Times* and the *Daily Telegraph* supported the police as a whole: "Deep searching of hearts, humiliation of spirit, and sorrowful reflection over the causes which make these unspeakable atrocities possible, would be more seemly than cheap declamation about the short-comings of the police" (*The Times*, November 11). This kind of sober appeal to good manners was shunned for a more direct, vituperative, and entertaining style by the *Daily Telegraph*. Upholding the police force, it chose its black sheep and criticized mercilessly: "We have had enough of Mr. Home Secretary Matthews, who knows nothing, has heard nothing, and does not intend to do anything" (September 19); "Mr. Secretary Matthews, who would make an admirable president of an asylum for deaf mutes, or consulting physician to a hospital for incurables" (September 24); "Our Home Secretary is a perverse and stubborn official" (October 2).

The irony displayed in all these criticisms of the police both in the French and English press produced a sense of community between the readers and the writers of papers, who together looked condescendingly on the shortcomings of specific individuals. This outside look of irony allowed savage criticism to be distributed randomly, without any implication into the problem: never were any possible solutions suggested, nor even were the major difficulties outlined. Irony allowed the press to discuss the problem without ever implicating itself. Other textual strategies achieved the same effect: a leader article in *The Times* (September 10) was entirely spent in repeating descriptions of the murder, its motives, and the panic it generated (which had already been given twice in the same issue), and in categorizing the crime with the usual clichés: "worse than fiction," and "unique in the annals of crime." The ultimate importance of such an editorial was that it allowed the paper to act as arbiter in the crisis, and fit the events within the parameters of reality/fiction, reason/madness, humanity/animality: to sound the voice of authority. Similarly, the police were constantly arresting people without any connection to the murders: "During yesterday several arrests were made but after a short examination in all cases the persons were set at liberty, as it was felt certain they had no connexion with the crime" (*The Times*, November 13); two days later: "During yesterday several persons were detained by the police on suspicion of being in the Dorset-street murder, but they were, after a short detention, allowed to go away" (*The Times*). Both kinds of activities enabled a practice of authority without any other aim or effect than its maintenance; power exists in its exercise.

Economic pressures also contributed to the flow of discourse. Because the Ripper murders were hot stories, newspapers wanting to keep their circulation numbers had to keep their readers informed: after the murders had been described in detail several times by several witnesses, after all the police efforts had been duly noted, after the coroner's inquests had been reported verbatim, newspapers had to find something else to say. The *Daily Telegraph* added visual representations to their efforts: sketches of what the Ripper might look like, facsimiles of his letters, and maps of the area where the murders had occurred, with daggers indicating the precise spot. The publication of letters to the editor provided an ongoing forum on the murders which allowed daily coverage even when the latest news was no news at all:

> Tuesday Morning (1:30 A.M.)
> Upon inquiry at Scotland Yard and at the City Police Office this morning it was stated that no additional information had been obtained, and that no further arrests were made. The bodies of the victims remain unidentified [*Daily Telegraph*, October 2].

The excessive violence used in the murders demanded attention and gave new dimensions to the meaning of dying in London slums. A significant shift can be noted in *The Times*'s way of describing the victims. At first they were referred to as "the woman" or "the deceased," and described as "one of the class called unfortunates" (September 10). In the October 1 report of the double murder the characterization changed to "the victim . . . [belonged] to the same unfortunate class"; finally, the words "unfortunate woman" were used—the discovery of a series of mutilated bodies had eventually humanized an occurrence otherwise considered both common and inevitable.[36] Moreover, after the "Maiden Tribute" agitation of 1885, the working-class demonstrations in London's West End in 1886, and their climax on Bloody Sunday, November 18, 1887, the murder and mutilation of five prostitutes working in the poorest districts not only revived, but also seemingly provided the ultimate justification for all the old fears that vice, crime, and revolution would grow from working-class depravity and threaten order and civilization. This led to an exceptional press discussion of crime in the London slums which articulated the ideological maxims on common criminals and the appropriate methods of treating them which were normally presupposed in the reports of court or police proceedings. For the purposes of clarity and convenience of analysis, I shall first examine how the innumerable arguments set forth in these letters (and in the editorials discussing them) reified the crimes, their victims, and the perpetrators through spatialization and identification, to see how the knowledge thus produced confirmed existing relations of power and knowledge by instituting a consensual opposition to criminality.

If the killings are usually remembered today as the Ripper murders, or the story of Jack the Ripper, in 1888 they were known as the Whitechapel murders: from the start, they were recognized in spatial terms. For the French, they were the "London crimes"; for the Londoners, the space was narrowed down to a specific district. This was accentuated by the newspaper titles: the first murder happened during the night of August 31, and on September 1, the *Daily Telegraph* entitled its report: "Mysterious Murder in Whitechapel," while *The Times*'s headline was "Another Murder in Whitechapel." As denoted in *The Times*'s title, murders were not unheard of in Whitechapel; the ellipsis of the verb accentuated the relation between murder and the district. On Monday, September 3, both papers carried the same title: "The Whitechapel Murder." Already, the spatial identification of the event was complete: the ellipsis of both the verb and preposition and the inversion giving "Whitechapel" the role of adjective established an essential relation between the two terms, making Whitechapel an attribute of murder. The letters further narrowed the space. In Whitechapel only a few blocks were really dangerous; on these blocks the lodging-houses caused all the problems; among the numerous lodging-houses, only a few were rookeries, "hotbeds of vice and crime" (*Daily Telegraph*, October 3), and the murders took place in the worst spots: "The courtyard where this crime was committed is only frequented by the lowest class of men and women" (*Le Temps*, November 11).

This narrow spatialization of the murders secured the rest of the city in respectable and safe surroundings, isolated the crime area, and thus denied its position within society as a whole; this reification in turn allowed numerous solutions to be proposed, which, logically enough, never involved social structures:

(1) *More light in the district*: "It was estimated in New York that every

street electric lamp saved one policeman and was less expensive to maintain. If every street were well lighted, and every court and alley were brilliantly lighted, deeds of darkness would be diminished and morality promoted" (letter to *The Times*, October 3).

(2) *The removal of the slaughter-houses*: "At present animals are daily slaughtered in the midst of Whitechapel, the butchers with their blood stains are familiar among the street passengers, and sights are common which tend to brutalize ignorant natures. For the sake of both health and morals the slaughtering should be done outside the town" (letter to *The Times*, September 19).

(3) *Rubber soles for police officers in the district*: "all the police boots should be furnished with a noiseless sole and heel, of indiarubber or other material, to prevent the sound of their measured tread being heard at night, which would enable them to get close to a criminal before he would be aware of their approach" (letter to *The Times*, October 3).[37]

The same pattern can be observed in the description of the inhabitants of Whitechapel, the "lowest classes." Although the need to distinguish the honest poor—the vast majority of East Enders—from the criminal poor was periodically expressed, it was generally agreed that all of them lived in conditions of filth, overcrowding, drunkenness, vice, and immorality. This led to biological analogies comparing the growth of crime in Whitechapel to that of pestilence from refuse:

We have long ago learnt that neglected organic refuse breeds pestilence. Can we doubt that neglected human refuse as inevitably breeds crime, and that crime reproduces itself like germs in an infected atmosphere, and becomes at each successive cultivation more deadly, more bestial, and more absolutely unrestrained? It is not that the amount of crime necessarily increases in proportion to the increase in its intensity. On the contrary, just as a house is all the cleaner because its rubbish and refuse have all been shot away out of sight, so society at large may show a smaller percentage of crime when its vicious and criminal refuse has all been segregated in particular spots [*The Times* editorial, September 19].

The argumentation in this paragraph gives a superb demonstration of how ideological knowledge is produced. The first sentence serves to establish the argument in authoritative knowledge, a scientific, proven biological law. The preterition introducing the second sentence, "can we doubt," allows a more forceful affirmation of the unprovable argument which follows. The syntagm "neglected human refuse as inevitably breeds crime" carries several presuppositions. It first presupposes the existence of "human refuse," thereby avoiding the need to define either its nature (which humans are garbage: the poor, the sick, the unemployed, the criminal?) or its origins (biological, social, economic, political?). This presupposition thus allows "human refuse" to be established as a broad category into which different social groups can eventually be classified for the sake of argument. "Human refuse" in its turn presupposes an organic degeneration among the poor, which would justify their position as outcast. "Neglected" presupposes that supervision could correct deviance, and "breeds crime" presupposes a biological origin for crime. These multiple presuppositions make the rest of the sentence plausible: *The Times* editorial could then *explain* the Ripper murders by comparing successive generations of germs to successive generations of progressively more bestial criminals, without ever demonstrating either that criminals bear criminals, or that children of criminals are more criminal than their parents, or finally that criminals are bestial.

Although useful to bypass the demonstration of an organic cause to crime, the analogy between pestilence and crime "more absolutely unrestrained" carried the dangerous implication that crime could be spreading throughout society. The third sentence categorically denies this implication: "It is not that the amount of crime necessarily increases in proportion to the increase in its intensity." However, to prove the contrary, that crime diminishes as it intensifies in brutality, a whole new analogy is required; this time, that of a clean house with dirty spots which are kept out of sight. The advantage of this analogy is that the value of segregating "human refuse" in out of the way places in the city is increased by its comparison to common housecleaning practices. The argument thus presupposes the inevitability of "human refuse" (which accumulates like rubbish and refuse in a house) while avoiding the discussion of its social, economic, and political origins. The strength (and danger) of such argumentation is that it "makes sense," even though social organizations are unlike houses and criminals are not rubbish and refuse. Through this system of presuppositions, implications, and analogies, the text can provide plausible explanations for crime without any demonstration of the unsaid ideological maxims which sustain them, and authorize the obvious solution—tighter controls—to be forcefully stated as a "matter of fact" a little further down: "In these infamous dens are bred and nurtured the miserable wretches to whom at last such crimes as those of Whitechapel become possible. Humanity there loses its native stamp and takes on the temper and impulse of a beast. This is a matter for improved and extended police supervision."

The identification of the Ripper victims as prostitutes probably helped the discussion of the murders, as their trade in sex provided the proof that crime derived from a physical love of vice: "And, such as the homes are, so will from them filter forth into street life the same race of beings, bred in all that can make them ignorant of God, defiant of all law, revellers in the profligacy which taints the scenes where they congregate with crimes which, however repulsive to the ordinary mind, are in their own estimation just the issues of the life they best enjoy" (*The Times* letter, September 18). The victims were dehumanized by the press, described not only as "miserable creatures," "bestial" and "degenerate," but also "unsexed": "how many of them are altogether unsexed, have no one element in character with female feeling?" (*The Times* letter, September 18). This general reification of prostitutes was strong enough to allow *Le Temps*'s correspondent to state that the very identity of the victims was meaningless:

> It is believed possible to establish the identity of the victim of Mitre square: she would be a woman named Kelly, several times convicted for drunkenness and detained in a police station a few days before she was assassinated. These identifications are without real importance. We know the business of all these unfortunates who after midnight beat the pavement in Whitechapel; but we never know where they come from and what their real name is; they are without fixed domicile, and when they do not have enough to pay for their night, they sleep under covers in the horrible dead-ends that abound in Whitechapel [October 5].

The *Daily Telegraph* described Kelly as follows: "The dead woman had, in fact, belonged to the lowest class, and frequently was without the money to obtain admission to the common lodging-houses. . . . She was accustomed to live on the streets from hand to mouth, and did no honest work whatever" (October 3). However, in an amazing paradox, these descriptions were gainsaid by the newspaper reports on the coroner's inquest, during which witnesses stated that "she was a

woman of sober habits," who "used to get a living by going out hawk-
ing" or "charring." "She was not often in drink," and was a "very jolly"
woman, "often singing." Friends and acquaintances testified that she
had been deserted by her husband, and had spent her last seven years
living with a man named Kelly, in the same lodging-house, coming
home every night between 8 and 9 P.M. The inquest also revealed how
desperate everyday life was for casual laborers in London. Kelly had
pawn tickets on her, as she had been forced to pawn a pair of boots to
buy tea and sugar; she spent her last night in a casual ward, because
they had run out of money. On the day of her murder she was arrested
for drunkenness (not a few days earlier, as reported in *Le Temps*) and
released in the middle of the night as soon as she was sober, as was
the usual practice with poor prisoners, who were not given shelter any
longer than necessary. Forty-five minutes later her mutilated body was
found. These aspects of her story, however, were not pertinent to the
story.[38] *The Times* repeatedly described Kelly as a prostitute, and ma-
nipulated the testimony given at the coroner's inquest so that it would
tend to prove her profession. A comparison of the articles in the *Daily
Telegraph* and *The Times* shows how differently the same inquest could
be "fully" reported:

> He [John Kelly] did not know that she ever went out for immoral
> purposes; he had never allowed her to do so. She was not in the
> habit of drinking to excess, but occasionally she did so. She had
> no money about her when witness parted from her. Her object in
> going to Bermondsey was to see if she could find her daughter
> and get a little money from her, so that she need not walk the
> streets.
> Mr. Crawford—You were asked before if she walked the streets,
> and you said she did not.—Sometimes we were without money to
> pay for our lodging, and we were at the time I speak of [*The Times*,
> October 5].

> I [John Kelly] never knew she went out for any immoral purpose.
> She occasionally drank, but not to excess. When I left her she had
> no money about her. She went to see and find her daughter to get
> a trifle, so that I shouldn't see her walk about the streets at night.
> What do you mean by "walking the streets?"—I mean that if
> we had no money to pay for our lodgings we would have to walk
> about all night. I was without money to pay for our lodgings at
> the time [*Daily Telegraph*, October 5].

The Times preferred the image of Kelly as a drunken prostitute, because it fitted the pattern, and narrowed the field of victims of criminal activity to the immoral or undeserving poor.[39] The victims were accused of helping the murderer: Warren wrote in *The Times* that "Statistics show that London, in comparison to its population, is the safest city in the world to live in. . . . In the particular class of murder now confronting us, however, the unfortunate victims appear to take the murderer to some retired spot and to place themselves in such a position that they can be slaughtered without a sound being heard" (letter to the chairman of the Board of Works in the Whitechapel district, published in *The Times*, October 4). One letter went as far as to accuse the victims of being murderers. The author estimated that as "the wages of sin have fallen so low" competition could "beget murders": "There are, I have no doubt, plenty of women of this class known for their violent temper, with physical power to commit such a deed" (*Daily Telegraph* letter, September 12). By always recognizing in both the criminal and the victim a deliberate choice to lead an immoral life, poverty, vice, and criminality were blended into a kind of moral affliction, with little or no relation to economic, social, or political factors: "The more we purify society at large, the more certainly does its impure remnant sink to the bottom and form a sediment of concentrated depravity. We speak and think far less often of the moral residuum ever present with us, though, as we may hope and believe, slowly decreasing in quality, in which lust and vice are altogether unbridled and even crime is almost unrestrained" (*The Times* editorial, September 19).

The constant repetition of arguments presenting the "necessitous and dangerous classes" as the residuum of society (this time compared to a volume of water chemically purified) and their identification with the "plague spots" of the East End made the notion of "semi-criminality" not only possible, but commonplace. Letters to the editor routinely suggested measures "for the accommodation particularly of those who are regarded as outcasts and semi-criminal" (*Daily Telegraph*, September 21); "vast numbers who would have been enlisted in the ranks of semi-criminality" (*The Times*, December 26); "single rooms at as low as 1s 8d per week rent, cater for the semi-criminal" (*Daily Telegraph*, September 22). Now one is either in or out of the law: it is logically and legally impossible to be a semi-criminal. However, ideological knowledge characterized by spatialization and identification, and produced through a complex system of presuppositions, implications, and rhetorical devices, allowed this notion to be not only plausible but true: semi-criminals were a fact of life which had to be countered.

If the ultimate solution rested in "personal service and the care of individual by individual. Social fellowship . . . being after all, the true remedy for social disease" (*The Times*, September 19), a great number of more practical measures were demanded in the face of the "disorderly and depraved lives" (*The Times* letter, November 13) revealed by the murders. The lodging-houses were of most concern: these should be closely supervised by appropriate landlords and constantly visited by the police, who should obtain the names and descriptions of all lodgers daily; the sexes should be separated to assure modesty; beds should be isolated by partitions eight or nine feet high "roofed-over with galvanised wiresetting, to prevent intercommunication" (*Daily Telegraph* letter, September 26). Last but not least, the children should be taken away, institutionalized, and released once they could be of service to the state and the middle classes:

> The population in such localities being of the very worst character, surely the first duty of the State is to prevent the increase of it. And this can only be done by withdrawing from such a criminal and vitiated atmosphere the neglected children, of whom there are hundreds in every such locality. . . . A very large number of children would be saved from destitution and crime; intelligent boys, fairly educated and properly trained, would be available for the army, navy, or any other service. Fairly educated and respectable girls would be of invaluable assistance in our colonies as well as in home domestic service, while the cost of our criminal establishments would in time be very greatly reduced, and our criminal system would be stamped with a Christian, parental, and reformatory character [*The Times* letter, September 26].

The advantages were tremendous: the notion of semi-criminals allowed all the "lower classes" to be treated *as if* they were criminals and processed more efficiently. The high acceptability of the notion of semi-criminals made such calls for supervision and control appear reasonable. It also quite successfully erased all economic and political dimensions of crime, paradoxically reified into a moral *and* biological issue. As most ideological maxims on the nature of crime and criminals were expressed metaphorically, and through intricate plays of presuppositions and implications, no demonstration was ever required, and any contradiction could always be resolved by a rhetorical switch, a change of metaphor or analogy. These processes of reification amounted to a dichotomous categorization of the population into us/them groups, where the out-group lost all intrinsic value: "The fact is that no remedy strikes at the root of the evil—the cheapness of human labour and human life. Still we may mitigate the misery by compelling order, decency, and cleanliness, by refusing indiscriminate charity, and by discouraging the influx of foreigners and rustics to London and, above all, to its East-end" (*Daily Telegraph* editorial, October 3).

The Ripper murders not only served to justify measures which would secure the established order, but also surprisingly provided an excellent opportunity for attempts at acquiring capital. Some were rather small in scale, like the case of the bloodhound trainer who took advantage of a large and captive audience to advertise the value of his dogs for detective work in a letter to the editor of *The Times*. Shortly after the publication of this letter, an article explained that Mr. Warren had "witnessed a private trial of bloodhounds in one of the London parks," and gave long descriptions of the dogs' exploits. Other trials were announced, and one fateful day the dogs were reported lost: "if seen anywhere, information is to be sent to Scotland-yard" (*The Times*, October 19).

Quite a few philanthropic individuals started new charity funds and societies, and in the process were attacked by the already existing agencies, quite unwilling to share available monies with aspiring newcomers: "every single agency suggested for the amelioration of Whitechapel is already in existence. . . . What then is needed? I reply, the strengthening of existing agencies, and the more active and sympathetic support of those who are devoting their best energies to making the lives of their poorer brethren happier and more hopeful" (*The Times* letter, October 29). Many decried the entire proceedings, claiming that charity only bred more poverty: "The number of lazy people that the clergy and their friends have attracted to London is very great, and the lower classes are becoming demoralized and pauperized to a fearful extent. The hypocrisy and hatred of honest work which have been engendered are inconceivable without an extensive acquaintance with the poor" (*The Times* letter, October 4).

The most elaborate ploy was a move by "philanthropic gentlemen" to acquire real estate at reasonable prices. The surface argument was that the present landlords of Whitechapel were immoral and bad managers; that, if they were arrested for keeping disorderly houses, Whitechapel lodging-houses could be bought at a fair price (because in their present use, they would be forbiddingly expensive, in view of the high profits reaped by vice); finally, the new group of moral land-lords would keep their houses clean, their tenants quiet, and make a profit! The ploy was denounced by a single reader (as a blatant move to acquire property) but otherwise generally accepted, as it provided a total solution for the entire problem of poverty and immorality, all within the parameters of free enterprise. The *Daily Telegraph*, whose series of articles on the subject were entitled "A Safe Four Per Cent" expressed its usual enthusiastic support:

> Millions and millions of money are eagerly seeking profitable in-vestment in these days of diminished returns from almost all good securities; and people send it abroad to foreigners, sink it in bogus companies, lend it to wild-cat speculators, while, all the time, a perfect mine of gold exists in undeveloped London at their back-doors . . . here is one enterprise which, with proper management and wise administration, would be better than preference shares in the best railways, or Prussian stock, or any foreign rentes. A net and safe four per cent is something to be desired. . . . What London wants she can pay for . . . to transform the slums into decent, commodious, lofty, healthy ranges of edifices, sheltering a cleanly, orderly, and contented proletariat. "A Safe Four Per Cent." There is the charm which, by the magic of financial arith-metic, ought to regenerate the poor quarters of the Metropolis [editorial, September 22].

Arguments claiming that the principles of free enterprise, com-bined with wise administration and adequate legislation, would solve the housing problems of the "lower orders" had been circulating since the 1840s, even though experience in the development of model dwell-ings had repeatedly disproved their validity. Their constant reiteration however, not only in the press but in the reports of commissions of in-quiry (like the 1885 Royal Commission on Housing), of philanthropic organizations (following the Octavia Hill scheme), and of sanitary en-forcement committees (like the Mansion House Council), increased their plausibility and truth value. Gareth Stedman Jones documents how measures informed by such principles (the Torrens Act of 1868 or the Artisans' Dwelling Act of 1875) systematically failed, and how, "despite voluminous evidence which might have suggested the contrary," the same solutions continued to be offered and accepted as valid.[40]

This surprising stubbornness in error becomes more understandable when it is considered that from another perspective, such measures succeeded brilliantly, as they authorized the clearance of large slum areas (thereby segregating the poor into smaller sections of the city), allowed the reallocation of land for the construction of railways, docks, and warehouses (as in Whitechapel), and, in some cases, substantially rewarded slum owners (as with the Artisans' Dwellings Act).[41] Moreover, these measures began to draw distinctions between the deserving and undeserving poor, those who could be counted on to live the closely supervised life of the model dwellings, and those who could not. Similar effects were achieved by the many legal and philanthropic campaigns against prostitutes: Judith Walkowitz has shown how the Contagious Diseases Acts and complementary legislative measures (the Industrial Schools Amendment Act of 1880 and the Criminal Law Amendment Act of 1885), as well as the cleanup campaigns of social purity groups, radically transformed the social position of prostitutes within their working-class communities, and segregated them into an under class.[42] Through such measures the "residuum" was formed, and allotted its place within constant reach of the criminal justice system. Perhaps more importantly, the identification and exclusion of this "residuum" allowed a consensual "we" to emerge: the poor themselves learned to shun the prostitute and the habitual criminal, all of these well-known characters of social discourse (maintained today in the deprived/depraved distinction).[43]

An analysis of the newspaper reports of the Ripper murders shows how effective the press could be as a tool of social integration: through various textual strategies (the constant use of irony, the focus on the incompetency of specific individuals, the spatialization of the crimes, and the identification of the victims as an outcast and worthless group), this discursive practice not only united the public in its abhorrence of the crimes, but also reiterated all the truths about the "lower orders" which supported established relations of power, while making substantial profits in the process. Moreover, just as objective information allowed the press to deny its implication in power and knowledge relations, so it authorized readers to observe the world from a distance, as bystanders, a consensual community united by a common "shrill of horror," by an enjoyable, ironic perspective on bungling police offi-

Figure 4   Press Grid

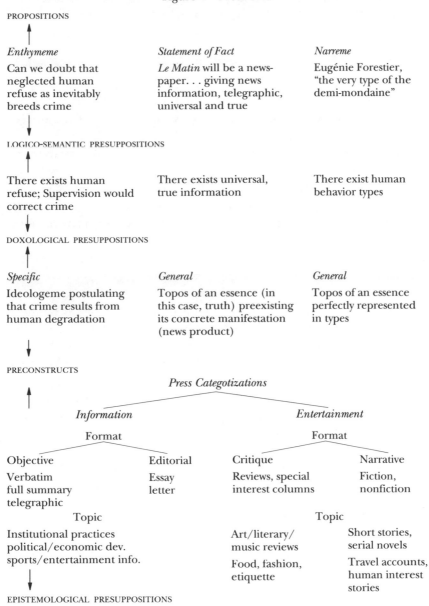

PROPOSITIONS

Enthymeme

Can we doubt that
neglected human
refuse as inevitably
breeds crime

Statement of Fact

Le Matin will be a newspaper. . . giving news
information, telegraphic,
universal and true

Narreme

Eugénie Forestier,
"the very type of the
demi-mondaine"

LOGICO-SEMANTIC PRESUPPOSITIONS

There exists human
refuse; Supervision would
correct crime

There exists universal,
true information

There exist human
behavior types

DOXOLOGICAL PRESUPPOSITIONS

Specific

Ideologeme postulating
that crime results from
human degradation

General

Topos of an essence (in
this case, truth) preexisting
its concrete manifestation
(news product)

General

Topos of an essence
perfectly represented
in types

PRECONSTRUCTS

Press Categotizations

Information

Format

Objective

Verbatim
full summary
telegraphic

Editorial

Essay
letter

Entertainment

Format

Critique

Reviews, special
interest columns

Narrative

Fiction,
nonfiction

Topic

Institutional practices
political/economic dev.
sports/entertainment info.

Topic

Art/literary/
music reviews

Food, fashion,
etiquette

Short stories,
serial novels

Travel accounts,
human interest
stories

EPISTEMOLOGICAL PRESUPPOSITIONS

Reality is a given—truth is absolute and cumulative; language is transparent

Most important object of knowledge produced: objective information, which ensured the
economic and political position of the press, and allowed the construction of a consensual "we,"
the public, united in its opposition to criminality in all its forms (the common criminal, the
master swindler, and the exceptionally depraved criminal as exemplified by Jack the Ripper).

cers, and a sad but superior attitude toward the "class of unfortunates." Armed with such knowledge, what could "we" want to do? Read the next story.[44]

◆

Summary   The first part of this study concluded that one of the primary functions of discourse on "criminal man" was to authorize repressive measures against the "lower orders" in times of organized protest against established power-knowledge relations. Such measures were met with silence: working-class groups did not voice any systematic opposition, as no one could effectively side with criminals in social discourse. This led to the hypothesis that criminality played an extended role of mediation: opposition to criminality in all its forms served not only to segregate the "residuum," but also to constitute a consensual "we," a public united in its need for protection from criminal deviance.

Part two examined the redistribution of knowledge and power relations which took place with the emergence of the public in national education systems and a mass-produced press articulated as defense mechanisms against the spread of criminality, a category which could include everything from thefts to strikes to sexual deviance. Textual analyses of the press outlined how the knowledge produced by this discursive practice reiterated hegemonic truths about the "lower orders" in general and the "residuum" in particular; the "nation as a whole" could stand in its opposition to crimes, secure in the knowledge that such exceptional circumstances proved the validity of established institutions.

The two discursive practices studied so far thus illustrate complementary processes in the articulation of knowledge and power in discourse. Authorizing negative measures of regulation and repression, criminology served to legitimate the broader development of social management policies for the supervision, discipline, and control of the "lower orders" through better knowledge of deviance in all its forms. The press, on the other hand, worked to incite, entertain, and distract the public into recognition of hegemonic truths. Crime reports were central in this process, as they provided the grounds for economic and political stability: they both increased circulation and allowed the reiteration of norms through the presentation of crimes as scandalous deviations from the recognized order of things. Whereas the production of "criminal man" as an object of knowledge elicited

technologies of power in legislative, judiciary, police, and penitentiary systems, the production of "objective information" elicited forms
of knowledge (the public views of society, democracy, and the crimes
of the "lower orders") which sustained strategic relations of economic,
political, and cultural power. Together, these processes represent the
positive (to produce truths, to induce the recognition of the "world as
it is," and promote appropriate practices) and the negative (to restrain,
limit, cauterize deviance) forms of power-knowledge relations which,
according to Foucault, are always interconnected.

Critics of Foucault have charged that his understanding of power
is guilty of preemptive totalization: his model is said to preclude any
form of resistance to power and negate the possibility of radical sys-
temic transformations.[45] Foucault, however, argues specifically that
power relations necessarily imply forms of resistance, which are *not*
"only reaction or rebound . . . doomed to perpetual defeat." Relations
of resistance are multiple in nature and location, and arise within individuals as well as institutions: "Just as the network of power relations
ends by forming a dense web that passes through apparatuses and
institutions, without being exactly localized in them, so too the swarm
of points of resistance traverses social stratifications and individual
unities. And it is doubtless the strategic codification of these points of
resistance that makes a revolution possible, somewhat similar to the
way in which the state relies on the institutional integration of power
relationships."[46]

Foucault often turns to literature to provide a paradoxical example
of resistance. At the end of *The Order of Things*, literature is presented
as the place from which the glimmerings of a new order of thought
can be detected—the space where language can dislodge "man" from
its central position in the *episteme* and yield the possibility of transgression.[47] Reading Mallarmé, Roussel, Kafka, Bataille, and Blanchot, and
their relations to Nietzsche allows Foucault to surmise the grounds of
another mode of thought, a thought of the other and of difference, as
meaning-event. On the other hand, toward the end of *Discipline and
Punish*, the novel is inscribed in the general production of the individual as case story, an indispensable process in disciplinary societies.[48]

Literary critics working within this framework have usually insisted
on the latter interpretation of literature as subjection. In *La production
de l'intérêt romanesque*, for example, Charles Grivel identifies the novel
as the primary means for the dissemination of ideology. He argues
that the interest for the story produced in the reader by the novel

also produces the added value (interest in the economic sense) of re-inforcing established relations of knowledge and power: "Through the novel, the class in power withdraws the right to speak of the dominated class in order to teach it the truth of its own discourse: the text implants a knowledge, the text silences another knowledge which cannot be born."[49] D. A. Miller argues along similar lines in *The Novel and the Police* when he states that "the point of the exercise [novel reading], relentlessly and often literally brought home as much in the novel's characteristic forms and conditions of reception as in its themes, is to confirm the novel-reader in his identity as 'liberal subject'," this identity serving in turn to discipline or police individuals into their assigned social position.[50] Such interpretations thus usually oppose a single dominant ideology to the dominated class, or to the (male generic) liberal subject. I would argue that Foucault's model allows for differences between subjects (and within subjects) to appear, and precludes the positing of a single, monolithic ideology. The following part of this study will attempt to substantiate this claim by studying novels dealing with crime and showing how, while literature is inextricably linked to both negative and positive processes of power-knowledge production, it also can allow for resistance and, at times, open the space where otherness can be glimpsed in transgression.

III LITERATURE

The emergence of literature in the modern sense is usually situated toward the end of the eighteenth century, and understood as the result of two broad developments concerning the conditions of cultural production and the definition of its product. The virtual disappearance of patronage (surviving only in the form of government funds or sinecure positions doled out to a few well-established authors) brought writers to address an impersonal market rather than a restricted circle of patrons and peers: writing and publishing a new work became a venture defined not only in political and aesthetic terms, but in economic ones as well.[1] It was also at this time that literature came to mean works of fiction rather than any text of erudition: this autonomization of literature as a distinct field of endeavor (a separation largely enacted by the Romantics) required the determination of its function within social discourse. A century-long debate on the nature and role of literature and of the novel in particular, coupled with the rapid expansion of the literary market into an important and lucrative one, eventually led to the institutionalization of literature as a discursive practice: by the last quarter of the nineteenth century specialized circuits were established in the publishing industry, the "man of letters" gained prominence in learned journals and in the daily press, writers joined in professional associations, university programs were set up, government funds allocated, and a new brand of literary experts emerged, the academics and students actively expanding their field.[2]

However, whereas the press and criminology held clear mandates as discursive practices, no consensus was ever reached concerning the mandate of literature. All those involved in the debate agreed that literature must play a major role in the organization of society and the founding of the nation, but this horizon accommodated all political programs: whereas the Romantics wished to establish "high" literature and its criticism as the place for resistance to the economic imperatives of capitalist society and its standardized mass-market cultural products, realist writers such as Dickens and Balzac strove to capitalize their mass readership to promote social reform. The "social question," it was argued, could be addressed more effectively in fictional narratives than in political tracts or detailed reports of commissioned inquiries, as widely circulated novels could rouse their readers' interests and emotions and thus provoke speedier resolutions.[3] Governments came to identify the teaching of a national literature as a useful weapon in the fight against social strife, when religion was losing its hold on the masses; conversely, certain types of fiction (naturalist in particular) were feared for their degenerative effects. Variously identified as the locus for the practice of radical critique, progressive reform, or the promotion of the established order, literature was known by all to be potentially dangerous—even if, after all, it was only literature.

The following chapters will explore this paradoxical position of literature in social discourse. Its preconditions of emergence (which largely overlap with those of the press) will first be outlined with a rapid sketch of the economic, political, and epistemological developments which served to delimit its sayable. A chapter on the conditions of emergence will further specify the position of literature within social discourse, and the members and missions of various schools (or individuals) within the literary institution. Finally, textual analyses will examine several strategies adopted by novels in their apprehension of "criminal man," (ranging from the scientific to science-fiction), in order to evaluate their role in the production of knowledge and power relations.[4]

7 Preconditions of Emergence: The Promise of National Literatures

◆

The development of marketable literary products   Launched onto the market as a commodity, the literary work was exposed to the same economic and political pressures as those exerted on the press. The need to increase sales made all the time-honored marketing tricks previously reserved for the promotion of cheap literature now acceptable for "quality" goods: books were given new titles and covers to obtain a better reception the second time around; smaller editions were printed to make a novel bear the sign of popularity at a faster rate; gifts, prizes, and price wars were turned to in the 1890s.[1] Advertising costs steadily increased until they reached 25 to 50 percent of production costs by mid-century.[2] Whereas the publishing industry traditionally had been "long on expertise and short on capital," market conditions in the 1840s and 1850s required increasingly large capital investments in order to achieve profitability.[3]

   The scale of the capital and risk involved tended to encourage the reproduction of winning formulas, even in serious fiction (*Martin Chuzzlewit* was bought and sold as another manifestation of the "true Pickwickian style"[4]), and to require the censorship of all material possibly offensive to any section of the buying public, as aptly described by Grant Allen in 1895: "Most novels nowadays have to run as serials through magazines and newspapers; and the editors of these periodicals are timid to a degree which outsiders would hardly believe. . . . This story or episode would annoy their Catholic readers; that one would repel their Wesleyan Methodist subscribers; such an incident is unfit for the perusal of the young person; such another would drive away the offended matron."[5] In *Victorian People and Ideas* Richard Altick documents such censorship and states that "editorial squeamishness . . . seems to have reached its peak in the sixties and seventies."[6] Those involved in the sale and distribution of books were equally active in the determination of allowable directions for fiction. Bookstall firms such as Hachette in France and W. H. Smith in England banned books which they considered below acceptable moral standards (that is, harmful to sales or to the firm's reputation), and thus held devastating powers over the sale of books and subsequent careers of their authors.[7] Owners and directors of circulating libraries such as Charles Edward Mudie could literally "make or break an author's career" through their book purchasing decisions.[8] Those in charge of local or school libraries, Mechanics' Institute libraries, and the like also exercised their authority, often with great zeal.[9] In the face of such strong opposition to the circulation of books in any way deviant from established political, economic, and moral standards, one can only agree with Darko Suvin's estimation that "a rare conjunction of both author and publisher powerful enough to resist snobbery, ostracism from one's 'betters,' fear of financial failure and finally, in some cases, fear of legal prosecution, was needed to get such matters [subversive of the politico-economic system] into print, particularly into cheaper forms of print."[10]

The slowness of returns on capital investments (with many editions taking years, or a second generation of readers to turn a profit) favored the nurturing of a cultivated market, and this in turn sharply increased the importance of the literary reviewer, whose function it was to guide the reading market to appropriate works.[11] The forums available for literary criticism multiplied and diversified (in reviews, magazines, specialized journals, and the daily press), and the career of literary critic acquired new prestige: Jules Janin, "the Prince of Critics," provided *Le Journal des Débats* with a weekly *"feuilleton dramatique"* for forty years, and received 12,000 francs a year for his services; George Saintsbury and Ferdinand de Brunetière reached glorious heights as literary critics known through their collections of essays and criticism, their international speaking tours and courses.[12] The high profile of such experts favored mass sales of carefully chosen works; their position in social discourse thus produced fields of visibility, networks of shared cultural material which fit within the parameters of acceptable—and marketable—truths.

Apart from this sector, highly considered, tightly knit, and generally cooperative in the maintenance of high prices, a series of efforts were made to reach a wider audience: noncopyright works were offered in cheaper, often illustrated number publications or classic reprint libraries, and recent fiction reprints were sold in 5s or 6s volumes (as compared to 31s 6d for the three-decker new fiction volumes).[13] Massive readership and profits were finally obtained with the part publication of new fiction: Dickens's *Pickwick Papers* (1836) did for number publication in England what Sue's *Mystères de Paris* did for the *roman-feuilleton* in France. Serialization proved extremely lucrative for all concerned, and the fortunes amassed by popular writers like Dickens, Dumas, and Sue legitimized literary careers and greatly increased the status of fiction writers.[14] Such profits led most of the major publishing firms to expand and consolidate their operations, and those "who missed the period of flux were to a large extent excluded after the period of consolidation in the 1840s and 50s. . . . Between 1850 and 1880 there were few major producers of good fiction established."[15]

The turning point seems to have been reached in the 1850s and 1860s when the *scale* of operations changed dramatically. Routledge, for example, was able to turn out 10,000 copies a day of *Uncle Tom's Cabin* in the early 1850s.[16] The export trade grew until it could reach 30 percent of a firm's business by mid-century; Walter Besant calculated that the reading public for English books went from 50,000 to 120,000,00 between 1830 and 1890.[17] With the generalization of 6s reprints in mid-century, the increase of cheap classics in the 1860s and 1870s, and the price wars of the 1880s, the price of fiction decreased until the eventual disappearance of the three-decker in the 1890s.[18] Similar expansion and consolidation took place in France: a *"littérature industrielle"* (in Sainte-Beuve's words) started to expand in the 1840s, and dramatically enlarged its scale of operations in the second half of the century.[19] Sharp increases in total output from 1875 to 1890 led to a glutted market in the 1890s: 14,849 books were copyrighted in 1889 (as compared to 5,442 in 1812), a total which would not be reached again until the 1960s.[20] From 1891 to 1893 two out of three books lost money for their publishers, and underselling brought prices down to ludicrous levels: from 3.5 francs to 60 centimes per volume, to 45 centimes for every 500-volume purchase.[21]

Thus, through the application of marketing methods proven successful in the most popular shares of the readership (serialization, part publication, cheap reprints) and the establishment of efficient networks of production (with capital and machinery intensive organizations), distribution (with railway bookstalls, circulating libraries, and a brisk export trade), and advertisement (and the promotion of "proper culture" for the middle and lower middle classes), a market for quality fiction was demarcated by mid-century, and actively developed thereafter. All of these factors worked to limit the sayable of fiction into the innocuous "interesting to all, offensive to none" category previously outlined for the press. Widely disseminated, this kind of knowledge favored the emergence of a consensual public in social discourse.

◆

The nature and function of a nation's literature   Whether held as the last bastion for the expression of visionary truths in capitalist societies (Coleridge, Carlyle, Balzac) or as the "recognized amusement of our lighter hours" (Trollope), whether condemned as "instruments of abomination and ruin" (the *Evangelical Magazine*) or hailed as a powerful motor for promoting social reform (Dickens, Zola), literary works were typically evaluated—their nature and function determined—within the framework of the nation. Arnold argued that the teaching of literature would elevate the lower classes, civilize the middle classes, and fuse all into a common nation under the guidance of the state.[22] English and French literature were indeed first taught in Mechanics' Institutes and Working Men's Colleges, in elementary schools, and in girls' schools—in short, to all those who could not be expected to learn the classics but needed to be moralized into acceptance of their social position.[23] Governments adopted various methods to promote the production of appropriate literature. Apart from the usual powers of censorship and taxation, the French established a *Commission du Colportage* to establish a list of permissible works, and the government went as far as to offer money for the production of good material: in 1851 prizes of 3,000 to 5,000 francs were offered to works which would "serve to educate the laboring classes by the propagation of healthy ideas and the spectacle of good examples."[24] A similar program was outlined in the 1855 East India Company report, which held that administrative posts should be awarded to men who knew English literature well, and could display this "superior" cultivation to the people of India, presumably to facilitate submission to British rule.[25] Thus, literature in the restrictive sense emerged with the modern chronotope of the nation, the alibi which unifies the time and space of social conflicts between divergent classes into the single evolution of a people in its motherland.[26]

Novels were particularly suited for this integrative purpose, not only because of their popularity (extending to all classes), but also because of their textual construction. Indeed, the narrator in realist novels produces the textual equivalent of the "nation," as it allows the limited perspectives of the characters to be united in an overarching structure of understanding. The narrator, as origin of the tale, is able to order facts in a causal chain of events. Barthes has shown how technical devices such as the use of the third person or the preterit allow this power to be manifested: "by its preterit, the verb implicitly takes part in a causal chain, it participates in a set of solidary and directed actions, it functions as the algebraic sign of an intention maintaining an equivocation between temporality and causality, it calls for a development, i.e., an *intelligibility* of the Narrative."[27] Barthes pointed to Balzac and Michelet as similar makers of self-enclosed, autarchic worlds, and recognized their shared preference for the narrative form as the "choice or expression of a historical moment"—for other periods could write novels in letter form, or history as chronicles. The moment in question is that of positivism, and its affirmation that the progressive development of knowledge would eventually allow "man" to understand and dominate external reality. The conventions of nineteenth-century realistic narrative allow this program to be enacted, as they work to produce a "genial consensus" which, according to Elizabeth Deeds Ermarth, implies "a unity in human experience which assures us that we all inhabit the same world and that the same meanings are available to everyone. Disagreement is only an accident of position."[28] This consensus is achieved (or rather simulated) by the narrator's ability to bridge the gaps between the characters' limited perspectives.

This position is also the one held by the state, theoretically and pragmatically, in its recognized responsibilities toward all citizens (as told in the narrative of national needs), and in its systematic attempts to supervise, normalize, and control the population as a whole. Miller has demonstrated how Victorian novels display these disciplinary processes, and police the reader in the reading process: "the novel encourages a series of deferential cathexes—all the more fundamental for being unconscious—onto various instances of authority. What is promoted in the process is a paternalism that, despite the dim view the novel takes of the power structures of the British state, can only be useful in maintaining such structures."[29]

However, unlike the state, the narrator achieves this position of dominant knowledge and power at a significant price, described by Ermarth as the "price of disembodiment": "standing forever in a continuous actual present that has no concreteness or measurable change and consists only of remembering, the narrator has no perceptible identity. . . . Like time and consciousness, the narrator is everywhere and nowhere, suspended from participation in actions and choices by the very reflective consciousness that presumably makes reasoned choice and action possible."[30] The invisibility and ultimate passivity of the narrator in relation to the events it recalls is reduplicated in the reader of realistic narratives, who is also trapped into passivity by the conventions of realism (and thus holds the same position as that produced for the reader of a press engaged in the production of a consensual "we"). Miller argues similarly when he states that the novel's "discourse on power only comes to light in (as) a discourse on 'the way things are.' 'Revealing' the character of modern power only insofar as it 'masks' it as an ontology, [the novel] is thus perfectly obedient to the imperatives of such power . . . the novel's discourse on power must finally be taken as a discourse of power."[31] The function of such discourse, according to Miller, is to produce subservient subjects.

It is at this juncture—when literature was championed by many in positions of authority as a useful agent for the founding of a unified nation, when the novel, in particular, was seen as providing the grounds for a common culture cutting across class barriers, and when the narrator of realist novels both enacted this political program and produced a passive position for itself and the reader—that the rhetoric of gender was modified in its application to literature. The role of literature was now described as feminine (to "mother" the nation, "civilize" the lower and middle classes, and reintegrate the emotional and spiritual dimensions of life in societies increasingly dislocated by the effects of industrial capitalism), and thus designated women as particularly well suited for the profession of literature teachers.[32] This feminization of literature corresponded to the reconceptualization of reading as a passive form of learning. D. J. Palmer and Lionel Gossman have argued that, whereas during the seventeenth and eighteenth centuries reading had been linked to writing and to the learning of rhetoric as means for an effective participation in public affairs, reading literature in the nineteenth century was promoted as a form of communion with the great minds of the past: "The reader's relation to books was thus no longer in the first instance that of a potential writer, a producer, an equal; it was that, at best, of an adept or worshipper, at worst, of a consumer."[33]

The feminine characterization of literature was furthermore a powerful means to limit its sayable. "Woman" and "literature" were at times practically collapsed as equivalent classes in their constitution of the concept of the "feminine," for both included beauty and disinterestedness as their primary objects. A widely used French textbook entitled *L'Instruction morale et civique des jeunes filles* (1882) insisted that a woman must never forget that "what men require above all in a woman, is that she be feminine in virtues and appearance."[34] Such requirements parallelled those placed by men in positions of authority on literature: that it be literary in virtues and appearance. Gustave Flaubert's *Madame Bovary* was not criticized—and prosecuted—for being untrue, but for incorporating truths which were out of place, untrue to the mission of art. During Flaubert's trial the prosecutor quoted the description of a waltz and declared: "I know very well that one waltzes a little in this manner, but this does not make it moral."[35] He concluded with a revealing comparison: "Art without rules is no longer art; it is like a woman who would take off all her clothes. To impose on art the unique rule of public decency, is not to subjugate it, but to honor it."[36] True literature should not be allowed to explore or reveal reality "as it was": its proper mission was to represent beauty and guide readers to a "higher truth." As women should have "no right to meddle with public affairs, no right to follow professions, no right to occupy themselves with any really intellectual pursuits," literature should not deal with social or political controversies: "we admit that Mr. Dickens has a mission, but it is to make the world grin, not to recreate and rehabilitate society."[37] If women needed education, it was "not only to show them what they can do, but what they cannot do and should not attempt": "the great fault in a woman is to want to be a man, and to want to be learned is to want to be a man."[38] Similarly, novels should not be cluttered with medical, architectural, economic, sociological, or political knowledge alien to the nature of art; realist descriptions which incorporated such matters only managed to substitute clinical observations for artistic sensitivity. Works by Flaubert or Eliot were constantly being accused of performing inhuman dissections: "Mr. Flaubert is not only a painter disguised as a novelist, but a surgeon who has missed his vocation. . . . He does not hear the cries of the patient that he is dissecting. One would think he is working on a cadaver."[39]

Throughout the century, writers resisted the limits imposed on the sayable of literature. Charlotte Bronte doubted the very possibility of writing within boundaries recognized as "feminine": "Come what will,

I cannot, when I write, think always of myself and what is elegant and charming in femininity; it is not on these terms, or with such ideas, that I ever took pen in hand." [40] In a scathing article entitled "*De la moralité*," Zola denounced the social hypocrisy of newspapers which purged narrative fiction of material routinely published in police columns and reports of court proceedings. [41] Why should descriptions of the "lower orders" or of criminals and prostitutes be widely disseminated in newspaper reports, bluebooks, and medical and sociological treatises but rejected in fiction? Close textual analyses will serve to clarify the reasons for this particular trauma over what literature could say, but it can be noted from the outset that descriptions allowed the novel to operate the intertextual rewriting of commonly held discursive truths; the very choice of objects worthy of description hinged on other practices. [42] A born criminal's description in a naturalist novel such as *La bête humaine* would thus almost necessarily include a reference to a prognathous jaw, as this anatomical feature was systematically recognized by criminologists, anthropologists, sociologists, and newspaper reporters. However, novels could then use this scientific truth to other ends, in the narrative context, and thereby display discursive modes of knowledge production—a process potentially threatening to the maintenance of established knowledge and power relations. As it was through their scientific and impersonal descriptions that novelists articulated their texts to the latest discoveries, and thereby claimed to produce scientific truths themselves, the battle over their right to include such material involved high stakes: not only the status and mandate of their discursive practice, but also the epistemological grounds for the production of knowledge in the age of positivism.

Those who worked to limit the sayable of narrative fiction usually did so in the name of taste and morality: "If Mr. Zola lacks taste and spirit, just as if he lacks psychological finesse, it is because Mr. Zola lacks a moral sense. . . . The moral sense, for us, is therefore strictly speaking the human sense, or, to speak more clearly, the sense of what in man is superior to nature. For rather than being a part of nature, man separates and distinguishes himself from her." [43] As usual, class distinctions were inscribed in the concept of morality:

Mr. Zola, who barely knows the meaning of words, has evidently never known the value or the power of words. If he were writing for workers, we could let him get away with it; but he is writing for the bourgeois; and if he believes that an ignoble blasphemy or a dirty insult have the same signification for a bourgeois who reads them printed in a book as for a peasant or a worker who utters them unknowingly, as he swallows a glass of wine or a bowl of cider, I can assure him that a "writer" or a "naturalist" could not be more mistaken.[44]

Whereas the "lower classes" enjoyed rough manners and crude entertainment, and were therefore closer to nature in their life-style, the bourgeois had developed taste, spirit, and psychological finesse, and had thus lifted themselves up from this primary state: the bourgeois had a moral sense which Zola—and his readers—could not grasp. Zola committed the unpardonable outrage of believing the bourgeois to be determined by the same natural forces as those affecting the "lower orders": "Are we considering high society through open doors, or high society behind closed doors? If we are curious, if we look through the cracks, I suspect that we will see, in the distinguished classes, what we saw in the people, for the human beast is everywhere the same, only the clothes are different."[45] By denying taste, defined by one critic as "the free will of the intellect," Zola destroyed the grounds for bourgeois distinction and authority. Naturalist writers were also greatly handicapped by their popularity: recognizing their worth would have been tantamount to acknowledging the discernment of hundreds of thousands of readers. For the cultured elite, as for penitentiary scientists and anthropologists, morality served as the point of dispersion of "man," the point where distinctions according to class, race, or gender could be recognized within the category of "universal man"; it also provided the grounds for the dominant classes to claim power, both physical and spiritual, over reality, through this indescribable sense.[46]

The epistemological basis for this articulation of power first to "man" and then to specific categories of men qualified with a distinct moral sense (or men of distinction) can be drawn from Foucault's analysis of an epistemological break occurring at the end of the eighteenth century, which placed "man" as the origin and measure of meaning. Whereas classical thought recognized living beings existing in nature in an ordered relation to meaning as determined by the will and wisdom of God, modern thought perceived the meaning of existing economic, linguistic, and life systems as deriving from their respective development in time. The shift, therefore, was from an *episteme* founded on the principle of order to one based on history and centered on "man," as it was through human labor that meaning was established, languages developed, riches accumulated, and history registered.[47] The study of legal, criminological, educational, and press discourses has shown that "man" was also the telos of knowledge production: each of these discursive practices defined its ultimate goal as increasing the knowledge, and power, of "man." Institutions established to regulate the distribution of knowledge, wealth, and political authority according to differences of class, race, and gender were all theoretically imposed for the protection of human rights and the enrichment of human nature. "Man" became the center through which power could be exercised.

However, the *episteme* which placed "man" at the origin of meaning also paradoxically revealed his inevitable domination by exteriority: language, labor, heredity, and environments overdetermined human nature and behavior. The power of knowledge at once revealed the finitude of "man": "Man's finitude is heralded—and imperiously so—in the positivity of knowledge; we know that man is finite, as we know the anatomy of the brain, the mechanics of production costs, or the system of Indo-European conjugation; or rather, like a watermark running through all these solid, positive, and full forms, we perceive the finitude and limits they impose, we sense, as though on their blank reverse sides, all that they make impossible."[48] What appropriate literature and criminology (the psychological novel, or the French sociological criminology) provided was room for an *indescribable*—and therefore unknowable—uniqueness in "man." Referred to euphemistically as the moral sense, the human sense, the soul, or free will, this quality endowed certain men with the power to choose and thus regain power over themselves and the environment.

Within this context, the narrative fulfilled two essential functions in the production of positivist truths. First, it emerged as the most appropriate medium for the investigation of "man": George Meredith voiced a widespread conviction when he stated that the aim of the novel was to present "the natural history of man."[49] G. H. Lewes went so far as to assert that the novel's intrinsic rules were universal in application, because they derived from human nature itself: "The art of novel-writing . . . is founded on general principles, which, because they have their psychological justification, because they are derived from tendencies of the human mind, and not, as absurdly supposed, derived from 'models of composition,' are of universal application."[50]

Moreover, the narrative served as a stopgap in the production of the ultimate blanket of positivist knowledge. Previous analyses have shown that narratives were vital for the elaboration of scientific criminology, for whenever an essential theoretical point could not be proved by measurement or argument, it was demonstrated in a short tale. Similarly, medical theories on heredity could rest on crime stories taken from the *Gazette des Tribunaux*. History as practiced by Macauley or Michelet incorporated narratives to order facts into meaningful representations of their author's philosophy. Paleoanthropology made extensive use of the narrative to elaborate its knowledge on prehistoric man: from the discovery of bones or flintstones elaborate stories of everyday life were drawn, including the details of eating and dressing habits, and sexual behavior.[51] The emergence of new fields of scientific investigation into the various dimensions of human nature (criminology, sociology, psychology, and prehistoric anthropology) was generally accompanied by the development of equivalent narrative subgenres. Criminological research into the influence of heredity and milieu on the behavior of the "lower classes" was doubled by equivalent interests in the naturalist novels of Zola, Rosny Aîné, and Gissing, with *La bête humaine* (1889–90) exemplifying their symbiotic development. Forensic and police sciences were established along with *romans judiciaires*, *romans policiers*, and detective novels. Claude Bernard's efforts to institute experimental medicine in the 1860s were duplicated in the Goncourt brothers' attempts to develop clinical novels studying temperaments. Prehistoric anthropology was institutionalized when Rosny Aîné, H. G. Wells, and many others were writing their apeman stories. Psychology was recognized as a science when the psychological novel was gaining prominence; the first French psychology laboratory was established at the Collège de France in 1889, the same year that Bourget published his most celebrated *Le Disciple*.[52] Thus, an extensive use of the narrative form throughout social discourse was coterminous with the apprehension of "man"; or perhaps better stated, "man" was known through narratives which took charge of times past, present, and future and aligned events in an order representative of the human scale.

The wide circulation of the narrative throughout social discourse increased the value of the novelist's work, for while short tales could be incorporated into scientific discourse as valuable tools for knowledge production, it was in novel-length stories that the ultimate desire for a total apprehension of "man" could be enacted. Only in the novel could the influence of heredity and environment be followed and fully documented in an individual's life story.[53] Said Zola, "If my novel must have a result, it will have the following: to tell the *human truth*, dismantle our machine, show its secret hereditary mechanisms, and make clear the influence of environments."[54] Narratives could eliminate within their sphere that great enemy of positivist thought, doubt. When asked what would be his greatest sorrow, Zola answered "To be in doubt."[55] Jevons explained in his *Principles of Science* (1874) that a scientific or "truly philosophic" mind could not tolerate doubt because it was "the confession of ignorance and involve[d] a painful feeling of incapacity."[56] Narratives allowed this thirst for absolute certainty—and power—to be temporarily quenched.

This capacity of the narrative form would perhaps explain its prominence in such a place as the *Gazette des Tribunaux* (started in 1825), the paper which scientists and novelists alike pillaged for material for their work. Whereas matters of civil court were presented concisely (lists of pertinent articles quoted in italics, precedents, and technical reports on matters of litigation), reports of criminal court proceedings were strewn with entertaining descriptions of defendants and witnesses, long narratives of the lives which led to criminal activity, and full reproductions of exciting testimony or stirring summations. As the outcome of the trial was life or death, guilt had to be established *beyond reasonable doubt*—and the *Gazette des Tribunaux* often opted for the narrative form as the most appropriate means to transmit information about the defendants. Indeed, the paper had no interest in casting doubt on criminal proceedings, and the narrative allowed "true accounts" of the life of the accused to be entirely molded by ideological maxims on criminal behavior. On January 1, 1856, the paper reported the trial of Rose Berlioz on counts of attempted abortion, infanticide, and poisoning. The report stated that Antoine Maubleu had married her even though she was an unwed mother, in the hope that she would soon settle down. The narrative continued:

> Unfortunately these hopes were dashed, and the Maubleu woman continued to abandon herself to her evil instincts. The profession she exercised [midwife], by allowing her to go out at all hours of the day and night, favored her misconduct, and the well-founded advice and reprimands of her husband only provoked insults and contempt on her part. The disorderliness of the conduct of Rose

Berlioz did not cease to increase, and, when a detachment of the army of the Alps was stationed in the commune of Saint-Etienne-de-Crossey, the profligacy of this woman knew no limits.

With this kind of presentation, reasonable doubt could be effectively dispelled. Novelists, sociologists, and medical doctors gathered much of their knowledge of the "lower orders" from these detailed narratives of the everyday life of peasants, workers, thieves, and murderers. Stendhal described the paper as "the golden book of French energy in the nineteenth century."[57] The obvious fascination this publication held for many of the learned elite probably also derived from their recognition of the tribunal situation as the epitome of their own search for truth. The *juge d'instruction* had to confront facts, sort them in an ordered chain of events, and discover their single true meaning in order to exercise his power effectively.[58] The encounter between judge, defendant, and jury involved social definitions of right and wrong, truth and falsehood: knowledge of "man" and society held in the balance. Finally, the exchanges taking place in a court of law had to end with an absolute conclusion, excluding the possibility of doubt. Whether applied to the discovery of human nature (in anthropology, sociology, criminology, psychology, and medicine) or in the determination of guilt or innocence, whether used in scientific treatises, the press, or in novels, realist narratives seemed endowed with a unique capacity to determine essential truths.

The institutionalization of literature was thus made possible by the convergence of multiple economic, political, textual, and epistemological factors. Economic imperatives sketched the boundaries of the sayable for literature, which largely overlapped with those of the press, and worked to forge a consensual "we," often identified with the ideal family circle. Political imperatives favored the cross-class dissemination of this material, to institute the nation; textual conventions allowed the enactment of this political program, through the narrator, and the passive position it assigned to the reader. In an age (or an epistemological configuration) recognizing "man" as the origin and telos of knowledge, novels, which were said to relate the natural history of "man," were valued as privileged means for the production of truth. Novels which foregrounded morality would be most prized by those holding positions of authority, as this sense—defined as their sense—served to found their privilege on biosocial grounds and deny the finitude inscribed in their knowledge and power. But if "man" was the origin and goal, "criminal man" would be the means, the discursive object allowing the narrative process to begin, and the nature of "man" to be implied. Indeed nineteenth-century novels began with a crime, lack, or scandal (the "narratable") whose narrative development allowed an originary positivity to be known, *a contrario*; as argued by Charles Grivel, "the disorder of the novel is only legible because it signifies, in depth, the generalized acceptance of the positivity [of hegemonic truth] and implies the adequation of the reader to this positivity." [59]

8 Conditions of Emergence: Disciplinary Limits

◆

The implications of institutionalization: receding realist narratives
Once institutionalized, most disciplines ceased to define their mandate of knowledge production in relation to "man"; physicians, historians, sociologists, philosophers, and literary experts painstakingly began to delimit specialized fields of interest and to expulse the narrative from their operations. Claude Bernard's *Introduction à l'étude de la médecine expérimentale* (1865) thus relegated most of Lucas's work outside of the realm of science. Whereas the *Traité philosophique et physiologique de l'hérédité naturelle dans les états de santé et de maladie du système nerveux* (1850) strove to incorporate medical facts into a broad conception of the universe of God and "Man," the *Introduction* carefully circumscribed a narrow field of experimental concerns which ignored primary causes but allowed mastery over particular processes.[1] Whereas Lucas wove narratives, religious precepts, press reports, judicial principles, and physical examinations into a single medical analysis, Bernard expelled all that could not be precisely measured and verified. From this perspective, narratives, however realistic, became literally meaningless for the scientist.

Similarly, history was transferred from the hands of amateurs following in the wake of Scott's popularity to those of academics intent on gathering all the facts and presenting them objectively, "as it actually happened."[2] Rather than search for the historical laws of the development of mankind or draw a philosophy of history, scientific historians concentrated their efforts on the discovery and impartial presentation of facts, and found relatively little value for the narrative in their work.[3] Literary studies were gradually transformed from the study of the lives of authors (Sainte-Beuve) or of peoples (Taine), to bibliographical and philological research (Lanson); the promoters of literary science at the *Nouvelle Sorbonne* developed a specialized vocabulary along with the *laboratoires* and *travaux pratiques* still in vogue today.

In his lecture, *Our Knowledge of the External World as a Field for Scientific Method in Philosophy*, Bertrand Russell reiterated this need to develop specific expertise: "Philosophy is not a short cut to the same kind of results as those of the other sciences: if it is to be a genuine study, it must have a province of its own, and aim at results which the other sciences can neither prove nor disprove."[4] Philosopher/mathematicians like Russell and Gottlob Frege before him worked to develop specialized tools and a precise methodology for philosophy, and applied these to objects of limited scope: for example, they tried to reduce complex sentences to logical atomic sentences stating primary truths, in order to discover the logical structures of thought shaping ordinary language. The gulf separating the method of Durkheim from the stories of Mayhew attests to analogous trends taking place in sociology.

This new specialization, identified with functionalism, transformed the relation between knowledge and social values, or, in Durkheim's words, between discipline and morality:

> Gone are the times when the perfect man seemed to be the one who, knowing how to interest himself in everything without tying himself exclusively to anything, capable of tasting everything and of understanding everything, managed to reunite and condense within himself all that was most exquisite in civilization. This general culture, highly praised in former times, today strikes us as a soft and slack discipline. . . . We rather see perfection in the competent man who tries not to be complete, but to be productive, who has a delimited task at hand and who dedicates himself to it, who renders service, traces his own furrow. . . . In a word, by one of its aspects, the categorical imperative of the moral consciousness is taking the following form: "Make yourself able to perform usefully a determined function."[5]

Early positivism, in Comte's formulation, strove to answer the social question through the development of a comprehensive knowledge of "man" and society which would provide the grounds for a secular deontology: the industrial capitalist order would thus paradoxically be naturalized and moralized, through positivist knowledge.[6] However, toward the end of the century a general redistribution of knowledge and power relations cleansed knowledge of its apparent relation to power or values (see chapter four): the new human scientists could produce empirical facts about human and social phenomena, but their value could not be determined within their field of investigation. As argued by Eliséo Véron, Western industrialized societies then clearly distinguished the production of empirical facts from the determination of values, and assigned the latter to "the political order of industrial 'democracy,' the field of public opinion in a pluralist society."[7] And indeed only the state and the press, those working with and from public opinion, and acting as mediators in the forum of social values, could still champion scientific knowledge as the royal road to happiness. The chemist and life senator (from 1881) Marcelin Berthelot, who edited the science column of the *République Française*, thus promised in his *Science et morale* (1896): "Such are the consequences of the scientific method, consequences that we pursue and that we realize, in the moral order as in the material order, in spite of all opposition: it is thus that the universal triumph of science will arrive at ensuring the maximum of happiness and of morality for mankind."[8]

Scientists engaged in the development of their newly instituted fields of inquiry, however, had turned their backs on "man" to concentrate on more limited, discipline-specific problems, which eventually rejected the positivist notion of truth (as the discovery of objective reality) and redefined the entire process of knowledge production. Just as in the 1840s and 1850s they had ceased to regard the explanations of the Old Testament as factual accounts, scientists in the last decades of the century started to abandon the belief that their theories constituted a faithful representation of reality as it was. Prominent physicists (J. C. Maxwell, W. Thomson, and E. Mach) and mathematicians (P. Duhem and H. Poincaré) began to question the postulates of scientific realism and to consider scientific theories as models which served to increase knowledge and shape experiences, but which did not necessarily represent objective reality.[9]

The epistemological implications of these and other scientific developments (theory of relativity and quantum mechanics) would radically alter the subject and object of cognition, and the cognitive process itself. Positivist thought, encountered here in the discursive practices of criminology and the press, considers truth to arise when the subject adequately represents objective reality in language; in other words, positivism rests on the epistemological presupposition that reality is a given, truth is absolute and cumulative, and language is transparent. Reiss described this epistemological model as characteristic of analytico-referential discourse, which

> assumes that the world, as it can be and is to be known, represents a fixed object of analysis quite separate from the forms of discourse by which men speak of it and by which they represent their thoughts. . . . Equally basic is the assumption that the proper *use* of language will not only *give* us this object in a gradual accumulation of detail (referentiality), but will also *analyze* it in the very form of its syntactic organization. . . . The assumption of objectivity and the consequent exclusion of whatever cannot be brought to fit its order are necessarily accompanied by the occultation of the enunciating subject *as discursive activity* and, therefore, of its responsibility for the status of the objects of which it speaks.[10]

The "new scientific spirit," on the other hand, perceives its object not as form or substance but as a complex of relations which includes and transforms the subject. Bachelard described this epistemological reconfiguration in terms of a project ("in scientific thought, the meditation of the object by the subject always takes the form of a project") necessarily social and polemic in character: "Objectivity cannot be detached from the social character of proof. . . . Scientific observation is always a polemical observation; it confirms or infirms an anterior thesis . . . it recognizes the real after having reconstructed its schemata. . . . Science calls forth a world, not by a magical impulse, immanent to reality, but rather by a rational impulse, immanent to the mind."[11] Parallel developments were taking place in the literary field, and can be traced in the internationally famous debate between Walter Besant, Henry James, and Robert Louis Stevenson on "The Art of Fiction." The debate is particularly pertinent to this study in that the positions taken by each of the interlocutors manifest the effects of these general epistemological and institutional reconfigurations for the emergence of literature in the modern sense.

When Besant, cofounder and chairman of the Society of Authors, presented his address on "The Art of Fiction" to the Royal Institution on April 25, 1884, his aims were largely practical: he wished to gain official recognition for this art form. Therefore, he used the most effective (and by now familiar) argument in nineteenth-century social discourse: the novel was valuable because it increased knowledge of "man." Placing "man" as both the origin and telos of the novel, his positivist description both naturalized and moralized its object: the novel had arisen along with a new faculty in human nature, that of recognizing "the real indestructible man beneath the rags and filth of a common castaway"—that is, the ability to discern "man" even in the "lower orders."[12] Described as a "tremendous engine of popular influence," the novel could moralize the masses: "can we not . . . say with truth, Let him who pleases make the laws if I may write the novels?"[13] Besant argued that the novel's effectiveness would be increased if novelists were granted national distinctions (titles, peerages) and if they organized themselves into academies and associations— only then would the art of fiction acquire its well-deserved status in society. The novel's champion was more than willing to accept the implications of professionalism, the first one being the recognition of rules to be followed by all practitioners of the art and taught to aspiring novelists. His list of rules worked to ensure that the novel give a "simple and faithful story, truly and faithfully told": "everything in Fiction which is invented and is not the result of personal experience and observation is worthless."[14]

Besant's lecture is typical of the positivist model of knowledge production. Novels are described as the true reflection of an external reality; the transmission of this knowledge is worthwhile because it increases "reverence for man," and provokes a "deepening and widening of the civilization of the world."[15] The consensual "we" is reiterated through an art form whose main effect is to produce a passive, silent recognition: "as for the great Masters of the Art . . . there is nothing . . . that we can give them but admiration that is unspeakable, and gratitude that is silent."[16] The sociocultural conditions of knowledge production and distribution are thus first erased by a model where universal truths are gradually discovered and disseminated through language. However, specific imperatives (technical, moral, national) are soon inscribed in the process: faced with an "inexhaustible and bewildering mass of things," the "observant and trained eye" of the writer must *choose* in order to make the world "dramatic by his silences, his suppressions, and his exaggerations."[17] Such selection is directed by morality, and morality collapsed onto the nation: modern developments such as "the growing reverence for the individual" and "the sense of personal responsibility among the English-speaking races . . . are all forces which act strongly upon the artist as well as upon his readers, and lend to his work, whether he will or not, a moral purpose so clearly marked that it has become practically a law of English fiction." [18] Sociopolitical and technical pressures, at first rejected from fiction as "simple and faithful story," thus return with a vengeance.

In September 1884 Henry James published a response to Besant's article under the same title. Willing to take for granted what Besant was still fighting to achieve, James agreed that fiction should be "reputed very artistic indeed," but wondered at the reasons for uttering such a self-evident notion.[19] Whereas Besant insisted that the public needed to take fiction seriously, James argued that fiction "must take itself seriously for the public to take it so," and thus began to shift the focus away from the public forum of values to more discipline-specific concerns.[20] These remained articulated to life and "man": "the only reason for the existence of a novel is that it does attempt to represent life . . . as the picture is reality, so the novel is history."[21] Like Besant, James considered the novel to be "a personal, a direct impression of life," but refused to recognize any social determinants to this impression, defining experience as "the very atmosphere of the mind."[22] The novel's only obligation was to be interesting, and the "ways in which it is at liberty to accomplish this result . . . are as various as the temperament of man, and they are successful in proportion as they reveal a particular mind, different from others."[23] The author's experience and execution were entirely personal, as were the reader's acceptance or rejection of the novel. Thus, James specifically denied any social interference in the process of literary production, first by describing its subject as the mind of the writer and the "temperament of man," and then by naturalizing its product as an organic life form: "a novel is a living thing, all one and continuous, like any other organism."[24] The novel, therefore, could not be bound by rules: "the good health of an art which undertakes so immediately to reproduce life must demand that it be perfectly free."[25]

A novel endowed with organic unity and freedom displayed that "supreme virtue," an "air of reality" that allowed it to "compete with life" and become a distinct experience in itself, as shown in James's final address to young writers.[26] Whereas Besant was eager to pass on the tools of the trade, James advocated a manner of living with and through art: "'Enjoy it as it deserves,' I should say to him: 'take possession of it, explore it to its utmost extent, publish it, rejoice in it. All life belongs to you. . . . Be generous and delicate and pursue the prize.'"[27] For James the organic novel allowed a special kind of life experience and possessed its own inner truth. This allowed the temporary bypass

of the contradictions of his position, which both recognized the subject and the practice of writing, but denied any social determinants
for either: "in proportion as in what she [Fiction] offers us we see life
without rearrangement do we feel that we are touching the truth; in
proportion as we see it *with* rearrangement do we feel that we are being
put off with a substitute, a compromise and convention." [28]

Robert Louis Stevenson aptly entitled his article (published in November 1884) "A Humble Remonstrance," for it scolded its predecessors and proposed a more humble view of the nature and function of
fiction. He began by specifying the object of contention along disciplinary lines, stating that it was not fiction in general, but rather "the
art of *fictitious* narrative in *prose*," and continued by separating such
objects from life:

> A proposition of geometry does not compete with life; and a
> proposition of geometry is a fair and luminous parallel for a work
> of art. Both are reasonable, both untrue to the crude fact; both
> inhere in nature, neither represents it. The novel, which is a work
> of art, exists, not by its resemblances to life, which are forced and
> material, as a shoe must still consist of leather, but by its immea-
> surable difference from life, which is designed and significant,
> and is both the method and the meaning of the work.[29]

The value of the novel derived not from its capacity to give a true representation of life or to compete with life, but rather from its power
to produce truth within its sphere of exploration. Stevenson proposed
a model theory of literature which appraised narrative texts on their
structural efficiency and their ability to awaken emotions and stimulate the intellect. Unlike James, he recognized classes of novels (and
categorized James's works as novels of character), each endowed with
its own technical requirements achieving specific effects. A novel of
adventure, for example, could not bear too many character traits, for
these would distract and dilute the reader's interest.[30] Stevenson's rules
were structural and pragmatic rather than professional (as in Besant's)
or organic (as in James). If literature imitated at all, it was "not life
but speech: not the facts of human destiny, but the emphasis and the
suppressions with which the human actor tells of them." [31] Besant's
call for a general recognition of rules of fiction writing and for the
establishment of awards for those who complied to such procedures
was met with silence on Stevenson's part, for the material conditions
of literary production, the financial and political positions of writers,

the sale and distribution of their work, and other such considerations were literally unthinkable within a model theory of literature (or of science).[32] Literature by the 1880s had become a field, with its special learning and its—quite limited—range of action.

Within this general trend toward the specialization of discursive practices, the program set forth by literary realists and naturalists appears as the last manifestation of positivist hopes rather than the beginning of modern scientific literature, as Zola affirmed in *Le roman expérimental* (1880). The leader of the naturalist school positioned their work within the general development of scientific truth bringing power to "man": "we work along with the century in a great oeuvre which is the conquest of nature, the power of man increased tenfold."[33] Zola argued that the experimental novel "continues and completes physiology, which itself rests on chemistry and physics; it substitutes for the study of abstract man, of metaphysical man, the study of natural man, submitted to the physical and chemical laws determined by the influences of the environment."[34] Like criminologists (also devoted to the study of "concrete man"), novelists applied the relevant findings of all sciences to their particular field of inquiry. Naturalism was also praised by Zola as the cure for—what else?—criminality: "To be masters of good and evil, to regulate life, regulate society, resolve in the end all the problems of socialism, most of all to bring solid bases for justice by resolving through experience the questions of criminality, is that not to be the most useful and most moral workers of human labor?"[35]

The rejection of the narrative from scientific research and the abandonment of the possibility of achieving an all-encompassing knowledge of "man" eventually made the notion of scientific novels unthinkable. Novels turned from vast studies of mankind (Balzac's *Comédie humaine* and Zola's Rougon-Macquart series) to close explorations of the narrative form and its potentialities.[36] How could such texts open the space for otherness to arise?

◆

The production of literary meaning   Not easily. Literary meaning was not just circumscribed by the general sociocultural determinants outlined above; the range of topics and genres open to individual authors also depended on their economic and cultural background, as demonstrated by Rémy Ponton and Christophe Charle in their analyses of French literary schools.[37] Zola's choice of the novel as genre, for example, was about the only one available to an ambitious young man with no higher education, no economic prospects, and no relations to facilitate his entry into literary circles. A reputation in poetry, the most prestigious genre, could only be achieved with a long-term commitment, and offered no financial rewards. Moreover, this genre led to few career opportunities, as all major honorific positions (in newspapers, the *Académie*, and so on) were occupied by the Parnasse school, then at the peak of its glory. Fame and fortune only materialized when Zola turned to the burning social questions of the day—poverty and alcoholism in the "lower orders" (*L'Assommoir*) and prostitution (*Nana*). Aspiring novelists started to congregate around the best-selling author, and a collective publication (*Les soirées de Médan*, 1880) and theoretical manifesto (*Le roman expérimental*) ensued, establishing naturalism in the French and international literary networks. Having served its purpose, that is, having launched obscure writers and increased Zola's credibility and visibility in the literary industry, the school began to dissolve shortly thereafter.[38] The second generation of naturalists counted great numbers of lower middle-class graduates of secondary schools, who could not afford to enter the professions. Their path was made more difficult by Zola's prodigious output and sales, and they often had to resort to publicity stunts (as the *Manifeste des Cinq*, in 1887, which denounced Zola's *La Terre*) or to mass production (J. H. Rosny wrote 130 novels alone or with his brother, and 55 others in collaboration) in order to survive.

Meanwhile, another group of writers (P. Bourget, A. France) with far different credentials (higher education, upper-class backgrounds, and family associations with the cultural elite) was also in need of a literary outlet. In what Ponton described as a "reconversion strategy," they applied their "distinction" to the novel, and explored the minds and souls of the complex few rather than the bodies and instincts of the "lower orders." The novel was thus made acceptable to the literary establishment, and important allies representing conservative religious and political interests in the press rallied to the side of the psychological novel, and its writers were eventually accepted in the *Académie*.[39]

All of these forces worked to ensure that literary texts reiterate norms. Grivel made this point by describing the novel as a version of a society's dominant ideological field (or general Text): "The novel is not and could not be critical. Essentially confirmative, it answers for and guarantees its origin (its archetypal base). Instrument of conservation, closely linked to the unconditional repetition of meaning (to its authoritative and exclusive dictation), it locks the user in the circle of reproduction (of redoubling): *the reader is only the replica of what he reads (from birth)*. In the novel, it is language which is prevented from thinking (the novel opens only on the novel)."[40]

And yet, the novel must constantly confront the materiality and historicity of language in ways that texts from the human sciences or the press and political forums usually avoid. As previously noted in the discussion of descriptions, the practice of novel writing can alter the pertinence of accepted truths by highlighting alternate semes through textual manipulations. Through the multiple, differing uses of the word "beast," as well as through plot and character elaborations, the narrative development of *La bête humaine*, for example, allows the animality of criminals asserted by criminology to be linked to technological and political factors specifically excluded from the criminological field, but nevertheless fundamental to its elaboration of truth. The intrinsically intertextual nature of narrative objects has been forcefully argued by Mikhail Bakhtin:

> Instead of the virginal fullness of an inexhaustible object, the prose writer is faced with a multiplicity of routes, roads and paths that have been laid down in the object by social consciousness. Along with the internal contradictions of the object itself, the prose writer comes to discover as well the social heteroglossia that *surrounds* the object, the Tower of Babel confusion of languages that goes on around any object. The dialectics of the object are interwoven with the social dialogue surrounding it. For the prose writer, the object is a condensation of heterological voices among which his own voice must also resound; these voices create the background necessary for his own voice, without which his literary nuances would not be perceived, and without which they "do not sound."[41]

This description reiterates Stevenson's point about literature imitating speech, "not the facts of human destiny, but the emphasis and the suppressions with which the human actor tells of them." Bakhtin defines the novel as "a diversity of social speech types . . . and a diversity of individual voices, artistically organized."[42] Stevenson's notion of classes of novels, each structured according to its intended effect, equally parallels Bakhtin's discussion of genre as a modeling system, which makes sense of reality through structured finalization: "every significant genre is a complex system of means and methods for the conscious control and finalization of reality"; "the artist must learn to see reality with the eyes of the genre."[43] Speech genres thus dislodge "man" as origin and measure of meaning, now identified as the always provisional result of sociocultural conflicts.

Indeed, unlike Stevenson, Bakhtin insists on the immediately sociohistorical dimension of literary models, or of any speech genre. There can be no disinterested discovery of truth for Bakhtin: "I call meaning the *answers* to the questions. That which does not answer any question is devoid of meaning for us."[44] The meaning of texts derives from their intervention in social discourse, that is, from their existence as *utterances*. Bakhtin recognizes two aspects in every utterance: "that which comes from language and is reiterative, on one hand, and that which comes from the context of enunciation, which is unique, on the other."[45] The historical dimension of the text as utterance connects it to social values and allows differences to be inscribed.[46] While every utterance is directed toward a social horizon of meanings and values, literary utterances can address several horizons simultaneously by displaying the dialogical confrontations between discourses, as further textual analyses will illustrate.

Therefore, Bakhtin's analysis of the semiotic process includes the subject and its sociohistorical position in the production of meaning. Friedrich Nietzsche made this point in *The Genealogy of Morals* (1887), when he mocked those who claimed to accumulate objective facts and thereby achieve pure knowledge, unaffected by the producing subject. He described their work as a *petit faitalisme*, and warned them of its fallacies:

Henceforth, my dear philosophers, let us be on guard against the dangerous old conceptual fiction that posited a "pure, will-less, painless, timeless knowing subject"; let us guard against the snares of such contradictory concepts as "pure reason," "absolute spirituality," "knowledge in itself": these always demand that we should think of an eye that is completely unthinkable, an eye turned in no particular direction, in which the active and interpreting forces, through which alone seeing becomes seeing *something*, are supposed to be lacking; these always demand of the eye an absurdity and a nonsense.[47]

However, this perspective on the cognitive process, which includes the social subject in the apprehension of the object (described as the "new scientific spirit" by Bachelard), was not adopted by most human and social scientists during the last quarter of the nineteenth century. Specialization was considered as a guarantee against subjectivity: the adoption of scientific methods assured historians, anthropologists, sociologists, and philosophers of their effectiveness in gathering objective facts about the world. Russell's theory of descriptions, for example, was based on the belief that the hidden logical structure of language revealed ontological structures of reality. The analysis of the sentence "The present king of France is wise" into atomic sentences:

(1) There is a king of France
(2) There is not more than one king of France
(3) There is nothing which is not the king of France and not wise

and the formal notation of this analysis as:

$$(\exists x) [\phi x \cdot (y) (\phi y \supset y = x) \cdot \psi x]$$

allowed certainty to be achieved, as outlined by Arthur Jacobson: "Only in the appropriate formal notation do we remove all possibility of ambiguity. We not only express what we mean but reveal, by the structure of the expression itself, the structure of the world about which we speak."[48] Discussing Russell's theory of knowledge, Albert Einstein rejected the possibility of this kind of certainty: "the concepts which arise in our thought and in our linguistic expressions are all—when viewed logically—the free creations of thought which cannot inductively be gained from sense-experiences. This is not so easily noticed only because we have the habit of combining certain concepts and conceptual relations (propositions) so definitely with certain sense-experiences that we do not become conscious of the gulf—logically unbridgeable—which separates the world of sensory experiences from the world of concepts and propositions."[49] The theory of relativity and quantum mechanics clearly illustrated this point, as highly successful theories which did not claim to give an objective representation of reality. Thus, whereas scientists recognized an inevitable disjunction between their theories and an "external world," human scientists and philosophers often kept the search for objective truth as their goal, however distant.

Both Frege and Russell recognized the difficulties arising from such a position. In his 1892 article "Über Sinn und Bedeutung," Frege argued that propositions had both a reference (the relation to an external object) and a sense (the description of the object): "The reference of 'evening star' would be the same as that of 'morning star' but not the sense."[50] The notion of sense thus included social discourse in the production of knowledge, as discussed in detail by Timothy Reiss in his article "Peirce and Frege: In the Matter of Truth": "The proposition was that referentiality *must* pass through sense, and because sense is the possession of all those 'familiar with the language,' the result of previous conceptualization, there can be no royal way to the grasping of objects. Sense is already and always caught in established discourse."[51] Russell's work on presuppositions could have opened to a discussion of the power yielded by their strategic use in argumentation; these aspects, however, held relatively little interest for the philosopher in search of logical certainty.[52]

Reiss argues that the difficulties encountered by traditional epistemology stemmed from its reliance on a binary logic: propositions were true or false (*tertium non datur*) depending on their relation to the external world; objective facts established outside of discourse. This dilemma was "solved" by Charles S. Peirce with his definition of truth as process.[53] The semiotician worked from the assumption that no facts could be established objectively: "Not only is every fact really a relation, but your thought of the fact *implicitly* represents it as such."[54] Peirce proposed a triadic definition of signs which accounted for the sociohistorical development of meaning and truth. A sign consisted of the relation between an object, a representamen, and an interpretant: "My definition of a representamen is as follows: A REPRESENTAMEN is a subject of a triadic relation TO a second, called its OBJECT, FOR a third, called its INTERPRETANT, this triadic relation being such that the REPRESENTAMEN determines its interpretant to stand in the same triadic relation to the same object for some interpretant."[55] Thus, meaning became the ever evolving process of "the translation of a sign into another [sign or] systems of signs," as outlined by Reiss: "Once a triadic relationship exists . . . it can no longer be separated from the evolutionary nature of the actual. The excluded middle can no longer hold, because the 'truth' expressed is never limited: it is not an either/or but rather the point of departure for a thought activity in the world."[56] Peirce underlined the relation between power and knowledge relations when he stated that ideas have "more or less [the] power

of working [themselves] out into fact" and "ideas utterly despised and
frowned upon have an inherent power of working their way to the
governance of the world, at last."[57]

Nietzsche shared the belief that meaning is developed through social
praxis. He insisted that the meaning of a concept or custom (good and
evil, or punishment, for example) did not reside in a primary origin
(whether historical or metaphysical) or in a hidden essence, but in the
power relations it established: "Thus one also imagined that punishment was devised for punishing. But purposes and utilities are only
signs that a will to power has become master of something less powerful and imposed upon it the character of a function; and the entire
history of a 'thing,' an organ, a custom can in this way be a continuous
sign-chain of ever new interpretations and adaptations. . . . The form
is fluid, but the 'meaning' even more so."[58]

It is within this context that literature in the modern Western sense
could emerge paradoxically as an institutionalized, discursive practice
and as a constant challenge to hegemonic values: as both the ultimate
justification of the elite's superiority (in carefully selected classics and
appropriate new products) and as an object of anxiety and censorship
(in new works or interpretations which challenged recognized truths).
The paradoxical position of literature in social discourse stemmed
from the inevitable ambiguity of its truth. Referentiality to an objective reality could not be simulated as in history or sociology: no matter
how true to the scientifically determined characteristics of the born-
criminal type, Jacques Lantier of *La bête humaine* remained "untrue,"
a nonexistent, and yet present reality. Literary texts are at once true
and false. Moreover, their structural capability of simultaneously presenting multiple interpretations of the "same" reality undermines the
notion of an essential truth fundamental for the defense of hegemonic
values. Narratives necessarily represented their facts as enmeshed in
interpretation by the narrator or the characters, thereby displaying
Peirce's contention that meaning is entirely produced by the process
of translating signs into other signs, or systems of signs. His analysis
of knowledge production as the triadic relation between representamen, object, and interpretant can be applied to novels apprehending
human nature through its opposition to criminal nature: "criminal
man" (the representamen), subject of a triadic relation to a second,
"man" (the object), for a third, the narrator (the interpretant), such
that the representamen determines the interpretant to stand in the

same triadic relation to the same object for some interpretant (in this case, the reader):

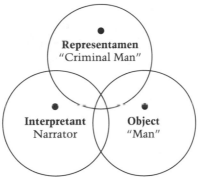

Reiss, who devised the tricircular model for the representation of Peirce's semiotic process, defined the area of overlap as "representing habit, belief, truth," and further specified that "the arena of the social is made possible by the combination of habit and the circulation of signs. For Peirce, this essentially discursive practice and the forms taken by it (what he would probably refer to as an endless process of semiosis) replaced the whole epistemological concept of truth."[59]

Literary texts can display the possibility of producing otherness, of transforming accepted truths and interfering in social habit, as argued by Godzich: "Poets are dangerous, then, because they give being to that which does not have it. . . . They serve as constant reminders of the fact that otherness, constitutive or otherwise, is a human production, and thus they empower us to think, to know, to give meaning, and to act upon our society."[60]

9 Textual Construction: Truth-Producing Fiction

◆

Presenting the facts: naturalist novels on "criminal man": *La bête humaine* **by Emile Zola** By its method of composition and its textual elaboration, Zola's *Bête humaine* followed contemporary rules for the discovery and dissemination of truth. Like the criminologists and journalists of his day, the novelist began by collecting all the facts. He completed his knowledge of crime first acquired in the works of Lucas, Morel, Létourneau, and Moreau de Tours by studying the 1887 French translation of Lombroso's *L'Uomo delinquente*. Accepting the view that born criminals were atavistic throwbacks of prehistoric men, the novelist set his tale in the railway *milieu*, which could represent both the material and cultural march of civilization: the railway not only provided physical proof of scientific and technological progress, it also served to break down regional barriers, accelerate communication, and allow national unity to be achieved. Pol Lefèvre, assistant director of the *Compagnie de l'Ouest* and author of *Les chemins de fer* (1889, closely studied by Zola) helped the novelist by giving him a detailed tour of Saint-Lazare station, arranging a similar visit at Le Havre, and sharing anecdotes about railway workers and their way of life. Zola was authorized to ride on a locomotive on April 15, 1889, between Paris and Mantes, to observe the tasks performed by driver and fireman, feel the train's rhythm and speed, absorb the view. His preparatory dossier also included train schedules and press reports of train accidents. Zola guaranteed the authenticity of his narrative crimes by deriving their main characteristics from very well-known murders: the Fenayrou, Barrême, and Poinsot affairs.[1] Always a shrewd publicist, he described his murderer Jacques Lantier as similar to Jack the Ripper during a press interview, thereby taking advantage of the international interest sparked by the murders.[2] Readings on the magistrature during the Second Empire ensured accurate descriptions of criminal investigation procedures and court proceedings.

Once he had accumulated all these facts, Zola's task was to let them "speak for themselves." By beginning his novel *in medias res* he was able to present his text as the mere transcription of a preexistent reality. Frequent use of free indirect discourse similarly affected the author/ text relation by simulating a relative autonomy of the object vis-à-vis its producer.[3] The inclusion of popular sayings or beliefs distanced the narrator from the text by letting common knowledge, the *doxa*, motivate narrative development:

> —Say quickly: my little gift.
> He was also laughing, like a good fellow. He decided to go along:
> —My little gift.
> It was a knife that she had just bought him, to replace the one that he had lost and had been lamenting, for the last fifteen days. He cried out, found it superb, that beautiful new knife, with its ivory handle and its gleaming blade. Right away, he was going to use it. She was delighted by his joy; and, jokingly, she made him give her a sou, so that their friendship not be cut.[4]

In the first four lines of this passage, the characters speak for themselves while the narrator speaks of them, describing their thoughts and actions to the reader. Objectivity is staged in a straightforward way, true to naturalist precepts, with the narrator merely registering developments for the passive reader:

$$\text{World} \longrightarrow \text{Reader}$$

[Characters speak]   Text   [registers]

[Narrator relates]

However, the following paragraph allows the narrator's presence to be distanced through the gradual use of free indirect discourse and the final introduction of the *doxa*. The first sentence is ambiguous, for the narrator could be either describing the scene or transcribing Séverine's words, which would be "It is a knife that I just bought you to replace the one you lost and have been lamenting for the last fifteen days." Apart from the clause "He cried out," the next two sentences transcribe Roubaud's words, feelings, and intentions rather than the narrator's perception of them. The numerous inversions and reiterations break the rhythm and present the character's speech pattern as well as his difficulties of expression: "found it superb, that beautiful new knife, with its ivory handle." The third person is used not to refer to a character but rather to transmit his thoughts and personality.[5] The sentence "Right away, he was going to use it" allows the reader to hear Roubaud without the narrator's clear interference as in direct, or even indirect discourse: "He said that he was going to use it right away." Such a statement of fact would destroy the sense of a scene developing in time and witnessed by the reader rather than registered by the narrator. The clause "She was delighted by his joy" returns to the paragraph's opening ambiguity (transcription or description of Séverine's words?), while the final coordinated clause allows the narrator to disappear behind Séverine's good humor toward the popular superstition she grudgingly observes. At this point, the narrator seemingly manages to close the gap between its perception of the characters' world and their own, and thus confront the reader directly with this reality.

La bête humaine was published in serial form in *La vie populaire* from November 14, 1889, to March 2, 1890. The novel attracted a large audience because, like the papers, it offered "something for everyone." It was packaged and promoted for a mass audience, with publicity campaigns promising violent domestic scenes, brutal train accidents, bloody murders, and a fine melodramatic weaving of individual tragedies. The readers' thirst for knowledge and culture could be satisfied by detailed descriptions of the century's great invention, the train, and by insights into the lives of various railway workers. The novel also allowed readers to keep abreast of the latest criminological theories, in the never ending debate on the relative influence of heredity and environment. An article by Paul Ginisty, editor of *La vie populaire*, carefully outlined all of these aspects four days before the novel's publication: Zola's principles and scientific methods were discussed, as well as his affiliation to Lombroso. The novel was thus clearly "in the know": it used all the latest scientific discoveries on the nature of "criminal man" to create an electrifying *fait divers*. Yet, even though the story was timely, up to date, exciting, and "true" (because of its exploitation of both actual crime stories and scientific explanations of criminal behavior), it was widely criticized for its exaggerations.

Criminologists discussed the scientific value of Zola's characters as representatives of various criminal types: was Jacques Lantier truly a born criminal, was Roubaud an occasional criminal, a semi-criminal, a criminaloid? If J. Héricourt, Ferri, and Lombroso disagreed with Zola (and with each other) on some aspects of his characterizations, all found many truths. Héricourt was particularly impressed by the novel, and found Jacques's personality and crime well established in scientific fact.[6] Although professing to be a great admirer of Zola's work, Lombroso noted several mistakes in the novel's depiction of criminals, and suggested that a lack of direct observation might have been the cause of these errors: "His criminals have that undecided and false air of certain photographs taken of portraits and not of originals. Thus even though I have studied thousands of criminals, I could not classify his Roubaud."[7] Lombroso argued that because of conflicting physical and mental traits, Roubaud could not be classified as a born criminal, an occasional criminal, or a criminal of passion. The problem, of course, was that Roubaud's great resemblance to Fenayrou prevented the criminologist from dismissing him as an impossible character, even though he seemed unclassifiable. Lombroso "solved" this dilemma somewhat surprisingly by devising a new category for *Fenayrou*, the "semi-born-criminal."[8] Lombroso rejected Lantier's good manners, his remorse, and his tenderness toward Séverine: born criminals were analgesic, and could therefore neither feel nor respect other people's emotions. His strongest objection was to Zola's description of atavistic murder instincts as a male desire for revenge against the harm inflicted by females: "We have here a factual error. Primitive women never hurt men: weaker than they were, they were always their victims."[9] Finally, the intricacies of the plot seemed highly improbable to the scientist from a statistical point of view: what were the odds of having the same knife serve two different murderers, or of several crimes occurring in such a restricted space?[10]

As usual, established literary critics decried Zola's lacks (of taste, talent, and moral sense) and his disrespect for the limits of literature: certain brutal aspects of life were not to be included in literary texts, under any circumstances. The numerous descriptions of landscapes, locomotives, train schedules, and stations (closely verified for their accuracy) were equally denounced as unliterary: their presence merely managed to choke the story and bore the reader.[11] Thus, it is apparent that Zola's text did more than "borrow" facts from scientific treatises or press reports. How were the facts processed by the novel?

Zola presents the opposition between "civilized man" and primitive "criminal man" as a social and biological phenomenon: most of the criminals are from the lower classes, and their deviance is a function of instinctive urges, lust and rage. Their bodies display the well-known stigmata of criminality (such as prognathous jaws or low foreheads), and this physical difference extends to their mental constitution. When a train is stopped by a snowstorm near the signal station, the encounter between travelers (those who are carried by the advances of progress) and workers (those who merely tend to the material requirements of this movement) is described as follows: "And here it was that, in the snow, a train landed at their door: the natural order was perverted, they peered at the unknown people that an accident had thrown on the tracks, they contemplated them with the wide eyes of savages running up to the shores where Europeans had shipwrecked" (p. 227).

However, the coupling of the civilized to the primitive is pervasive in Zola's novel, occurring within each individual and saturating institutions. Grandmorin's murderers, Roubaud and Séverine, are first presented as good human beings rather than lowly deviants. Happily married, they are tender and attentive to each other's needs. If Jacques Lantier represents the born-criminal type who kills by instinct and with pleasure, he also feels within himself "civilized man . . . the strength acquired through education, the slow and indestructible scaffolding of transmitted ideas" (p. 288). If he cannot deprive himself of the pleasure of killing Séverine, he also cannot convince himself of the right to murder, and refuses, against his better interests, to kill Roubaud. Moreover, several characters also feel the attraction of death in sexual pleasure. Thus Roubaud: "And, in the troubled night of his flesh, at the bottom of his soiled, bleeding desire, the necessity of death suddenly stood before him" (p. 74). Flore recognizes the same necessity when her love for Jacques is refused. In Zola's text the *"bête humaine"* is everywhere, in spite of appearances: a difference in degree, not in kind, distinguishes the desires of Grandmorin and Lantier toward Séverine, and the violence they take pleasure in inflicting on her. The narrative context, therefore, modifies the meaning of Séverine's murder: to the manifestation of atavistic violent instincts is added the representation of a fundamental struggle between sexual love and hate, life and death, reappearing throughout the text, in different degrees of intensity, between several characters.

Order and civilization are achieved not so much by an opposition to criminal instincts as by their secret integration (and systematic denegation) throughout social, economic, political, sexual, and family structures, as figured in the relations of Grandmorin to the characters and institutions of the novel. Grandmorin is influential in the novel's judicial circles (as the retired head of the Cour de Rouen), political circles (through his professional and personal contacts, his position in the Conseil Général, and his title of Commandeur de la Légion d'Honneur), in the railway company (as a member of its board of administration), and in the social life of the upper classes (through his wealth and his sister's role as host for the Rouen magistrature in the family château). The beast within him manifests itself through his habit of exacting sexual favors from young women in his employ. In exchange for this sexual domination, Grandmorin gives professional and political protection, thus extending his power to every facet of his victims' lives. Most of the characters are in this way indebted to and abused by Grandmorin. Séverine, the daughter of Grandmorin's gardener, is raised by him after the death of her father and in return for quasi-incestuous relations receives a dowry and a promise of inheriting the house where she was first violated at sixteen, the Croix-de-Maufras. Grandmorin gives her husband a job as deputy stationmaster at Le Havre, and protects him when his republican political opinions threaten his position (p. 60). He provides lodgings and employment for Séverine's wet nurse, la mère Victoire, and thus helps to sustain her marriage to Pecqueux, whom she bribes with extra money for drink. Grandmorin also protects Pecqueux from being fired because of his drunkenness (p. 116). The president is equally connected to the gatekeepers of the small signal station near the Croix-de-Maufras, Phasie, Misard, and their daughters Flore and Louisette, for his actions toward Séverine are known to Flore, and his sexual abuse of Louisette, the youngest of the family working as his maidservant, eventually leads to her death in the arms of Cabuche (an incident which will later contribute to his wrongful conviction for the murder of Grandmorin). Expelled at the very beginning of the novel, appearing only briefly as a shadow in a train station and then as a body, the character of Grandmorin is nevertheless essential to narrative development, as it allows Zola to postulate a supersaturation of social organizations (familial, sexual, economic, political, judicial) by criminal instincts, and to construct his novel as the gradual discovery of the truth of this postulate: "And so it was that the presumed crime of a small deputy stationmaster, some shady, low, and dirty story, went back through complicated cogwheels, shaking the enormous machine of a train company, upsetting even its higher administration. The jolt went higher still, reached the ministry, threatened the State, in the political malaise of the moment: a critical hour, when the smallest fever in the great social body hastened its decomposition" (p. 178). The precariousness of the social order derives from its foundation on a denegation of criminal instincts which cannot be continuously maintained: the discovery of Grand-morin's sexual crimes determines the sequence of narrative events, while the novel as a whole registers the repercussions of the circulation of this information.

The first effect of the irruption of truth is to destroy the social equi-librium by transforming the meaning of all its constitutive relations. Séverine's involuntary confession to Roubaud in the opening scene of the novel inverts the meaning of each event and relation previously described: Grandmorin's generosity toward Séverine and all those sur-rounding her, as well as her marriage to Roubaud, result from sexual and economic oppression authorized by the president's position *and* by the dissimulation of his abuses. Objects themselves are transformed: the knife which had allowed the couple to express tenderness (the "small gift" given as a surprise to Roubaud, who praised its qualities and used it to please and calm Séverine when she was upset, pp. 58, 65), becomes a lethal weapon, used to kill Grandmorin (and eventually, Séverine herself).

Each group reacts to the discovery of Grandmorin's criminal abuse according to the choices made available by its social position. The lower classes react first with violence and then with relative indifference, while the upper classes maneuver to redefine the event appropriately, that is, in a way which can promote or consolidate power. If the gov-ernment wants to "discover the truth, the better to hide it if necessary" (p. 133), the opposition uses the affair as a "war machine" against the Empire, to criticize both the moral standards of the elite and the com-placency of the police and magistrature at the eve of the elections; the magistrate Denizet wishes to dispose of the matter in order to be called to Paris after many long years of unfulfilled hope (due to his lack of economic and professional influence); Mme. Bonnehon works to cleanse her brother's reputation in order to maintain her prestige within Rouen society; and finally, the Lachenaye try to inculpate the Roubauds to recuperate the Croix-de-Maufras. For all these groups the fact of Grandmorin's murder acquires meaning only in relation to power. Thus, Zola's text manifests that every fact is a relation, a point of departure for further interpretation, in a never ending struggle for power through knowledge. This is reiterated by the "mise en abyme" episodes of Phasie-Misard (where Misard slowly poisons his wife who refuses to let him know where she hid 1,000 francs) and of the Mère Lebleu (who obsessively seeks gossip in order to keep her dominat-ing position and her apartment). If the sought-for power is limited (a little money, a better view), the stakes are enormous, for losing means death: "Yes, she had been enraged by not finding anything between them, and had died for it" (p. 355).

La bête humaine thus displays the social determinants of knowledge production, and goes so far as to draw an inverse relation between the capacity to discover truth and the institutional elaboration of knowledge: it is when Denizet is the most perspicacious, when he follows all the rules of the art of judicial inquiry to construct a "masterpiece of fine analysis" (p. 359), the greatest triumph of his career, that he is wrong—and right, since his false judgment is seen as true, and the innocent Cabuche is recognized as the "very type of the assassin" (p. 371) and condemned, while Jacques remains invisible.

The disorder started by the irruption of truth is temporarily neutralized by the circulation of a series of false stories converging to produce hegemonic truth—not the closest approximation of an exterior reality, but rather the various understandings corresponding to economic, political, and social power relations. Grandmorin's reputation is vindicated, Cabuche is convicted along with Roubaud, Jacques is only seen as a kind and tender man, Flore's wilful sabotage is understood as a terrible accident, and Misard's careful poisoning of his wife remains largely unnoticed and unpunished. The cycle of violence and murder, however, is continued with Jacques, Pecqueux, and Philomène, and this time generalized on an international scale, the "*bête humaine*" becoming the "*bétail humain*," the trainload of drunken soldiers transported for slaughter in the 1870 war, racing into the night without a driver after the double murder of Jacques and his coal heaver Pecqueux. This final murder, presenting an extended and more horrific version of the initial one, confirms the text's basic postulate, enunciated by Phasie: "Oh! it's [the train] a nice invention, there's no doubt about it. You go faster, you get smarter. . . . But savage beasts stay savage beasts, and they can invent even better machines. There will always be savage beasts underneath them" (p. 88).

If criminological texts describe crimes and their authors as temporary social or hereditary aberrations in the progressive development of civilization, Zola's novel finds some criminal in each individual, and at the basis of every social relation, as an integral force of (human) nature. The risk taken by this text is to inscribe crime as an unknown value in a four-term equation:

$$\text{Power} : \text{Knowledge} :: \text{Order} : (\text{Crime})$$

Two hermeneutic quests motivated by the will to maintain order over-determine the narrative development, one public (who killed Grand-morin?), and one private (Jacques trying to understand the reasons for his desire to kill women). The proairetic sequence (started by Séverine's confession) allows these quests to develop links between past private sexual crimes (Grandmorin's abuses) to future public international crimes (the 1870 war). The unfolding of narrative scenes allows various personal and institutional relations to be drawn between these forms of disorder: it allows diverse meanings to be attributed to each term of the equation. The end of the text marks a new beginning for the cycle of violence, and the unknown value is found in the eponymous title: crime is the "*Bête humaine*" (the beast within "man," created by "man," and bringing him to his future, in an endless repetition of his violent past).

And yet the narrative text is there to break the cycle, to establish a difference by revealing the processes working to dissimulate truth, by capturing its presence ("There was the truth, silently passing by," p. 373), and by offering a totalizing vision of the interrelated conflicts preventing its general recognition. Moreover, the text produces its own truth through the eventual realization of a series of predictions, the repetition of crucial scenes, the redoubling of narrative events, which together allow the text to operate a constant confirmation of its premises, and to unfold as the progressive establishment of truth. Thus, Misard's searches (pp. 92, 102–3), the installation at the Croix-de-Maufras (pp. 188, 297), Phasie's death and the train passengers' indifference to it (pp. 88, 297), the train accident (pp. 89, 312), the fight between Lantier and Pecqueux (pp. 354, 380–81) are all predicted or prefigured before their eventual realization; the confession scene between Séverine and Roubaud is repeated and completed with Lantier, in the same overheated room, after an impromptu meal provided by the men (Roubaud bringing only the savory, Jacques only the sweet), while the Dauvergne sisters sing and play the piano; Séverine's murder takes place in the room where Grandmorin first violated her, and both are killed with the same knife, by "the same blow," at "the same place, with the same rage" (p. 348): in a hallucinating image, their bodies are found in the same position, Séverine on her back, Grandmorin on his stomach, in a differed embrace produced by the text (pp. 104, 349). Events are thus inscribed in a reiterative series extending in time. Through this nexus of predictions and repetitions, the forces of determinism are textually transformed into fatalism.

The convergence of all the characters' destinies at the Croix-de-Maufras allows this transformation to be complete. The house is first mentioned as Séverine's inheritance, as though she (and, by extension, all women) had inherited her fate of being abused and killed by men, who in turn inherit the need to dominate and kill. It is because of the house that the Roubauds are suspected of murder; as it will not sell, it ties them together, for Séverine will not leave the husband she hates without capitalizing on her inheritance (p. 283). The first thing seen by Séverine after she has killed Grandmorin is the Croix-de-Maufras (p. 254); every time she travels on Jacques's train, she is compelled to look at the house, and this need makes her noticeable to Flore, who then suspects their relation (pp. 228, 281). The house haunts and attracts Jacques (pp. 92–93). It is there that he almost kills Flore and does kill Séverine. Cabuche must roam around the house because of his love for Séverine, and this leads him to be accused of her murder. The Croix-de-Maufras allows all characters and events to be interrelated, and ultimately linked to an animal sexual passion for death. This postulate is validated through the series of predictions and confirmations, repetitions and reenactments which display the inexorable unfolding of fate. In the process, language loses its simulated transparency: no longer the neutral transmitter of facts, it can serve to conceive and produce new realities.

It was this structural development of *La bête humaine* which scientists and many critics at large found intolerable. From their perspective, this contrived aspect of the novel diminished its worth as a representation of reality, and made it untrue to life—the novel was overly "*romanesque*." Ironically, Zola's novel was blamed for taking advantage of the freedom allowed for literary texts. It was by producing such a closed and tightly meshed universe of discourse that the author was able to confront various social perspectives on a single event, and thus both explore the limits of truth and propose new interpretations. Such discursive strategies also allowed the text to question its own epistemological foundations.

Reality is a given. This epistemological presupposition is maintained by Zola's working methods (basing his text on a series of previously accumulated "facts"), by diverse stylistic devices suggesting the presence of a preexistent reality (the beginning *in medias res*, the use of free indirect discourse and the inclusion of the *doxa*), and by the achievement of a totalizing vision allowing the narrator and reader to understand the events as a whole, with their causes and effects, as though reality could be grasped from the outside, with an impersonal eye (in Nietzsche's formulation).

The presupposition is also denied by the text, as all the crimes remain obscure and ill understood, as false interpretations manage to be recognized as true and thus become reality, and as most characters never begin to understand—let alone dominate—their own reality.

Truth is absolute and cumulative. Confirmed by the use of scientific, technical, and journalistic reports for the production of an experimental and true novel, this epistemological presupposition is also denied by the denunciation of the inevitable blindness of institutional knowledge and by the revelation of the political, economic, and social factors determining the conditions for the production of hegemonic truths.

Language is transparent. Simulated by diverse stylistic devices allowing the narrator's presence to be erased and the reader to be confronted directly by narrative scenes, this presupposition is also denied by a series of predictions, repetitions, and prefigurations which scan the text and underline its capacity to produce another reality, where the forces of determinism are transformed into fatalism, and where personal struggles recall ancient struggles between love and hate, life and death.

These diverse narrative strategies allowed Zola to use current apprehensions of "criminal man" to begin a reinterpretation of the nature of "man" and of social organizations, in the positivist hope that the knowledge so produced would authorize the creation of new and better realities: "Our real labor is there, for we the experimental novelists, to go from the known to the unknown, to render us masters of nature. . . ." [12]

Dans les rues by J.-H. Rosny Aîné　*Dans les rues* was published in 1913, at a time when both naturalism and the born criminal were no longer controversial issues. Decades of debate on the relative influence of heredity and environment on criminal behavior prevented yet another novel on the question from achieving a "*succès de scandale.*" Efforts to secure the widest possible audience can be traced in the introductory "warning" which served to arouse the reader's curiosity (with promises of painful investigations into the "lower orders") while situating the novel in a strategically safe place, in between the naturalist and psychological schools. As a naturalist narrative, Rosny's text recorded objective observations of the effects of environmental pressures on street gangs living in the *faubourgs,* and so examined the social origin of crime and the nature of "criminal man." This entailed abundant physical descriptions where the noxious influence of family and *milieu* could be read in the ugly, diseased, and deformed bodies of the protagonists. As a psychological novel, it also included the unformulated thoughts and fears of the characters and underlined their physiological origins: Gobiche, the main character's friend, is said to feel "towards Jacques the admiration of the flaccid for the nervous and of the inert for the impulsive."[13]

The narrator is usually present and addressing himself directly to the reader in this text, guiding its understanding of the events with brief analyses such as the following evaluation of the Lérande family instincts: "the scale of instincts decreased from Jacques to Maurice. Jacques was at the level of brute instincts; in Adrienne instincts were complicated with sociality [*socialité*] and empty mysticism; in Jeanne thought emerged as trickery and scheme; in Maurice, thought dominated even his dreams, it accompanied each act" (p. 56). When the characters are made to speak, the narrator (or author?) is careful to footnote the slang words his cultivated readers cannot be expected to understand.[14] Rosny's novel is thus constructed as a dialogue between a truly knowledgeable narrator and the acquiescent reader. This consensus is derived from the text's recourse to hegemonic ideological maxims, scientific precepts, and narrative techniques. *Dans les rues* uses recognized truths without questioning or transforming them in any way. The "lower orders" are shown to be like cavemen who are like anthropoids who are like workers; the author probably knew as many workers as prehistoric men—he had, however, acquired a textual knowledge of them, in a series of contemporary sociological, political, and journalistic texts.

Dans les rues tells the story of how Jacques Lérande evolves from a juvenile delinquent with a bad conscience to a hardened criminal. The narrator first presents him as poised "at the crossroads of the instincts" (p. 33). His violent nature (clearly visible in his curled up lip, à la Lombroso, p. 13) is barely contained by his civilized manners, and the novel demonstrates how the environment causes his gradual devolution into a thieving and murderous anthropoid. *Dans les rues* would at first appear to be Rosny's answer to *La bête humaine*: by underlining the influence of *milieu*, the author would have tried to give a more complete view of "criminal man," showing his Jacques (same first name, similar last name) to be the result of social as well as hereditary forces. Like the French criminologists, Rosny managed to balance the forces of heredity and environment in his text in a manner which recognized criminality as a physical attribute while paradoxically maintaining the principles of free will and personal responsibility needed to justify class domination. Thus, if Jacques prefers to roam the streets looking for trouble, his brother Maurice can choose to work hard, study, and spend all of his energies trying to build a better life for his family (p. 18). Moreover, it is only once Jacques has committed his first important and premeditated theft that his physical attributes begin to change, until his very bone structure becomes that of a criminal:

> Even his bones have become scoundrelly. He holds his head and mostly his chin forward; he has the curves of a watching animal or of a prowling hooligan. The freshness in the face is fading. A smoky skin is covering it, tightening and petrifying. The eyes have grown pale and, at times too mobile, at times fixed and devouring, vacant and prying, they bewilder gentlefolks. Blond weeds sprout on his lip and only the hands are fresh, almost charming, if it wasn't for their gestures, which reveal the predatory beast [p. 187].

This description ascribes Jacques's revolting appearance to his newly acquired criminal habits rather than to his original physical constitution. His eyes are frightening because they have become pale (revealing a disorderly and drunken existence) and furtive (in their service for criminal activities), his hands, which could be charming, belie a rapacious nature. Further proof of the predominance of the will over nature is given by Gobiche who, although born in the "lower orders" and enrolled in a street gang, gradually evolves toward honesty, and improves his physical appearance in the process (pp. 148–49).

Whatever the influence of heredity and environment, an individual's moral and physical nature ultimately reflect his or her personal choices. These choices are then paradoxically associated with biological factors, as social distinctions are transformed into racial ones: middle-class values are constantly described as "illusions of the race," and lower-class values as "horde morality," or "Apache customs." Characters define crime according to their social and racial background: street dwellers and "regulars" have entirely different notions of acceptable behavior, and neither group is capable of understanding the other's values. Whereas the "Apaches" lead parasitic lives, stealing and preying on the needs and weaknesses of others, the bourgeois support themselves through hard work, self-help, and self-discipline.

Jacques, who strives for rapid wealth and increasing power in the streets, cannot understand his brother's love for books or his subservient behavior at work. Conversely, Maurice cannot even imagine his brother's way of life (pp. 298–99). In the face of economic and political turbulence, the morally fit struggle and survive, while all others follow the path of devolution into "natural" primitive criminal behavior (p. 18).

Although each race and class has its own value system, the novel constantly reaffirms that only one path leads to truth: society on the whole is well established, and those who follow its rules—the bourgeois—are right. The few institutions that are shown in the novel are shown to work: thieves and murderers get caught. On their way to this ultimate destiny, they can be saved by the intervention of philanthropic organizations, as carefully noted by the narrator ("It was still time for philanthropists to intervene," p. 61). Salvation of the individual by the individual is the only social reform program recognized as necessary in the text. The narrator assures the reader that even Jacques's devolution could have been halted before his transformation into an anthropoid, if only Maurice and Adrienne had been more perceptive, more capable of curbing his will, or if only the father had not died (p. 377). Those who accept social rules are justly rewarded. In spite of several setbacks, Maurice's patience and hard work are recognized in the end, and duly recompensed in the form of personal advancement, salary increases, and even bonuses. Throughout his difficult times, when the family is reduced to starvation, Maurice is heartened by his social sense, that profound knowledge that all is ultimately well with the world (p. 337).

If hard work and sheer will are necessary prerequisites for success, happiness comes mainly from knowing one's destination or place in society: if Maurice, Adrienne, and even Gobiche stand a good chance of making their dreams come true, it is because they have tailored them to suit their station in life. To keep a steady job, rent a small house in the country, or sell chestnuts on the street are proper goals, whereas to aspire to the "good life," to money and power, as Jacques and Jeanne do, is to overstep class boundaries and condemn oneself to a deviant life. Crime derives from an unwillingness to accept the place nature and a just society have determined.

Of course, the difficulty inherent in such a view is to show this just society. Apart from Maurice's employers, the novel gives little material proof of social justice. Whereas evil is graphic (rotten souls in rotting bodies), good is always vaguely expressed by such euphemisms as "social weight," "illusion of the race," "long heredity," "caste," "very social," "the good of the descent," and the like. The narrator describes the look between Jacques and his mother as follows: "Their fiery gazes met, strangely similar, yet one very 'social,' the other already wild" (p. 39). Evil is also expressed with difficulty, for apart from a seemingly endless series of nauseating physical descriptions, its presence is usually manifested by variations on the word "scoundrel" (*crapule*): "Even his bones have become scoundrelly" (p. 187); "He was dreadfully obscure, scoundrelly and menacing" (p. 359); "From time to time, Jacques would relate an anecdote, at times colorful but scoundrelly" (p. 363); "Frequenting scoundrels had given him all kinds of disgusting habits and ignoble twitches" (p. 373).

The unquestioning transcription of hegemonic values ultimately reduces the text to silence, for very little can be said when all of reality must be contained by the opposition of two equally vague terms, "social" versus "scoundrelly," and their variations: good versus bad, us versus them, and so on. The text blindly reaffirms ideological maxims and scientific precepts which are politically, economically, or socially useful for the maintenance of the established order, and ends with the affirmation that good and evil (so defined) exist in the world because . . . they do:

> He felt too well that we are miserable almost as we are ugly, rich almost as we are handsome, triumphant in the way we are healthy, defeated in the way we are sick. What have we done to be men rather than horses?
>
> . . . .
>
> —We could not be dishonest!
> He felt that there was their profound truth. They could not! It is the truth that goes beyond everything—for the supreme, dazzling, and unanswerable reason that, *it is* [pp. 410, 412–13].

Like newspaper reports, Rosny's novel accomplishes an ideological *coup de maître*: it manages to discuss crime in the poorest districts as the surface manifestations of an unchangeable (and largely unknowable) human nature, barely affected by transient social conditions, while providing a notion of "criminal man" entirely suitable for social repression.

A comparison of these novels by Zola and Rosny does more than outline the differences between a leader and his followers: it shows how the potential threats of a discursive practice can be successfully neutralized (see figure 5). Both authors accepted recognized scientific and ideological apprehensions of "criminal man," both identified his environment as that of the "lower orders," his nature as primitive, and his motivations for murder as instinctive, violent impulses. However, whereas Zola used narrative structures to demonstrate the limits of these truths, their effect on social organizations, and their role in establishing and maintaining oppressive power relations, Rosny transcribed them as the simple representation of a single and inalterable reality. In Rosny's narrative, truth prevails, one and indivisible, and knowledge of it belongs to those who deserve it, the bourgeois. This is perhaps why his work is so bad: not just because of the clumsiness of its style or the inanities of its plot or because of a systematic recourse to hegemonic values, but rather because the narrative ultimately has but one voice, able only to establish an equivalence between the forces of determinism and those of social conservatism.

◆

Dangerous knowledge and criminal behavior: *Le Disciple* by Paul Bourget   The publication of *Le Disciple* in 1889 provoked a high-level debate on science and morality during which scientists, literary critics, and philosophers discussed the proper production and distribution of knowledge in society. Should scientists publicize theories which might lead to antisocial behavior? If such theories were made public, could their producers be held responsible for the criminal activity of their followers? *Le Disciple* fuelled the ever present opposition to the spread of knowledge and democracy; it crystallized all the old fears that such developments would inevitably bring dissatisfaction and degeneration, not progress. Brunetière wrote a laudatory article presenting Bourget's work as a good deed, as well as a good novel. The critic began his appraisal with a rhetorical question: "Do ideas affect customs, or not?" Taking determinism as a case in point, the answer became obvious:

> Even if you were assured that "the struggle for life" is the law of man's development, as it is for the other animals . . . and that there is but one reason and one right in the world, that of the strongest, you should not say it, since to follow such "truths" to their last consequences would bring humanity back to its primary barbarism, as no one today can avoid recognizing. Even if you

Figure 5   Naturalist Novels Grid

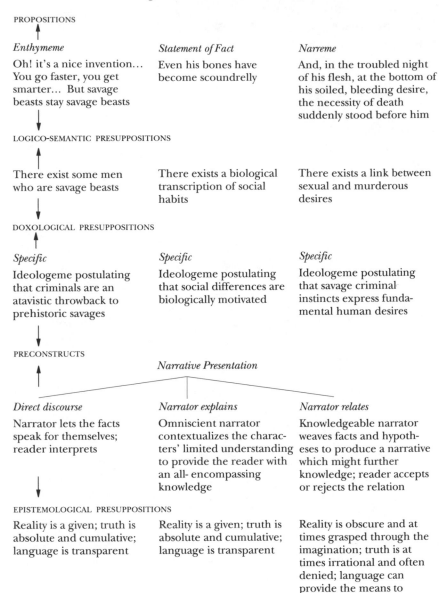

PROPOSITIONS

Enthymeme

Oh! it's a nice invention...
You go faster, you get
smarter... But savage
beasts stay savage beasts

Statement of Fact

Even his bones have
become scoundrelly

Narreme

And, in the troubled night
of his flesh, at the bottom of
his soiled, bleeding desire,
the necessity of death
suddenly stood before him

LOGICO-SEMANTIC PRESUPPOSITIONS

There exist some men
who are savage beasts

There exists a biological
transcription of social
habits

There exists a link between
sexual and murderous
desires

DOXOLOGICAL PRESUPPOSITIONS

Specific

Ideologeme postulating
that criminals are an
atavistic throwback to
prehistoric savages

Specific

Ideologeme postulating
that social differences are
biologically motivated

Specific

Ideologeme postulating
that savage criminal
instincts express funda-
mental human desires

PRECONSTRUCTS

Narrative Presentation

Direct discourse

Narrator lets the facts
speak for themselves;
reader interprets

Narrator explains

Omniscient narrator
contextualizes the characters' limited understanding
to provide the reader with
an all- encompassing
knowledge

Narrator relates

Knowledgeable narrator
weaves facts and hypoth-
eses to produce a narrative
which might further
knowledge; reader accepts
or rejects the relation

EPISTEMOLOGICAL PRESUPPOSITIONS

Reality is a given; truth is
absolute and cumulative;
language is transparent

Reality is a given; truth is
absolute and cumulative;
language is transparent

Reality is obscure and at
times grasped through the
imagination; truth is at
times irrational and often
denied; language can
provide the means to
grasp hidden realities

Whereas in Rosny the notions of "man" and "criminal" man serve to reproduce and reinforce
the value of established knowledge and power relations, in Zola they serve to expose social,
political, and economic contradictions and relate these to fundamental explorations about the
limits and possibilities of knowledge.

were assured that man is not free . . . you should not say it, since
the social institution and the whole of morality rest, as on their
sole foundation, on the hypothesis or the postulate of freedom.[15]

Le Disciple outlines the effects of the circulation of such ideas within
society through a series of imbricated narratives which establish a constant master/disciple relation between changing fictional characters,
and ultimately entangles the author and his actual readers in the implications of the novel. The title refers to Robert Greslou, a young,
middle-class student fascinated by modern theories of determinism.
His mentor, Adrien Sixte, who contemporaries recognized as a thinly
veiled portrait of Taine, is presented as one of the founding fathers of
scientific psychology. Sixte's faith in determinism is expressed in arguments bearing a striking resemblance to those of Lombroso, Zola, and
many social scientists of the day:

> If we really knew the relative position of all the phenomena which
> constitute the present universe,—we could, already, calculate with
> a certainty equal to that of the astronomer's the day, the hour,
> the minute when England will quit India, for example, or when
> Europe will have burnt its last piece of coal, when a certain crimi-
> nal, yet unborn, will assassinate his father, when a certain poem,
> not yet conceived, will be composed. All of the future rests in
> the present, as all the properties of the triangle are present in its
> definition.[16]

Sixte believes that France's future depends on a general recognition
of the findings of psychology (p. 49), much as Zola believed that it
depended on the wide acceptance of naturalism.

Whereas the master is content to remain in abstractions, the disciple
is eager to put theory into practice. Hired as a tutor by an aristocratic
family, Greslou decides to conduct a psychological experiment on his
pupil's sister, Charlotte: his aim is to seduce her and document each
stage of the development of her passion for him. Comparing himself
to Bernard, Greslou (like Zola) sets out to operate a "vivisection of the
soul" (p. 153), hoping to dismantle "cog by cog" (p. 120) the object of
his study. The impartial observer soon gets caught up in his experiment: in love with Charlotte but unable to marry because of their different social standing, he agrees to the double suicide pact she requires
as precondition for their love. After the love scene, however, Greslou
refuses to kill anyone, preferring that they run away together. Know-

ing her place in society, Charlotte resorts to suicide, leaving Greslou to be arrested as a prime suspect for her alleged murder, but sending a letter to her older brother, the Comte André de Jussat-Randon, explaining the circumstances of her death. As the available evidence against Greslou is circumstantial, the determination of his guilt or innocence must rest entirely on the findings of scientific psychology, and Sixte's expert knowledge is called upon to discover "criminal man" (p. 37).

Most of the novel is taken up by an autobiography written by Greslou in a desperate attempt to understand the unexpected outcome of his experiment. Still following the rules of scientific psychology, he details the hereditary and environmental influences which led him to his present condition. Greslou's self-analysis brings him to realize the futility of his scientific knowledge which cannot account for his personal feelings of anguish and remorse, let alone understand or direct the feelings of others.

The disciple's fate affects Sixte just as Charlotte's destiny affected Greslou (Charlotte : Greslou :: Greslou : Sixte). Indeed, Sixte at first considers his disciple as an interesting case, a possible source of documentation: he files his letters with others of the same type under the heading "Contemporary documents on the formation of spirits" (p. 24). When told of his disciple's involvement in a murder case, he welcomes this unexpected turn of events. Sixte hopes to find traces of Greslou's criminality in his physical constitution and his ancestry, à la Lombroso (and indeed, à la Greslou): "The reappearance of ferocious animality in civilized man would alone suffice to explain this act" (p. 51).

Sixte's interests in collecting documents soon backfires, for Greslou's text implicates him in deadly events which question the value of his life's work. His self-imposed solitary confinement of more than a decade, carefully described at the beginning of the novel, is interrupted for the first time by two letters, one from the investigating magistrate for Greslou's case, one from the defendant's mother, both asking the philosopher to account for the practical consequences of his abstractions. However, Sixte is as ill-equipped as his disciple to handle the effects of his theories, and finds himself in the predicament forecasted by penitentiary scientists who insisted on the necessity of dismissing scientific theories which provided no grounds for moralizing or rehabilitating a prisoner: how could Sixte condemn his disciple for actions dictated by the laws of heredity and environment? (pp. 260–61, 269).

The master's torment is presented to the reader as an interesting and authentic document on human behavior by the narrator: "Moreover the details of the life led by this man will provide those curious about human nature with an authentic document on a rather rare social breed, that of the professional philosopher" (pp. 3–4). The narrator knows more than any of the characters and is always careful to share this information with the reader, thereby reiterating the master/disciple relationship. When describing Sixte's theories and thought patterns, he clearly underlines their limitations (p. 50). Characters are explained through classification: Sixte is a "born-philosopher" (p. 18), the investigating magistrate is a "purebred magistrate" (p. 29), servants react as they must, being "of the people" (p. 53), and their lives are structured by their social position and occupation: "This caretaker—following the manners and customs of all caretakers in small apartment houses" (p. 6).

The narrator organizes its material to direct the reader toward proper comprehension: phrases such as "it is advisable to add right away that" (p. 1), "we will understand why" (p. 3), "would remain unintelligible if it was not remembered that" (p. 10), "it is indispensable to summarize here, in a few general traits, for the understanding of the drama" (p. 16), serve to outline the single meaning of events. These are always contextualized: the novel does not begin *in medias res* but rather with a story illustrative of the meaning of the one to follow:

> According to a legend that has not been refuted, the bourgeois of Koenigsberg had guessed that a prodigious event disrupting the civilized universe had occurred simply by seeing the philosopher Immanuel Kant modify the direction of his daily walk. . . . [S]everal inhabitants of Guy-de-la-Brosse street felt . . . a similar stupor when they noticed, around one o'clock, that a philosopher less illustrious than the old Kant, but just as regular, Mr. Adrien Sixte, the one the English gladly call the French Spencer, was coming out [p. 1].

The opening paragraph also indicates the target market for the novel: the educated classes, those who, like the narrator, are aware of their cultural heritage and interested in its development. This close relationship allows the narrator to appeal directly to the reader's common sense when wishing to establish the true meaning of the last scene, during which the master is humbled at the bedside of his dying disciple. Describing the scientific philosopher as perhaps incapable of recognizing God, the narrator assumes that the reader can, through rhetorical questions:

> and, for the first time, feeling his thought incapable of sustaining him, this analyst whose logic rendered him almost inhuman felt himself humbled, bowed, engulfed by the impenetrable mystery of destiny. The words of the only prayer he remembered from his distant youth, "Our Father, who art in heaven . . ." came back to his heart. Of course, he did not pronounce them. Perhaps he would never pronounce them. But if he does exist, that Celestial Father, towards whom great and small turn during the awful hours as though towards their only help, is this need for prayer not the most touching of prayers? And if this Celestial Father did not exist, would we have this hunger and this thirst at such hours? [pp. 293–94].

The novel as a whole is presented by the author to "a young man" as a case study of modern attitudes which must be avoided at all costs for the survival of the nation (author : young man :: narrator : reader :: Sixte : Greslou). The text thus presents gradually more restricted perspectives on a disruptive event, the death of a young woman and the trial (and subsequent assassination) of a young man for her murder. The author has the widest possible understanding, for he is able not only to explain the social and moral reasons for the event but also to trace its possible consequences on a national and international scale: he hopes in his preface that reading this story will remind young men of their duties to family, nation, and God. The narrator knows more than the characters and is able to discuss the limits of their science and to recognize its social and moral ramifications: human suffering, atheism, and crime. Sixte recognizes his disciple's perversion, accepts his social duties (for he intervenes in Greslou's defense by writing to the count), and begins to feel the need for God. Even Greslou, the one who understands the least, is at last able to see that his knowledge provides little control and less answers. Presumably the reader, the "young man" provided with this full understanding, will be able to avoid the errors of Sixte and Greslou and build a better future:

> You will find in *Le Disciple* the study of such a responsibility. May you find in it proof that the friend who is writing you these lines possesses at least one merit, that of believing deeply in the seriousness of his art.

—May you find in these very lines the proof that he is thinking of you, anxiously. Yes, he is thinking of you, and has been for a very long time [pp. i–ii].

Bourget's emotionalism was perhaps fueled by reasons a little more personal than patriotism, as one of his own disciples, Henri Chambige, had just been convicted of murder, and the prosecuting attorney had made reference to the Paris literary milieu as one of the factors contributing to his decadent behavior. In his preface Bourget disclaimed any allusion to notorious recent events (p. ix), but he later reversed this position in an interview in *Le Figaro*.[17] The resemblances between the two stories were in any case too numerous to be denied. The real Chambige and the fictional Greslou had both come to Paris for their studies, and there met their masters in psychology (Bourget, Sixte). Both had written on the ego, both had attracted first the pity, then the love of a wealthy and unattainable woman, and both agreed to a double suicide pact: the main difference was that Chambige shot his lover and then missed his own suicide. The international press seized the affair as the best story since Jack the Ripper. The pitch was heightened when, one year later, while *Le Disciple* was being published in the press, news of the double suicide of the Archduke Rudolph of Austria and his sixteen-year-old lover Mary von Vetsera was released. Was "Chambigisme" becoming epidemic? Stories following the same pattern were certainly multiplying in the press, both as factual reports of love-suicides and as novels on the subject.[18]

The popularity of Bourget's novel (and the acceptability of similar stories) probably derived from its ability to make all the dire warnings on the effects of widespread democracy and education come true. Indeed, in this text both the producer and practitioner of determinism and scientific psychology are "*déclassés*": their knowledge and perceptions are antisocial because they spring from the social movements initiated by the Revolution. Sixte is a philosopher by default: the son of simple artisans, his ascent into philosophy was provoked by public schooling and his parents' wish for social advancement rather than any "true destination" (the contemporary euphemism for social position). Such unnatural developments only lead to atheism and nihilism, as manifested in Sixte's first masterpiece, *Psychologie de Dieu*, which denies the existence of God and describes faith as a psychological response to "cerebral modifications."

Greslou's personal background provides a more complete sociopolitical statement on the harmful effects of revolutionary democratic movements and the wide distribution of knowledge in France. In his autobiography he notes that he suffers from "contradictory heredities," as his parents come from the incompatible regions of the North and South of France: "For the last hundred years there have been mixtures between provinces and races which have charged our blood, all of us, with overly contradictory heredities. . . . My mother and I are an example of this which I would qualify as excellent, were it not that the pleasure of finding the clear proof of a psychological law is accompanied by the bitter regret of having been its victim" (p. 81). Greslou blames the mother-son conflict on the fact that he has inherited his father's northern analytical skills and love for abstract intellectual work, both of which can neither be shared nor understood by his mother's basic southern mentality. It was through their keen intelligence and hard work that Greslou's father and grandfather rose, however briefly, in society: the peasant grandfather became a rich civil engineer only to lose his fortune in litigations, while the engineer father working for the government died very young, having lost his health trying to qualify for the Ecole Polytechnique (p. 73). From them Greslou inherited not only his intellect, but also his weak physical constitution, nervous disposition, and complete incapacity to act (p. 72).

Bourget's beliefs, briefly stated in the preface, are thus detailed in his novel (see figure 6). Revolutionary movements have brought disruption and disorder, giving peasants and artisans false hopes of social advancement. At first their efforts in this direction may seem to bring results (financial and social) but in time further generations develop false perceptions of reality because of their drifting social standing and failing physical constitution. Greslou recognizes no affiliation to religious communities (his analysis of the Catholic *milieu* results in his loss of faith, p. 98), political organizations (as he believes that only an oligarchy of scientists could run a country well, p. 135), and legal institutions (as he maintains that those who think should not submit to the same rules as those who do not, pp. 76–77). To the pure aristocratic virtues of duty and honor, respect for authority, patriotism, and religious faith, all manifested in the Jussat-Randon family, Greslou opposes egotism (pp. 93, 138), atheism, selfish pride (pp. 91, 99, 121, 138, 153, 166, etc.), and class *ressentiment* (which is described as the real reason for his conduct, pp. 122, 128–29, 145, 155). Once infected by this influence, honorable people of a pure race must defend them-

Figure 6   *Le Disciple* Grid

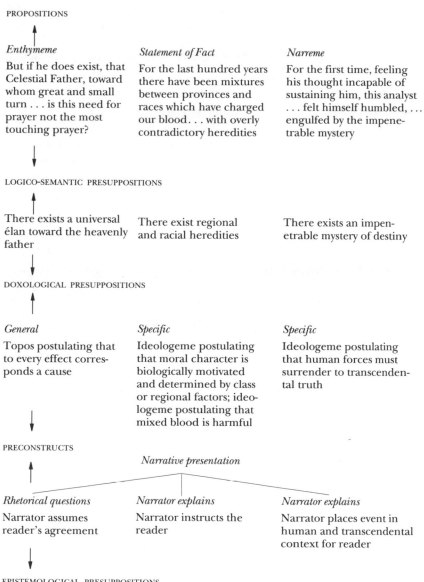

PROPOSITIONS

Enthymeme

But if he does exist, that
Celestial Father, toward
whom great and small
turn . . . is this need for
prayer not the most
touching prayer?

Statement of Fact

For the last hundred years
there have been mixtures
between provinces and
races which have charged
our blood. . . with overly
contradictory heredities

Narreme

For the first time, feeling
his thought incapable of
sustaining him, this analyst
. . . felt himself humbled, . . .
engulfed by the impene-
trable mystery

LOGICO-SEMANTIC PRESUPPOSITIONS

There exists a universal
élan toward the heavenly
father

There exist regional
and racial heredities

There exists an impen-
etrable mystery of destiny

DOXOLOGICAL PRESUPPOSITIONS

General

Topos postulating that
to every effect corres-
ponds a cause

Specific

Ideologeme postulating
that moral character is
biologically motivated
and determined by class
or regional factors; ideologeme postulating that
mixed blood is harmful

Specific

Ideologeme postulating
that human forces must
surrender to transcenden-
tal truth

PRECONSTRUCTS

Narrative presentation

Rhetorical questions

Narrator assumes
reader's agreement

Narrator explains

Narrator instructs the
reader

Narrator explains

Narrator places event in
human and transcendental
context for reader

EPISTEMOLOGICAL PRESUPPOSITIONS

Reality is a given—truth is absolute and cumulative; language is transparent

Bourget uses the concept of criminality to characterize modern democratic and scientific
developments. His novel identifies a conservative religious, political, and social order as the
only true reality for Frenchmen; to deny the value of this order is to be immoral and criminally
antisocial.

selves and their honor with the means available to them: Charlotte, full of "patrician pride" (p. 244), commits suicide, and her brother, wounded as deeply by this personal disgrace as by the national surrender in Metz (p. 277), revenges the family name by killing Greslou, whose actions are unpunishable by law, but more dangerous than any criminal act (p. 289). A trial set in motion by a libertine magistrate depending on scientific psychology to discover the criminal ends with the acquittal of the accused and the condemnation of his science and its social implications. If modern society is powerless to defend itself against such antisocial behavior, men of honor can still administer true justice; having secured Greslou's release simply by proclaiming his innocence (as the letter was destroyed, no material proof remains, p. 289), the count executes him forthwith, accepting his arrest with the words: "I have rendered justice" (p. 293).

Brunetière's article on *Le Disciple* embraced this analysis and insisted that destructive theories such as determinism were by definition antisocial and criminal, and should be censored. Stating that "Adrien Sixte is responsible for Robert Greslou's crime," he proposed the following guideline for the production of truth: "Every time that a doctrine will lead, through logical consequence, to call into question the principles on which society rests, it will be false, do not doubt it; and the error will have as measure of its enormity the gravity of the very harm it will be capable of causing in society."[19]

France took exception to this rule. Proclaiming the need for science to be free, he argued that "there could be no worse domination for pure thought than that of manners and customs."[20] However, the critic did not wish this freedom of thought to be translated into freedom of action. Science should not presume to govern society: "The rights of thought are superior to everything. It is the glory of man to dare all ideas. As for the conduct of life, it must not depend on the transcendental doctrines of philosophers. It must rest on the simplest morality."[21] Such a position brought the argument full circle, for who should determine simple morality? Bourget and Brunetière had no doubt: the good of "man," society, the nation, and God were best served under traditional, authoritative structures of power.[22]

Scientists defended determinism against *Le Disciple* and argued that science increased morality. At the first congress of psychophysiology held in Paris at the same time, both Ribot and Richet fought for the rights of science. An anonymous article in the *Revue scientifique* proclaimed the liberty of science to seek truth wherever it rested, whatever the consequences; great thinkers were always revolutionary. The author further argued that Greslou was a born criminal who would have found justification for his actions in Balzac or Tacitus just as easily.[23] In a presentation to the *Académie des Sciences morales et politiques* entitled "De la responsabilité philosophique à propos du *Disciple*," Pierre Janet tried to satisfy all sides by claiming absolute freedom for research within the confines of speculation, and moral responsibility when dealing with knowledge which could be dangerous if made available to the crowds.[24] Taine himself wrote to Bourget saying that he saw in the success enjoyed by *Le Disciple* a sure sign that times were turning against his generation: "Forgive me my opposition: it comes from the fact that your book has touched me in what is most intimate. I only conclude that tastes have changed, that my generation is finished, and I am going to sink back into my Savoie. Perhaps the road you are taking will lead you . . . to a mystical port, toward a kind of Christianity." [25]

Bourget's success with established authorities was thus rather predictable: not only did his novel capture their imaginations and enrapture their souls, it ratified their social and political ambitions in an unequivocal manner: both the author and the narrator presented the narrative as the simple transmission of the truth of the world as it was.[26] Resting squarely on the age's epistemological presuppositions concerning reality, truth, and language, *Le Disciple* used the correlated concepts of "man" and "criminal man" to define appropriate institutions for the distribution of power and knowledge in society. Elaborated from "authentic" interlocking documents on human nature, the novel ended with the discovery of the soul and the condemnation of knowledge which denied its existence: modern science and the institutions which promoted its development and dissemination were the criminal elements in *Le Disciple*. Bourget presented his case so well that most of the major articles and reviews identified Greslou's actions (seducing an aristocrat and *refusing* to participate in a double suicide) as criminal, while never taking notice of the count's premeditated, cold-blooded murder of his sister's lover—an action presumably justified within the context of the novel. The true criminal act was not to extinguish a soul, but publicly to negate its reality.

◆

A happy compromise: the Holmes and Watson team   In the midst of this wide debate on "criminal man," the proper means of social defense against his activities, and the advantages as well as the dangers of producing and circulating knowledge about his nature, the modern figure of the detective gained prominence in social discourse, principally through the press and literary networks. During the Ripper murders, when public controversy over crime and its prevention intensified with each new atrocity, editorials in *The Times* and the *Daily Telegraph* insisted on the vital role played by detectives in the maintenance of law and order and described in detail the ideal nature of such personages: "The official whom we really require, and who should be found at whatever outlay of expense or trouble, as a Director of Criminal Investigations, should certainly not be a soldier; he should be a civilian, a gentleman, if not a lawyer at least the possessor of extended legal training, a linguist, widely travelled, a man of the world, courageous, inventive, cool-headed, and indefatigable" (*Daily Telegraph*, September 12, 1888). Paradoxically, great acumen and worldly experience were deemed necessary for the capture of bloodthirsty barbarians.

A few months earlier Arthur Conan Doyle introduced Sherlock Holmes to the world in a novel entitled *A Study in Scarlet*, and although the great detective met and even surpassed all the widely recognized requirements of his profession (that is, even though the acceptability of such a figure for contemporary social discourse seemed assured), his appearance went relatively unnoticed. Refused by several editors, the novel was finally purchased for £25 by Ward Lock and Company, and published in *Beeton's Christmas Annual* in 1887. As it attracted some attention in the United States, Doyle was commissioned by Lippincott to write another Holmes novel. *The Sign of Four* appeared in 1890 with similar results. It was only when Doyle purposefully packaged his detective stories in a format which answered the needs of the publishing industry that he achieved his phenomenal success. Considering that serial novels were dead weight for the new monthly and bimonthly magazines (as readers inevitably missed an episode and then lost interest in the work), he decided to write a series of short stories featuring the same character, in order to promote repeat purchases from addicted readers. He submitted two stories to *The Strand*, a magazine started in 1890 by Newnes (of *Tit-Bits* fame) for the middle-class family market, and spectacular results ensued. Public demand for new stories remained constant until the author's death, and Newnes happily paid whatever price was requested for the resurrection of Holmes (at one time, £100 for one thousand words).[27] Once properly packaged, the adventures of Sherlock Holmes answered many needs: they satisfied a public interest in detection, provided a solid financial base for *The Strand*, and supplied their author with the income required to write serious (and largely ignored) historical novels.

In spite of this highly functional role, detective stories came to be generally described as a kind of aristocratic intellectual game. Holmes described his cases as little problems or games, and authors and critics accepted this view, eventually going as far as to lay down rules of fair play for the detective story genre. The virtual absence of the criminal was usually accepted as one of the requirements of the game. Thus, John Cawelti argued that the detective story could not include a criminal whose motivations and actions were not summarily recognized as evil, as this would "break up the formula."[28] From the time of their first appearance to the present day, most critics have agreed that by substituting the detective for the criminal as focus of attention, and by endowing him with reasoning powers strong enough to solve any case, such stories offer an optimistic, conservative view of an orderly world where the good are always victorious and the evil inevitably punished.

These explanations present certain difficulties, the first one being that they seem circular (there are no criminals because it is a game, because there are no criminals). Moreover, the accepted "good always victorious over evil" model cannot account for the times when Holmes is defeated or for those when he solves problems which do not involve any criminal activity. In the first *Strand* story, "A Scandal in Bohemia," no crime is committed and the great detective is foiled by—of all things—a woman's wit. In "The Adventure of the Dancing Men," he is unable to prevent the murder of his client, even though his knowledge allowed him to anticipate the crime. Holmes readily admits past failures ("I have been beaten four times—three times by men, and once by a woman"), and his chronicler Watson tells his reader of cases which remain unsolved, and of others resolved by chance rather than analytical skill.[29] In view of these discrepancies, the wide acceptability of the image of Holmes as the invincible criminal catcher becomes suspect. From the outset it can be noted that the game theory allows other issues, such as the social and scientific apprehensions of "criminal man" presented in the Sherlock Holmes stories, to be silenced. A closer examination of Holmes's Science of Deduction and Analysis (referred to as SDA in this study) and the power it generates will help to clarify this issue.

The numerous correlations between criminology and the SDA allow the latter to be considered as a figuration of the former. Like criminology, the SDA is constructed as a *bricolage* of useful discoveries in other fields drawing its structural unity from its object: Holmes uses bits of chemistry, botany, geology, anatomy, law, politics, and criminal statistics to elaborate his special knowledge which derives its cohesiveness from its object, the apprehension of criminals. Before learning from Holmes the nature of his interest, Watson cannot perceive any connection between his disparate learning.[30] As in criminological studies, special attention is given to problems of identification and classification: ashes, footprints, tattoos, secret writings, and the various hand types of different trades are all categorized by Holmes.[31] In a newspaper article entitled "The Book of Life," the great detective states the basic tenets of determinism in terms similar to those used by criminologists and other social scientists (including fictional ones, such as Sixte): "From a drop of water, . . . a logician could infer the possibility of an Atlantic or a Niagara without having seen or heard of one or the other. So all life is a great chain, the nature of which is known whenever we are shown a single link of it" (*A Study*, p. 23). Like Bernard for medicine and Russell for philosophy, Holmes extols the virtues of achieving seemingly trivial discoveries:

> Like all other arts, the Science of Deduction and Analysis is one which can only be acquired by long and patient study, nor is life long enough to allow any mortal to attain the highest possible perfection in it. Before turning to those moral and mental aspects of the matter which present the greatest difficulties, let the inquirer begin by mastering more elementary problems. Let him, on meeting a fellow-mortal, learn at a glance to distinguish the history of the man, and the trade or profession to which he belongs. Puerile as such an exercise may seem, it sharpens the faculties of observation, and teaches one where to look and what to look for [*A Study*, p. 23].

If the theoretical ambitions of the SDA are vast, its actual state of elaboration leads to the identification of individuals as representative types—results homologous to those of criminology.

With his science Holmes can gather as much information from an old watch as Lombroso can from an enlarged occipital fossa and vermis: "He was a man of untidy habits—very untidy and careless. He was left with good prospects, but he threw away his chances, lived for some time in poverty with occasional short intervals of prosperity, and finally, taking to drink, he died. That is all that I can gather"

(*The Sign of Four*, p. 92). Just as criminologists are able to deduct past developments and predict future ones from their solidly established facts, Holmes can reconstruct past events and not only predict, but also provoke future ones by devices as simple as placing an advertisement in the local paper: "What should he do then? He would eagerly look out for the evening papers in the hope of seeing it among the articles found. His eye, of course, would light upon this. He would be overjoyed. . . . He would come. He will come. You shall see him within an hour" (*A Study*, p. 38). As criminologists discover the scientific truth in common knowledge about criminals (explaining proverbs, paintings, Bible passages, and stories), Holmes disentangles appearances and finds the true meaning of facts available to others (*A Study*, p. 24). The inquiry's dénouement represents the victory of rational thought and presupposes a direct relation between knowledge and reality. The problem-investigation-solution sequence reinforces the positivist belief in science as the answer to the social question. However, through the characterization of Holmes and his relationship to Watson, and through the social contextualization of the SDA (with subplots, descriptions, and surrounding characters), Doyle's detective stories alter the meaning of such knowledge production.

Whereas criminologists usually present themselves as humble servants of truth and their work as adequate means of safeguarding society by eliminating criminals, Holmes describes himself in professional terms (the world's best and only consulting detective) and his work as a source of personal income and pleasure ("The work itself, the pleasure of finding a field for my peculiar powers, is my highest reward," *The Sign*, p. 90). Holmes complains of a lack of criminals depriving him of the chance to prove his talents: " 'There are no crimes and no criminals in these days,' he said, querulously. 'What is the use of having brains in our profession?' " (*A Study*, p. 25). The scientist's work is shown to be a career more than a calling, a self-indulgent, joyful activity more than a public service. The hunt gives Holmes renewed energy, intellectual stimulation, and a kind of animal delight: "He trotted noiselessly about the room, sometimes stopping, occasionally kneeling, and once lying flat upon his face. . . . As I watched him I was irresistibly reminded of a pure-blooded, well-trained foxhound, as it dashes backward and forward through the covert, whining in its eagerness, until it comes across the lost scent" (*A Study*, p. 31). The "far-away expression" he bears when seeking a solution is grounded in practical considerations: "I depend upon them [his theories] for my bread and cheese" (*A Study*, pp. 23–24). In "A Scandal in Bohemia," Holmes sees his chance to profit ("There is money in this case, Watson, if there is nothing else" p. 163), and does not let it escape him:

"Then, as to money?"
"You have carte blanche."
"Absolutely?"
"I tell you that I would give one of the provinces of my kingdom to have that photograph."
"And for present expenses?"
The King took a heavy chamois leather bag from under his cloak and laid it on the table.
"There are three hundred pounds in gold and seven hundred in notes," he said [pp. 166–67].

In this case Holmes's investigations clearly draw the necessary inter-connections between intellectual, economic, and political power, links which remained unsayable for criminologists.

As Holmes is an "unofficial personage" (*A Study*, p. 2), he must stake his field on claimed territory. Fierce competition arises when the prac-titioner of a new science applies his knowledge on cases handled by the police, such as the Jefferson Hope case (*A Study*, pp. 30–32, 40–43, 49, 51, 83). In *The Sign of Four*, this competition is expressed as resistance to presumptuous theories and methods. The investigating police officer insists on the need to "apply common sense to the matter" (p. 113); the "bad business" allows only for "stern facts here—no room for theories" (p. 113). However, institutions are generally described as structurally incapable of discovering the truth. Holmes, who believes that "many men have been wrongfully hanged," must often break the law and take justice into his own hands to see its fulfillment.[32] Real criminals such as Professor Moriarty, "the Napoleon of crime," are protected rather than prosecuted by the law.[33] The possibility of insti-tutions producing true knowledge on the criminal is equally denied by the descriptions of the self-styled detective's knowledge as "queer," "eccentric," "out-of-the-way," and unlikely to allow "entrance into the learned world" (*A Study*, pp. 16, 20).

Finally, the stories' criminals are often good men who failed to adapt to the requirements of social organizations either through misfortune or misjudgment. In *A Study in Scarlet*, "victim" and "criminal" are float-ing signifiers, equally attributable to the same characters, depending on the social context. John Ferrier, a criminal according to Mormon rules, is also their victim, since he was forced to adopt them without believing in them. Drebber and Strangerson are justiciaries for the Mormons, criminals for Jefferson Hope, and victims for Scotland Yard. Hope, the victim of the Mormons (who cause the loss of his fiancée, his fortune, his health, and ultimately his life) is forced into crime because the justice system cannot prosecute Drebber and Strangerson; a murderer according to Scotland Yard, he considers himself to be the justiciary of John and Lucy Ferrier, working as the hand of providence (p. 81). A simple slip in social conventions is at times enough to throw a man's life into ruins, as shown in the introductory substory of "The Man with the Twisted Lip," which opens with the following description of a drug addict: "Isa Whitney, brother of the late Elias Whitney, D.D., Principal of the Theological College of St. George's, was much addicted to opium. The habit grew upon him, as I understand, from some foolish freak when he was at college . . . and for many years he continued to be a slave to the drug, an object of mingled horror and pity to his friends and relatives" ("The Man," p. 229). No one is safe from such falls from grace. Meditating on the fate of a highway robber and murderer whose identity he has decided to keep from the police, Holmes explains: "I never hear of such a case as this that I do not think of Baxter's words, and say, 'There, but for the Grace of God, goes Sherlock Holmes'" ("The Boscombe Valley Mystery," p. 217). Thus, criminality is often shown as the outcome of social rather than natural determinations, or as the consequence of ill fate rather than ill will.

Even those who follow social conventions are not necessarily rewarded. In "The Man with the Twisted Lip," Neville St.Clair, the son of a schoolmaster, receives an excellent education, training in drama, and eventually becomes—what else?—a newspaper reporter. He is sent on an undercover mission to gather the facts about begging in the city and is amazed to discover that, because of his special abilities as an actor with a talent for repartee, he is able to make his weekly salary (£2) in a day of begging. In spite of this realization, he dutifully returns to his job only to find himself served with a writ of £25 because of a bill he backed to help a friend. As a concerned citizen, a respectable, middle-class, *déclassé* reporter who helps to publicize the needs of the lower classes and assists his peers in their endeavors, St.Clair has no hope of finding the sum. However, by becoming Hugh Boone, the poor, cripple, beggar cum match-peddler, he is able to gain it in ten days. It is only by becoming a parasite by day that he can be respectable by night, and live the life of a rich country gentleman with a large villa and nicely laid grounds in Lee. Through a chance encounter, Mrs. St.Clair surprises her husband in between two identities, as he is changing from beggar back into gentleman in his unsavory rooms over an opium den. To avoid being caught in such shameful surroundings, he changes back into Boone and is arrested for the murder of St.Clair. Preferring to be executed rather than bring social ostracism on his children, he refuses to reveal his identity. Holmes exposes his scheme to the police, and arranges his release from prison.

The story is fascinating for it reveals the limits of both social conventions and the SDA—for what has Holmes managed to solve? With all his powers, he has done nothing more for St.Clair than what the rather dim-witted Watson had done at the beginning of the story for the opium addict: send him home without a solution to his problem. Watson determines his plan of action laboriously (hesitating on the proper course to follow, suggesting to bring the addict's wife with him on his search, and then deciding against) and executes it plainly (arriving dressed as a prim gentleman in an opium den), while Holmes resorts to fancy disguises and a dramatic dénouement (sponging Boone's face in front of the bedazzled Watson and police officer in charge), but the end results are equivalent. Both actions merely hasten the inevitable outcome of events, for the police would have insisted that Boone wash once his case had been settled (p. 241), and would thus have discovered his identity, and presumably the addict would have found his way home after his bout with opium, as he had done all his life.

Holmes's knowledge solves very little, even in his own life, where it serves mainly as a temporary escape from ennui. When no case is available, cocaine works just as well: " 'May I ask whether you have any professional inquiry on foot at present?' 'None. Hence the cocaine. I cannot live without brainwork. What else is there to live for? Stand at the window here. Was ever such a dreary, dismal, unprofitable world?' " (*The Sign*, p. 93). Holmes uses his cases for the same purposes as those outlined by Stevenson for narrative fiction: to awaken emotions and stimulate the intellect through sheer technical virtuosity. In some cases, narrative pleasure is Holmes's greatest recompense: "I have been at some small expense over this matter, which I shall expect the bank to refund, but beyond that I am amply repaid by having had an experience which is in many ways unique, and by hearing the very remarkable narrative of the Red-headed League" ("The Red-headed League," p. 189).

There is one story where all of these conditions are radically changed by Conan Doyle. In "The Final Problem," Holmes is faced with a dangerous criminal threatening society. Professor Moriarty, a man of "good birth and excellent education" (p. 470), combines genius (Holmes considers him as his "intellectual equal," p. 471) with an inherited criminal strain. Having such a formidable opponent, the head of a criminal organization responsible for most of the horrible London crimes, gives new meaning to Holmes's work: ridding society of this great evil will make his life worthwhile, and allow him to end his career (and perhaps indeed his life) in peace (pp. 470, 477, 480). This major departure from the usual "little problems" was necessary to justify Holmes's demise. If the great detective was to perish, it should be in the ultimate destruction of evil, rather than in the solving of an interesting puzzle. Holmes's final problem was meant to end Conan Doyle's problems with Holmes: now in possession of sufficient income, the author wished to concentrate on his "real" writing, his historical novels. Conan Doyle failed on all counts: not only was the story out of tone with the rest of the series (Holmes's sudden taste for a "placid life" [p. 470] being as out of character as the sudden appearance of an all-powerful evil organization was out of place), it did not succeed in ending the series. The public outcry was tremendous: letters poured in to protest Holmes's death, one starting with the words "You brute!"[34] Neither would the publisher allow a major source of income to run dry: Newnes kept increasing his offers until Conan Doyle finally gave in, and continued to produce Sherlock Holmes stories up to 1927, shortly before his death.

The Sherlock Holmes stories crystallized contemporary developments in social discourse. As a character, Holmes reproduced the trend toward specialization in knowledge production and the human limitations ensuing from this trend; as a literary phenomenon, his emergence and subsequent positioning as figurehead of a subgenre manifested the specialization of literature as a field and the economic limitations brought about by this transformation. "High" art had to be financed by other kinds of writing: if not journalism, then more popular stories, now described as para-literature, or something in between art and trash. This ambivalent status was at times discussed in the stories themselves. Holmes accused Watson of embellishing his tales which nevertheless publicized the value of both his science and his services. Neither artistic nor scientific, Watson's writings were useful and entertaining.

What is not often underlined is the immense freedom given to such stories because of their status. As a novel, "The Man with the Twisted Lip" would have most probably caused a tremendous outcry of public indignation, not only because of the necessary scenes in the lower quarters, but also because of its "immoral" suggestion that upper-class respectability and lower-class degradation were directly related. The story went further still by showing a gentleman unprotected by his blood against personal failure and deviant behavior in the drug underworld. Presented in a trivial story meant for entertainment, such issues could be raised without censorship in a family magazine—the format and the status of the story ensured that it really didn't mean very much.

And yet the series as a whole explores the personal and professional stakes involved in the production of knowledge and the political and social implications of these limitations. Truth and falsehood, respectability and criminality are shown to be determined by blind—but powerful—institutional processes. The stories also work to outline the limits of the basic epistemological presuppositions of analytico-referential discourse.

Reality is a given. This is entirely denied by the constant blindness of all characters save Holmes. Watson, although aware of Holmes's techniques, is constantly "in the darkness": "I had no doubt that he could see a great deal that was hidden from me" (*A Study*, p. 28); Holmes was "measuring with the most exact care between marks which were entirely invisible to me" (*A Study*, p. 31). Holmes continuously points out that knowledge produces facts: "You see, but you do not observe" ("A Scandal," p. 162). The detective discerns his facts through reasoning. In *A Study in Scarlet* he deduces the existence of poisonous pills before he finds them. When it appears at first that he is mistaken (because he tests a harmless pill set beside the deadly one), he is shaken in his beliefs, but only temporarily: "I ought to know by this time that when a fact appears to be opposed to a long train of deductions, it invariably proves to be capable of bearing some other interpretation" (*A Study*, p. 49). Truth cannot be simply collected: it must be grasped through knowledge. Speaking of an important French detective, Holmes points out: "He has considerable gifts himself. He possesses two out of the three qualities necessary for the ideal detective. He has the power of observation and deduction. He is only wanting in knowledge, and that may come in time" (*The Sign*, p. 90).

Truth is absolute and cumulative. This belief is maintained on one level through the cumulative elaboration of the SDA. Yet it is denied by its relatively small field of application: Holmes's ignorance is said to be "as remarkable as his knowledge" (*A Study*, p. 21). When Watson draws a list of the knowledge acquired by Holmes, he entitles it "Sherlock Holmes—his limits" (*A Study*, p. 21). The SDA is only capable of covering half of Holmes's "dual nature," as the emotional or illogical are part of another reality which remains out of reach for the problem-solving science ("The Red-headed League," p. 185). Finally, the SDA leaves Holmes without any answers toward life. After successfully solving his case in "The Adventure of the Cardboard Box," he turns to Watson in search of meaning: " 'What is the meaning of it, Watson?' said Holmes solemnly as he laid down the paper. 'What object is served by this circle of misery and violence and fear? It must tend to some end, or else our universe is ruled by chance, which is unthinkable. But what end? There is the great standing perennial problem to which human reason is as far from an answer as ever' " (p. 901).

Language is transparent. On one level, this belief is maintained as Watson sets his stories down plainly and straightforwardly, without omitting any details: "I shall be brief, and yet exact, in the little which remains for me to tell. It is not a subject on which I would willingly dwell, and yet I am conscious that a duty devolves upon me to omit no detail" ("The Final Problem," p. 477). This apparent transparency of Watson's writings to reality is denied by Holmes, who decries the fancy tales as exaggerated. Watson's reports are no more objective or complete then the conflicting press reports they sometimes contain, where facts are presented according to each paper's general political policy (*A Study*, p. 41). Language is thus shown to be a social practice rather than a "pure" and free transmission of truth.

If the basic plot development sequence (problem-investigation-solution) and the theoretical postulates of the SDA reproduce and re-inforce the age's positivist faith in science as a solution to social problems, the general hermeneutic quest for truth led by Holmes and the other characters calls into question the basic epistemological presuppositions of contemporary methods of knowledge production. By dwelling on Holmes's acumen and worldly experience (rather than on his science), by focusing on the game theory (rather than on the professional, economic, and social pressures involved in knowledge production), and by insisting on the absence of the criminal (rather than on his precise function of opening up a field of specialization for Holmes), critics were able to bypass the social, political, and epistemological questions raised by the texts. The stories show that in the end answers are as limited as their field of emergence. No matter how brilliant, scientific, successful, and true, the SDA ultimately reveals the limits of human nature—as outlined by Foucault, the finitude of "man" is inscribed in the very wealth of his knowledge (see figure 7).

Translated into several languages, transformed into movies and television programs, the Sherlock Holmes stories continued to gain momentum: the characters of Holmes and Watson are still used to sell anything from tobacco to personal computers. The continuing effectiveness of this double characterization can perhaps be explained by its particularly successful figuration of transformations in social discourse which started at the end of the nineteenth century but are still in process today: that is, the gradual erosion of positivist beliefs in the elaboration of an all-encompassing knowledge of life bringing happiness to mankind by the emergence of new kinds of specialized knowledge, bringing with them increased abilities in social processing, as well as growing anxieties about their effects on individuals.

Whereas Holmes the scientist experiments to discover the laws of nature and life, Watson the writer focuses on life experiences as means to better understand mankind. When first introduced to Holmes as a rather mysterious fellow, he seizes the opportunity to study him: "This is very piquant. I am much obliged to you for bringing us together. 'The proper study of mankind is man,' you know" (*A Study*, p. 19). Watson cannot help but describe his own moods ("with the unreasonable petulance of mankind," p. 23) and even the weather in terms of their relation to "man" and civilization: "All day the wind had screamed and the rain had beaten against the windows, so that even here in the heart of great, hand-made London we were forced to raise our minds for the instant from the routine of life, and to recognize the presence of those great elemental forces which shriek at mankind through the bars of his civilization, like untamed beasts in a cage" ("The Five Orange Pips," p. 218). During this storm Watson is reading a novel while Holmes sits "moodily at one side of the fireplace cross-indexing his records of crime" (p. 218). Holmes, who values statistics, experiments, and logical reasoning, criticizes Watson for cluttering his accounts with narrative, human elements extraneous to the process of detection:

> "Honestly, I cannot congratulate you upon it [*A Study in Scarlet*]. Detection is, or ought to be, an exact science and should be treated in the same cold and unemotional manner. You have attempted to tinge it with romanticism, which produces much the

Figure 7   The Sherlock Holmes Stories Grid

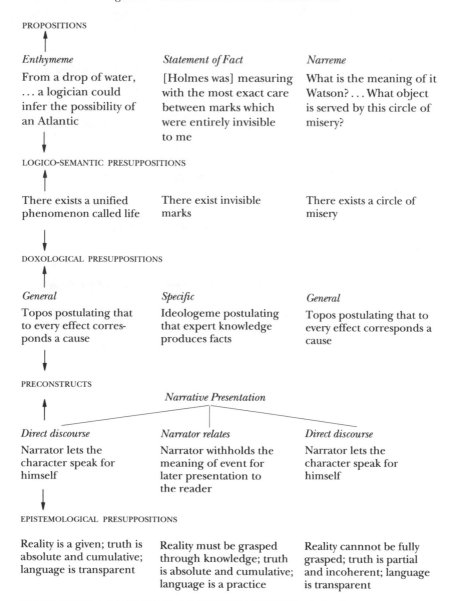

PROPOSITIONS

↑

Enthymeme

From a drop of water,
... a logician could
infer the possibility of
an Atlantic

↓

Statement of Fact

[Holmes was] measuring
with the most exact care
between marks which
were entirely invisible
to me

Narreme

What is the meaning of it
Watson? ... What object
is served by this circle of
misery?

LOGICO-SEMANTIC PRESUPPOSITIONS

↑

There exists a unified
phenomenon called life

↓

There exist invisible
marks

There exists a circle of
misery

DOXOLOGICAL PRESUPPOSITIONS

↑

General

Topos postulating that
to every effect corres-
ponds a cause

↓

Specific

Ideologeme postulating
that expert knowledge
produces facts

General

Topos postulating that to
every effect corresponds a
cause

PRECONSTRUCTS

Narrative Presentation

↑

Direct discourse

Narrator lets the
character speak for
himself

↓

Narrator relates

Narrator withholds the
meaning of event for
later presentation to
the reader

Direct discourse

Narrator lets the
character speak for
himself

EPISTEMOLOGICAL PRESUPPOSITIONS

Reality is a given; truth is
absolute and cumulative;
language is transparent

Reality must be grasped
through knowledge; truth
is absolute and cumulative;
language is a practice

Reality cannnot be fully
grasped; truth is partial
and incoherent; language
is transparent

Reproducing and reinforcing hegemonic values on "man" and "criminal man" through their
plot development and through the theoretical foundations of the SDA, the Conan Doyle stories
outline the limits of such values and question the age's epistemological foundations through
their characterization of Holmes and his relationship to Watson, and through the social
contextualization of the SDA (with descriptions, subplots, and surrounding characters).

same effect as if you worked a love-story or an elopement into the fifth proposition of Euclid."

"But the romance was there," I remonstrated. "I could not tamper with the facts" [*The Sign*, p. 90].

This conflict between Holmes and Watson reproduces a larger one opposing two modes of thought. Watson's aims are similar to those of the last writers of realist and naturalist fiction: to accumulate and present facts in order to gain a fuller knowledge of human nature. Holmes, on the other hand, is one of the new breed of scientists who reject the narrative as part of their domain, and work instead to develop precise methods allowing the attainment of narrow, specific, and verifiable results. If Watson is old-fashioned and endearing, Holmes is fascinating and in some ways fearful, the image of future power, the cold and yet patronizing "machine": "He was, I take it, the most perfect reasoning and observing machine that the world has seen. . . . Grit in a sensitive instrument, or a crack in one of his own high-power lenses, would not be more disturbing than a strong emotion in a nature such as his" ("A Scandal," p. 161).

For the moment, however, past and future are poised in present mutual service, as Holmes and Watson need and complement each other. They first meet because of financial necessity, neither being able to afford lodgings on his own (*A Study*, p. 16). This arrangement soon provides Watson's "comfortless, meaningless existence" (pp. 15–16) as a convalescent army doctor with a new purpose, that of assisting Holmes and chronicling his achievements, and thus provide the detective with the notoriety he deserves (and financially requires) (*A Study*, p. 86). Conversely, Holmes constantly requests the presence of his self-effacing friend, and values his help enough to arrange to have it full-time, in a most friendly and discrete manner:

> At the time of which I speak, Holmes had been back for some months, and I at his request had sold my practice and returned to share the old quarters in Baker Street. A young doctor, named Verner, had purchased my small Kensington practice, and given with astonishingly little demur the highest price that I ventured to ask—an incident which only explained itself some years later, when I found that Verner was a distant relation of Holmes, and that it was my friend who had really found the money ["The Adventure of the Norwood Builder," p. 496].

Thus if the Holmes-Watson relationship constitutes a successful instance of the modern team of specialists able to serve complementary interests, it also emblematizes bonds of friendship and respect. The wide fascination for this strange couple, as hopeful and desperate, as promising and barren as its time, perhaps derives from this mutual need: as long as Watson and Holmes are together, the choice between the old beliefs in truth and "man" and the new beliefs in operative models can still be postponed.

◆

The knowledge of fictitious narrative in prose: *Strange Case of Dr Jekyll and Mr Hyde* **by Robert Louis Stevenson** *Jekyll and Hyde* attracted a wide audience from its first appearance as a shilling shocker in 1886, and its lasting popularity eventually established the tale as something of a permanent cultural fixture, as well known as Holmes and Watson. Stevenson wrote on a theme as old as "man"—as Cain and Abel, as God and Satan, all of whom are written into the story. The fundamental opposition between good and evil, transposed in the image of the dual nature of "man," was particularly pertinent in the light of the nineteenth-century debate on "man" and "criminal man": the novel could emblematize the generalized efforts to define deviance and normality in a changing industrialized society.

The text's initial premise is simple: if science were powerful enough to apprehend "criminal man," what would it discover about him, and then about "man"? Edward Hyde possesses many of the usual physical and moral features of the scientifically determined, born-criminal type. He is small, ape-like, with bony and hairy hands, and an immoral, violent, and ultimately cowardly nature. The mere sight of him is enough to provoke extreme aversion, a reaction recognized by contemporary criminologists.[35] Hyde's crime, identified by Jekyll as a symptom of moral insanity ("no man morally sane could have been guilty of that crime"), brings disruption to a just and orderly world.[36] This is clearly illustrated in the murder scene, when Hyde brutally beats a gentle, handsome, and wealthy M.P., to the great horror of a truly happy and contented maidservant who witnesses the crime from her window:

> Never (she used to say, with streaming tears, when she narrated that experience), never had she felt more at peace with all men or thought more kindly of the world. And as she sat she became

aware of an aged and beautiful gentleman with white hair drawing near along the lane; and advancing to meet him, another and
very small gentleman, to whom at first she paid less attention. . . .
And then all of a sudden he [Hyde] broke out in a great flame of
anger, stamping with his foot, brandishing the cane, and carrying
on (as the maid described it) like a madman. . . . And next moment, with apelike fury, he was trampling his victim under foot
[pp. 46–47].

As Hyde corresponds to hegemonic apprehensions of the born-
criminal type, Jekyll presents the true image of the nondeviant. Like
most scientists of his time, he is male, white, and upper class. Not
only does he labor "at the furtherance of knowledge and the relief of
sorrow and suffering" (p. 81), he also engages in philanthropy. The
transformation of Jekyll into a savage criminal is described as a moral
choice on the doctor's part: "Had I approached my discovery in a more
noble spirit, had I risked the experiment while under the empire of
generous or pious aspirations, all must have been otherwise, and from
these agonies of death and birth I had come forth an angel instead
of a fiend" (p. 85). Destruction eventually comes to the disrupters of
social peace and sanity; both must die as Jekyll runs out of powders,
while his alter ego runs out of places to hide. On one level the message is clear: moral weakness or deviance from accepted standards of
behavior are gravely antisocial, and inevitably ruinous to those who
succumb to temptation.

The story is at once conventional and exciting, which is why it works
so well. The drama and suspense end with the confirmation of accepted truths on "man" and "criminal man," morality and sanity, social
conventions and peace. These features which make the story extremely
palatable, restful, enjoyable, were immediately recognized—*Jekyll and
Hyde* spoke the eternal truth about "man," even though it was only
an impossible romance. Such a perspective categorized the story with
many others expressing "eternal truths" or "anthropological myths."
By identifying *Jekyll and Hyde* as yet another expression of the transhis-
toric theme of human nature, critics occlude all that is original in the
story, and bypass the issue of its historical significance: what social relations made the expression of an abstract notion ("man's" dual nature)
work as an abstraction at the end of the nineteenth century? Why was
a slightly gruesome romance the proper vehicle for its expression? [37]

Jekyll is a man of his times insofar as he explores human nature through scientific methods, a preoccupation of nineteenth-century researchers in many fields. He is a man of his decade in that his science is transcendental, that is, oriented toward the irrational and incommensurable domains shunned by positivists. Lanyon describes Jekyll's theories as "unscientific balderdash" (p. 36), while his own views are criticized by Jekyll-Hyde in a manner reminiscent of the revolt against scientism which gained momentum in the 1880s and 1890s. Jekyll characterizes him as "an ignorant, blatant pedant" (p. 43), while Hyde takes pleasure in challenging his conventional knowledge: "And now, you who have so long been bound to the most narrow and material views, you who have derided your superiors—behold!" (p. 80). Jekyll's research disputes established views not only by its orientation (toward the transcendental rather than the material) but also by its motivation: Jekyll works not to understand "criminal man" and discover means to eradicate his presence from society (to ensure the triumph of good over evil), but rather to discover ways of allowing himself, an upright citizen, to become a criminal and enjoy deviance with impunity. This slight but all-important tilt in perspective allows the narrative to explore the limits of hegemonic views on "man" and "criminal man."

Jekyll's desires and eventual scientific discoveries demonstrate that human nature as a monolithic entity is a product of social conventions rather than the adequate expression of a preexistent reality. It is because Jekyll is a perfect example of the elite white male that he must hide his "natural" pleasures. His lifelong conformity to the rules of good behavior brings him considerable personal success, and makes any deviance—however small—perilous to his standing (p. 85). Jekyll describes his transformation into Hyde as a wonderful, "incredibly sweet" release: "And yet when I looked upon that ugly idol in the glass, I was conscious of no repugnance, rather a leap of welcome. This, too, was myself. It seemed natural and human" (p. 84).

Other characters behave in a manner which shows that Jekyll's love for lower pleasures is unexceptional. When Richard Enfield learns that Jekyll is willing to pay for Hyde's misconduct, he immediately suspects blackmail, and is not overly surprised (p. 33). When Utterson suspects the same, his first reaction is to look to his own past in search of irregularities, and be "humbled to the dust by the many ill things he had done, and raised up again into a sober and fearful gratitude by the many that he had come so near to doing, yet avoided" (pp. 41–42). When glancing at a police officer, Utterson is "conscious of some touch of that terror of the law and the law's officers which may at times assail the most honest" (p. 48). No one seems far removed from disgrace.

Like his friend, Utterson is attracted to forbidden pleasures and finds ingenious ways around the barriers of convention and conscience. Willing to forego theater entirely and to spend his Sunday evenings reading divinity works (retiring to bed, "soberly and gratefully," at the stroke of twelve, p. 33), he mortifies his taste for vintages by drinking gin when he is alone (p. 29). Wine acts for Utterson as the powders do for Jekyll; it dissolves his countenance and lets a hidden facet of his personality emerge, "something eminently human" which is specified as a tolerance for the evil in others providing vicarious satisfaction. Jekyll's satisfaction with Hyde is also described as the inebriating feeling of wine: "I knew myself, at the first breath of this new life, to be more wicked, tenfold more wicked, sold a slave to my original evil, and the thought, in that moment, braced and delighted me like wine" (p. 84). Thus, the doctor's deviant wanderings are not only readily understood, but in some ways shared by surrounding characters, and especially Utterson; in Jekyll's words, they are "as old and commonplace as man" (p. 89).

Jekyll's ultimate discovery concerns not only the nature of "man," but also the nature of knowledge about "man":

> With every day, and from both sides of my intelligence, the moral and the intellectual, I thus drew steadily nearer to that truth by whose partial discovery I have been doomed to such a dreadful shipwreck: that man is not truly one, but truly two. I say two, because the state of my own knowledge does not pass beyond that point. Others will follow, others will outstrip me on the same lines; and I hazard the guess that man will be ultimately known for a mere polity of multifarious, incongruous and independent denizens [p. 82].

Jekyll's knowledge is not absolute or true in a "real" sense (that is, in a positivist sense), for reality and knowledge are in constant mutual transformation: Hyde is made possible by Jekyll's scientific knowledge, and both keep evolving until their deaths. However, Jekyll only learns of the transient nature of knowledge and reality when it is too late. His initial plan is simply to conform to social definitions of "man" and "criminal man," to be truly good, and then truly evil, in order to satisfy all of his nature without losing his social standing. He shares the hegemonic view of human nature as an entity which can be divided into fixed realities, and is unprepared for Hyde's development. His initial joyful recognition of Hyde is gradually transformed into amazement (p. 87) and then horror (p. 95) at the extent of his growing evil.

When Jekyll tries to go back to his previous way of life, he finds it has become impossible: on the first occasion of moral weakness, when he indulges, as Jekyll, in forbidden pleasures, Hyde returns with increasing strength, against Jekyll's will. The dispersion of "man" into upright and deviant natures makes life intolerable. Jekyll's dry and good life becomes as unbearable as Hyde's sensuous and evil one. Jekyll's discoveries do not just reveal the limits of hegemonic truths on "man" and "criminal man," they also expose their positive role in the determination of reality, and warn of the dangers arising from the imposition of stultifying definitions and norms. These realizations make Jekyll's attempts to return to normal life hopeless—to develop scientific knowledge is not to discover reality but to engage in its ever evolving process of transformation.

These discoveries are revealed to the reader only at the end of the novel, in Jekyll's full statement. However, they are in many ways prefigured by Utterson's own quest for knowledge. Most of the novel is taken up by the lawyer's efforts to discover Hyde in order to save Jekyll's social credit. This double intention—know to help—provides an allegorical representation of the positivist faith in knowledge as a solution to social problems. The plot of the *Strange Case of Dr Jekyll and Mr Hyde* unfolds as Utterson's progress from ignorance to knowledge; the narrative as a whole shows how knowledge is produced and distributed in social discourse.

Utterson acquires his knowledge piecemeal, for information is never freely given; its distribution is regulated according to social and professional relations throughout the narrative. This general reluctance to speak out of turn or make information public is presented at the very beginning with Enfield's "Story of the Door" (his encounter with Hyde). Willing to detail the events of the evening in question and describe his own and everyone else's reaction to Hyde, Enfield refuses to name Jekyll as his associate, because of the doctor's reputation. Utterson listens to the story with particular interest (noted by the narrator through reference to his "slight change of voice," p. 31) because he knows that the door leads to Jekyll's laboratory, and that the doctor is a friend of Hyde's (through his will leaving all to Hyde in the event of his death or disappearance), but cannot understand the reasons for this association. Utterson cannot tell Enfield of Jekyll's relation to

Hyde, because of social and professional constraints (respect for his reputation and lawyer-client confidentiality). Listening to the story is an act of indiscretion on Utterson's part, as Enfield points out to him (p. 34).

Thus, the narrative starts with an exchange which can only be described as restrained. Enfield, who will not ask questions or name Jekyll, is incapable of describing Hyde: "'He is not easy to describe. There is something wrong with his appearance; something displeasing, something downright detestable. . . . No, sir; I can make no hand of it; I can't describe him. And it's not want of memory; for I declare I can see him this moment'" (p. 34). Conversely, Utterson cannot tell Enfield what he knows of the door or of Jekyll's relation to Hyde. The exchange ends with a lesson and a pact of silence: "'Here is another lesson to say nothing,' said he [Enfield]. 'I am ashamed of my long tongue. Let us make a bargain never to refer to this again.' 'With all my heart,' said the lawyer. 'I shake hands on that, Richard'" (p. 34). The novel begins with the silent recognition of an unsayable relation between an unnameable high personage and an indescribable creature; efforts to categorize this information carry it through to its conclusion.

Utterson cannot forget the story, for professional and personal reasons.[38] Jekyll's will obsesses the lawyer because it does not fit legal, social, or even rational guidelines: "It offended him both as a lawyer and as a lover of the sane and customary sides of life, to whom the fanciful is the immodest. And hitherto it was his ignorance of Mr. Hyde that had swelled his indignation; now, by a sudden turn, it was his knowledge" (p. 35). Relations of knowledge establish fields of visibility, as outlined by Foucault; Jekyll's will, described as Utterson's "eyesore" (p. 35), also determines his field of action. He turns to a mutual friend, Dr. Lanyon, for more information. Although ignorant of Hyde, Lanyon holds an important piece of the puzzle, for he knows of Jekyll's unconventional scientific interests. Utterson misinterprets the meaning of this new data: "'They have only differed on some point of science,' he thought; and being a man of no scientific passions (except in the matter of conveyancing), he even added: 'It is nothing worse than that!'" (pp. 36–37). His grasp of available information is always partial and his search for Hyde consists of a reinterpretation of already interpreted events rather than an objective accumulation of facts. Utterson goes through a sleepless night during which Enfield's story haunts his imagination. In the process the information gathered is transformed.

Enfield's description of Hyde trampling a little girl ("It sounds nothing to hear, but it was hellish to see. It wasn't like a man; it was like
some damned Juggernaut," p. 31) is altered in the remembrance: "Mr.
Enfield's tale went by before his mind in a scroll of lighted pictures.
He would be aware of the great field of lamps of a nocturnal city; then
of the figure of a man walking swiftly; then of a child running from
the doctor's; and then these met, and that human Juggernaut trod the
child down and passed on regardless of her screams" (p. 37). The process not only alters the perception of Hyde (from not human-damned
Juggernaut to human Juggernaut) but also transforms Utterson who
becomes consumed with "a singularly strong, almost an inordinate,
curiosity to behold the features of the real Mr. Hyde" (p. 38). This
desire to see redefines Utterson's identity: "'If he be Mr. Hyde,' he
had thought, 'I shall be Mr. Seek'"(p. 38). Discourse produces both its
subjects and its objects.

Seeing Hyde makes Utterson feel "hitherto unknown disgust, loathing and fear" (p. 40). Unexplained by any "nameable malformation"
(p. 40), these feelings in turn set him on a search for understanding
which takes the form of the social attribution of the proper term for a
hitherto unknown reality:

> "There must be something else," said the perplexed gentleman.
> "There *is* something more, if I could find a name for it. God bless
> me, the man seems hardly human! Something troglodytic, shall
> we say? or can it be the old story of Dr. Fell? or is it the mere radi-
> ance of a foul soul that thus transpires through, and transfigures,
> its clay continent? The last, I think; for, O my poor old Harry
> Jekyll, if ever I read Satan's signature upon a face, it is on that of
> your new friend!" [p. 40].

This striking passage reproduces the very process of meaning production. Direct discourse is used to describe the moment of apprehension;
however, the voice of the observer is presented and characterized by
that of the narrator—discourse refers not to reality, but to discourse
on reality. The initial perplexity, the actual questions, originate in a
"gentleman," a member of a social class, rather than the neutral "I"
(the objective eye) of criminologists; moreover, the will to know is
motivated by fear rather than by the free pursuit of truth for its own
sake. The auxiliary "must" states the necessity-probability-certainty of
the sought-for supplement. Neither given nor revealed, reality exists

within discursive praxis: "There *is* something more, if I could find a name for it." The difficulty of producing new knowledge is displayed in the syntagmatic development of this complex sentence. Starting as a statement of fact about reality ("There is something more"), its validity is immediately restricted by a conditional clause ("if I could find a name for it"). The stressed verb reiterates, at the presuppositional level, the speaker's will (previously posed by the auxiliary must). However, the conditional clause is grammatically incorrect, as the verbs do not agree: "there is . . . if I could!" To be correct, the sentence should either be "there *would* be something else if I could find a name for it," or "there is something else; if only I could find a name for it." The first version would state the power of language to produce reality; the second version would explicitly pose the speaker's will to find a name to express a previously existent reality. As it now stands, the sentence displays the speaker's mental process, presupposes his desires, and shows how objects of knowledge emerge from discursive praxis.

Meaning is first sought within a religious framework ("God bless me") in reference to the outside limits of human nature ("the man seems hardly human"). Once again, syntagmatic development produces semantic tension as the phrase "hardly human" partially negates the existential presupposition of "the man." The contradiction originates in perception ("seems") and is partly resolved by its very uncertainty (the man only appears to be hardly human), underlined by the exclamatory form. Language enacts the struggles of mind with uncertain perceptions and threads of ideas.

The following question ("Something troglodytic") activates the ideological maxim correlating biological and social deviance in a way that underlines its limitations and thereby undermines its foundations. The adjective "troglodytic" specifies "something" to be of a troglodyte or troglodytes. The latter noun refers to a genus of insessorial song birds from the Northern Hemisphere, the wrens, and then to a genus of anthropoid apes. The former noun refers to (1) a cave dweller or a member of an ancient or prehistoric people that lived in caves; (2) a hermit, recluse, or anyone living in a primitive low or degenerate fashion; (3) a wren; or (4) an anthropoid ape.[39] Presupposed in the first two sentences, the existence of "something" is thus eventually specified with an adjective referring to two nouns, with four possible meanings, depending on which of the absent nouns is selected. Placed as it is in a question form, the adjectival phrase lets several interpretations stand as possibly true:

(1) The ideological maxim conflating social and moral characteristics (Hyde as anthropoid ape/cave dweller/degenerate);
(2) The scientific explanation of Hyde as an atavistic throwback to prehistoric humanity;
(3) The discordant and yet revealing metaphorical representation of Hyde as songbird—a being with the instinct to voice (human) nature.

The meaning effect of Hyde is to circulate these interpretations without allowing one to take over as ultimately true. Recourse to the editorial *we* at the end of the question reiterates the class basis of knowledge production (previously presupposed by the "gentleman") and presents truths as matters of choice and consensus, not simple collection.

Two more alternatives are also introduced in question form. The "old story of Dr. Fell" indicates the ever present factor of already existent discursive interpretations: the story is old and presumed to be known, as it is introduced without further elaboration by the narrator—the reader is left to assume that the story fell into discredit, or at least into silence, as it is never mentioned again.[40] The following cleft sentence presupposes that something "transfigures its clay continent," and poses the radiance of a foul soul as a possibility. The sentence incongruously uses the light of the transfiguration of Jesus to describe the effects of a foul soul—whose very existence is only stated as a possibility, through the indefinite article. This tentative explanation is chosen as a matter of personal opinion, by an "I" speaker (as opposed to the gentleman and the "we") and justified—if such is the case—through a conditional clause, first introduced through parataxis with a semicolon and then immediately subordinated through hypotaxis with the preposition "for." This complex syntactical arrangement reproduces the difficulty of weaving relations between phenomena within discourse. The last cleft clause presupposes the existence of Satan's signature as well as that of a new friend of Harry Jekyll's. Utterson's final Calvinist explanation, which he assumes to be true (the evil soul transforming the body), is ultimately discovered as neither true nor false, for Hyde is not a different person (a new friend) but rather an inherent part of Jekyll's being, and while Utterson's interpretation is religious and metaphorical, Jekyll's experiments are scientific and material—his powders literally transform his body and soul.

Thus, Utterson's knowledge is not the end product of a progressive accumulation of true facts about an external reality: it is the social process of translating signs into other signs. This process never ends. Utterson's eventual discovery of Jekyll's experiments retroactively transforms the truth value of the second sentence, "There *is* something more, if I could find a name for it," for the novel ends without finding a name for the unsayable, without resolving the problem of the nature of "man" and "criminal man"—indeed its conclusion shows both categories to be inapplicable to participants in an ever evolving process of knowledge production. The conditional clause is thus transformed into a counterfactual conditional, and the presupposition "There is something" is (perhaps) denied by the novel's development.

The final explanation, given in "Dr. Jekyll's Full Statement of the Case," is constructed like a realist novel: the "I" narrator explains his origins and organizes his life as a chain of causes and effects leading to his ultimate demise. However, the narrator is not in control of either his environment or his knowledge—even his text is at risk of being destroyed. Jekyll presents his knowledge as partial, sure to be surpassed, and as much the product of chance than rational elaboration: as the initial powders were impure, the experiment cannot be repeated. Even if it could, its object has been so radically transformed (as Hyde is stronger and more evil) that a mere repetition of past procedures would no longer cause the same effect. The doctor's knowledge has transformed reality without giving its producer any control or even any greater understanding, for Hyde is and is not human. The dispersion of a complex process ("man" as an incongruous amalgamation of possibilities) in clear-cut, fixed entities ("man" and "criminal man," good and evil) is shown to be ineffective, harmful, and untrue; and yet the truth—or rather the process—uncovered by Jekyll is deadly. Instead of an increase of power and control commensurate to the development of a new understanding of "man," all that is left is the story of the *Strange Case of Dr Jekyll and Mr Hyde*: an unexpected occurrence, a bizarre experiment which had to be attempted as it was prescribed by the research of the period (part of the debate between transcendental and material science), and whose accomplishment has transformed reality without bringing any progress, power or happiness—rather than answer the social question, Jekyll's solution participates in its elaboration. As both Jekyll and Lanyon die from this discovery, the novel implies questions about future developments: what will become of Utterson and of the reader now that they too possess this deadly knowledge?

Had the novel ended with the initial narrator either summing up the action or describing Utterson's reaction to his new grasp of the situation, the reader would have been left with a far more conventional if somewhat gruesome crawler. However, the author does nothing of the kind: Jekyll's servants are left waiting, frightened and huddled by the fire, while Utterson and even the initial narrator disappear behind the documents left by the dead. Jekyll's statement ends the novel with a speech act, Jekyll ending Jekyll by resting his pen: "Here, then, as I lay down the pen, and proceed to seal up my confession, I bring the life of that unhappy Henry Jekyll to an end" (p. 97). Discourse is displayed as praxis, and the reader is involved. Indeed, the narrator manipulates information and disseminates clues which remain out of reach for all the characters, and therefore make sense only to the reader. For example, Hyde's shuffling walk is noted by different characters, and always charged with emotional values:

> Mr. Utterson had been some minutes at his post when he was aware of an odd light footstep drawing near . . . his attention had never before been so sharply and decisively arrested [p. 38].

> London hummed solemnly all around; but nearer at hand, the stillness was only broken by the sound of a footfall moving to and fro along the cabinet floor.
> "So it will walk all day, sir," whispered Poole; "ay, and the better part of the night. . . . Ah, it's an ill conscience that's such an enemy to rest! Ah, sir, there's blood foully shed in every step of it!" [pp. 68–69].

This characteristic then reappears in another context, when Utterson tries to make sense of Jekyll's relation to Hyde: "Ah, it must be that; the ghost of some old sin, the cancer of some concealed disgrace; punishment coming, *pede claudo*, years after memory has forgotten" (pp. 41–42). This slight transformation (literally a translation of signs into other systems of signs, of body language into a different semantic framework, in a foreign language) signals the process of meaning production to the reader.

On other occasions the reader is obliged to participate in this process. The names of the three main characters, for example, are not given outright but only eventually disclosed as part of particularly significant written documents. Jekyll is spoken of for a full chapter before his name is mentioned as written on an envelope: "Dr. Jekyll's Will." From the outset, Jekyll is associated to Hyde in death. Lanyon's full name appears posthumously, as the signature on his narrative, to reveal the character flaw which led the doctor to his demise. Indeed, Lanyon refused to be "wise" and "guided," and rushed into the "new province of knowledge and new avenues to fame and power" (p. 79) offered to him by an almost hysterical Hyde—only to suffer the consequences of being Hastie Lanyon. Utterson's full name is given at the end, on Jekyll's new will: "in the place of the name of Edward Hyde, the lawyer, with indescribable amazement, read the name of Gabriel John Utterson" (p. 72). The reader is left to determine whether or not Utterson will also die from his position in Jekyll's will.[41]

Religious references are numerous enough to provide the reader with another interpretation of the novel as a whole. Streets, people, and relations are all described in religious terms, with reference to Christian and pagan beliefs: "Street after street, all lighted up as if for a procession, and all as empty as a church" (p. 31; also pp. 29, 32, 33, 36, and so on). Several characters call to God in moments of fear or desperation: "'Utterson, I swear to God,' cried the doctor, 'I swear to God I will never set eyes on him again'" (p. 52). "'God forgive us! God forgive us!' said Mr. Utterson" (p. 61; also pp. 53, 63, 64, 65, 68, and so on). The accumulation of such references is only visible to the reader, and their interpretation is complicated by jumbled biblical references. The narrator's opening conventional description of Utterson is thus interrupted by the character's self-portrait: "'I incline to Cain's heresy,' he used to say quaintly: 'I let my brother go to the devil in his own way'" (p. 29). Cain's words to Jahveh, "Am I my brother's keeper?" are translated to suit Utterson's views. This variation starts the narrative ambiguously: will Utterson do as Cain, and kill his brother, or is he merely referring to a (false) position of noninvolvement? Both interpretations are possible, and both turn out to be at once true and false. In spite of all his efforts to get involved, Utterson remains aloof from Jekyll's experience, and indirectly brings his death by provoking a fearful Hyde to commit suicide. Ambiguities are multiplied by Utterson's name: the angel Gabriel and John the Baptist both announced the coming of the son of God, while Utter-son can only see Satan: "O my poor old Harry Jekyll, if ever I read Satan's signature upon a face, it is on that of your new friend!" (p. 40).

If no single, "true" meaning is attributed to Jekyll's experiments with Hyde, they are constantly shown to contradict existing moral, scientific, economic, political, and social guidelines of behavior. Reference to Jekyll's relation to Hyde is barred by professional standards (medical and legal) and social rules (of etiquette toward a person of standing), and any written statement concerning this offensive association is systematically reserved exclusively for Utterson, who always keeps such documents in "the most private part" (p. 35), in the "inmost corner" (p. 59) of his safe. Their relationship equally goes against local trends in social and economic development. The laboratory where Hyde is first released (and ultimately destroyed) is an ominous building which interrupts a perfect row of thriving middle-class shops (p. 30). Connected to the laboratory by a common courtyard, Jekyll's house around the corner similarly clashes with its environment. The prominent doctor, owner of "the pleasantest room in London" (p. 41), resides in a decaying neighborhood, where all other properties have been divided and relinquished to the dubious ranks of borderline professionals (p. 40).

Stevenson's novel provides a cluster of clashing interpretations; it translates hegemonic truths on "man" and "criminal man" in intersubjective, professional, social, economic, political, and religious terms, which multiply meaning—and ends with a speech act leaving the reader in the middle of an unexplained discursive event. This process perhaps finds its best illustration in the Peircian definition of the sign as a triadic relation between a representamen, an object, and an interpretant. The representamen, "criminal man" (Hyde), is identified as part of the object, "man" (Jekyll); both become the representamen of a new object, "man" as the continually changing participant in an ever evolving process of knowledge production. This new object, manifested in the sudden interruption of the narrator's presentation of Utterson's hermeneutic quest (and their subsequent disappearance) places the reader in the position of interpretant. The reader is left to determine the meaning of Utterson's discovery, and of the narrator's presentation of it:[42]

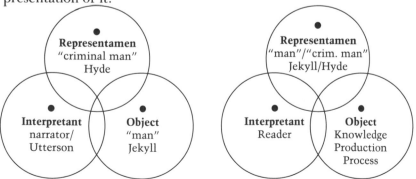

This semiotic process of translating signs into other signs allows Stevenson's romance to question the limits of the fundamental epistemological presuppositions of its time.

Reality is a given. This is denied by Jekyll's discovery of the possibility of producing new realities: his Hyde is "alone, in the ranks of mankind, pure evil" (p. 85). Furthermore, Jekyll, Lanyon, and Utterson are all transformed by their knowledge of this new and constantly developing reality—in Stevenson's novel reality and knowledge are mutually evolved and in constant transformation.

Truth is absolute and cumulative. This is denied by the above-described concept of reality. The novel presents the transformation of one set of truths determining possible actions (knowledge about "man" and "criminal man") by another ("man" as a "polity of multifarious, incongruous, and independent denizens," p. 82). "Truth" is constantly reinterpreted through this discursive praxis, the circulation and transformation of signs.

Language is transparent. This is denied throughout the text, where discourse is constantly presented as constrained by social, professional, and political barriers. The multifarious identity of Jekyll-Hyde is displayed in language, through the multiplication and conflation of "grammatical and narrative positions" in the "Full Statement."[43] It is also denied by the novel's textual construction as an operative model of knowledge production which ends by directly involving the reader in the discursive process (see figure 8).

Profound questioning of hegemonic truths and epistemological presuppositions can thus be found in trivial narratives marketed as pure entertainment. Because of their inferior position within the literary establishment and their foregrounded message of social integration, the Sherlock Holmes stories and *Jekyll and Hyde* were allowed great freedom to reveal the unsayable of social discourse. The lighthearted narratives exposed not only the social, political, and economic conditions of knowledge production, they also outlined the limits of contemporary apprehensions of human nature (in its criminal and nondeviant incarnations) and questioned the possibility of "man" ever grasping truth. Stevenson's narrative presented contemporary notions of "man" and "criminal man" as the products of an ever evolving social praxis, the discursive production of reality. Doyle and Stevenson were generously rewarded for their clear message of social integration; the liter-

Figure 8   Jekyll and Hyde Grid

PROPOSITIONS
↑

Enthymeme	*Statement of Fact*	*Narreme*
And carrying on (as the maid described it) like a madman. . . with apelike fury, he was trampling his victim under foot	Man is not truly one, but truly two. I say two, because the state of my own knowledge does not pass beyond that point	Here, then, as I lay down the pen, and proceed to seal up my confession, I bring the life of that unhappy Henry Jekyll to an end

↓

LOGICO-SEMANTIC PRESUPPOSITIONS
↑

There exists a phenomenon such as simious fury	There exists an entity such as man	There exists a person called Henry Jekyll

↓

DOXOLOGICAL PRESUPPOSITIONS
↑

Specific	*Specific*	
Ideologeme postulating that "criminal man" is an atavistic throwback to primitve brutality	Ideologeme postulating that human nature is comprised of separate identities	

↓

PRECONSTRUCTS
↑

Narrative Presentation

Narrator relates	*Direct discourse*	*Speech Act*
Narrator weaves the tale from existing network of narrations and interpretations; narrator/reader roles united in ever present discursive activity	Narrator lets character speak for himself	Character/narrator determines his own narrative end

↓

EPISTEMOLOGICAL PRESUPPOSITIONS

| Reality is a given; truth is absolute and cumulative; language is transparent | In narrative form: Reality is a given; truth is absolute and cumulative; language is transparent

In utterance: Reality is grasped through knowledge; truth is ever evolving; language is transparent | Discourse is praxis |
|---|---|---|

Stevenson's romance confirms hegemonic views of "man" and "criminal man" in its characterization of Jekyll and Hyde; Jekyll's quest for knowledge, reenacted by Utterson's own quest, outlines the limits of such views and denies the age's fundamental epistemological presuppositions.

ary and philosophic explorations in knowledge production presented in their narratives were not acknowledged.

Comparing the sayable of scientific, informative, and literary discourse on "criminal man" leads to the belief that only a discourse with no specific claim in the effective organization of people and products can explore the limits of hegemonic knowledge. Indeed, the closer an institution gets to effective social organization, the more its truth must be tendered as unified, essential, and inalterable; conversely, as an institution becomes farther removed from practical and immediate considerations, the presence of partial or contradictory information and conflictive interests can emerge and signal the unthinkable or unsayable of other discursive practices. Thus, criminology had to present itself as the simple compilation of undeniable truths in order to claim its right to define criminal nature and determine methods of social control designed to eliminate deviance. Similarly, newspapers had to market objective information in order to silence the political and economic relations which not only guided their choice and presentation of material but also allowed—or rather required—their very presence as information providers to the nation.

Literary discourse possesses no mandate in the organization of people or resources. Deriving both from the imaginary, and from political, economic, and social structures of production and distribution, literature holds a para-doxical position within the discursive production of knowledge, which permits it to present several layers of contradictory or correlated meanings, without having to provide a final resolution. Literature is thus distinguished by its capacity to reproduce the very process of knowledge production, from the unthinkable or unsayable. Traditional definitions of high literature as being the product of geniuses who saw better and more than their contemporaries probably follow from this special capacity: the particular vision afforded by *certain* literary texts (for many, like *Le Disciple* or *Dans les rues*, reiterate relations of power-knowledge) comes less from the miraculous intelligence of rare individuals than from the position held by literature in the general production of true discourse, which opens the necessary space for the exploration of the production of knowledge in its contradictions and limits.

CONCLUSION

◆

This discursive analysis of the apprehension of "criminal man" in nineteenth-century social discourse has foregrounded a web of concepts entangling several discursive practices in the establishment and maintenance of knowledge and power relations. The concept's infinitely expandable classes (semi-criminals, born criminals, occasional criminals, latent criminals, criminaloids, animal and vegetable criminals, master criminals, common criminals) could include any discursive object (women, children, the "lower orders," the "inferior races") and legitimate a wide variety of technologies of repression and control (in police, penitentiary, governmental, and philanthropic organizations). Discourse on "criminal man" served not only to generate and restrain a "residuum," but also to produce a consensual community defined by its difference from, and opposition to, criminality. National educational systems and the new, mass-produced press would further articulate the place and voice of "the public," usually defined in terms of "the nation."

Starting with an analysis of the production and dissemination of texts on "criminal man," this study thus yields a profile of the *ratio* of "man," the apprehension of deviance serving to elaborate the otherwise unsayable grounds of normalcy.[1] Indeed, the criminal, at first defined as the sum of his or her lacks (of morality, discipline, health), finally emerges as the firm figure of knowledge and power, while "man" appears to have been a fleeting phenomenon: once its contrastive function had been served, it could disappear into the unknowable background. The constant rumble of criminals in social discourse allowed the establishment of the main institutional frameworks for the production of knowledge and power relations in modern Western industrialized societies: not only police and penitentiary systems, but also national educational systems, welfare measures, and a mass-produced press were established in the name of "man" and for the progress of the nation, in their fight against "criminal man." Once in place, these discursive practices could turn to more immediate, discipline-specific concerns, only recognizing in "man" the distant original impulse for their endeavors.

To this historical process corresponded an epistemological shift altering the status of truth and knowledge: developments in the natural sciences and in philosophy and literature redefined cognition as a project engaging and transforming both the subject and object of knowledge. Truth was not discovered but produced in discourse, as praxis. Because it cuts across disciplinary and national boundaries, discourse analysis can yield fields of visibility where the interrelations between discursive objects, and their various appropriations and transformations by social subjects engaged in discursive practices, can be grasped. Thus, if discourse analysis notes that Holmes reads a watch like Lombroso does a skull, it also shows how the detective story exposes all that positivist knowledge obscures, underscores the limits of its power, and demonstrates the weakness of institutional means, while the criminological text asserts a monolithic truth in order to claim absolute power for knowledgeable men. Discourse analysis remarks the intertextual circulation of objects of knowledge and desire (by tracing the wide dissemination of the Allmayer story in the press, in novels, and in criminology, for example), and allows distinctions to be drawn according to the status and mandate of discursive practices. As the primary object of an emerging human science, the born-criminal type served to justify technologies of repression and control; as the object of a literary text, such as *La bête humaine*, it could both confirm scientific truths about the nature of the criminal (in the character of Jacques Lantier) and indicate their limits, by positioning the emergence of the born criminal within the parameters of normalcy, in a continuum originating with the secret sexual crimes of a leader of the community (Grandmorin's social position being roughly that of the inventors of the born-criminal type) and leading to the international crimes of wartime slaughter: in Zola's text, truth is always the object of desire, the result of struggles, and the grounds for power—it is never simply "discovered." *La bête humaine* inscribes criminality as the otherness lying within individuals, at the basis of their interrelations, and throughout social rituals and institutions: criminality as the unsayable requiring the entire social edifice to contain its frightening, threatening possibilities. Discourse analysis can relate the indescribable morality allowing men in positions of authority (criminologists, penal scientists, literary critics) to legitimate their place in the social order to the indescribable evil in *Jekyll and Hyde*, an unnameable, desirable otherness which undermines the possibility of solid social edifices, and projects the subjects and objects of knowledge in an endless discursive process involving technologies of power and strategies of control in life and death.

Discursive criticism seems particularly pertinent in this, the "Information Age,[4] when national boundaries are being redrawn by economic, political, and social pressures, when disciplinary limits are blurred by the emergence of new objects and methods of analysis (semiotics, cultural studies), when technological developments make the power of discourse go without saying—or more accurately, go constantly reiterated (with everything from superpower summits to soft drink publicity campaigns and wars being served up in the news as "well-staged media events"). Space insensitive (with economic, political, and cultural globalization) and time sensitive (with the most valued information circulating "live"), the chronotope of contemporary social discourse can no longer recognize the unifying principles of "man" or History as epistemological foundations. The practice of discursive criticism could work to disable these century-old alibis, and devise altering strategies of power-knowledge relations.

NOTES

◆

N.B. All translations are mine, unless otherwise indicated.

Introduction

1 W. R. Cornish et al., *Crime and the Law in Nineteenth-Century Britain* (Dublin, 1978), p. 170. See also Douglas Hay, "Property, Authority and the Criminal Law," in Douglas Hay et al., *Albion's Fatal Tree: Crime and Society in Eighteenth-Century England* (London, 1975), pp. 17–65; Michael Ignatieff, *A Just Measure of Pain: The Penitentiary in the Industrial Revolution 1750–1850* (London, 1978); D. Melossi and M. Pavarini, *The Prison and the Factory: Origins of the Penitentiary System* (London, 1980); Victor Bailey, ed., *Policing and Punishment in Nineteenth-Century England* (London, 1981); David Jones, *Crime, Protest, Community and the Police in Nineteenth-Century England* (London, 1982); and Clive Emsley, *Crime and Society in England 1750–1900* (London, 1987).

2 Michel Foucault, *Discipline and Punish: The Birth of the Prison*, trans. Alan Sheridan (1975; New York, 1979), pp. 222–24.

3 Many important works have cleared the way for this kind of research. M. Foucault in the archeology of knowledge; C. Lévi-Strauss and R. Barthes in mythology; L. Prieto in semiotics; M. Angenot, R. Robin, and D. Maingueneau in discourse analysis; P. Bourdieu, J. Dubois, and C. Duchet in sociocriticism; J.-P. Faye in the history of discourse; G. Genette, T. Todorov, and J. Kristeva in narrative semiotics: all have variously explored the horizons of a new perception of discourse, no longer considered as the expression or representation of reality, but rather as the very locus of its social construction.

4 The term *intertext* and its derivations have served as banners for a multiplicity of problems and methods of research. Within the field of literary studies, it sometimes serves to designate the transformations or repetitions operated by a text in relation to others which have preceded it: from this perspective, citations, variations on a theme or a character, and pastiches or the simple reproduction of the rules of a genre constitute an intertextual network linking the text to the literary field as

a whole. Other semiotic and sociohistorical studies reject this kind of analysis and use the term to designate the links between the literary texts and social discourse as a whole. For an account of the various appropriations of the word intertextuality, see Marc Angenot, "L'"intertextualité': enquête sur l'émergence et la diffusion d'un champ notionnel," *Revue des sciences humaines* 60, no. 189 (1983): 121–35.

5   Cesare Lombroso, *L'Uomo deliquente: In rapporto all'antropologia, alla giurisprudenza ed alla psichiatria*, 3 vols. 1 atlas. 5th ed. (1876; Turin, 1897), 1:278.

6   *Le Petit Parisien*, September 14, 1888.

7   Arthur Conan Doyle, *A Study in Scarlet* (1887; reprint of 1974 ed., London, 1976), p. 41.

8   See Patrick Tort, *La pensée hiérarchique et l'évolution* (Paris, 1983), for a discursive analysis of "evolution."

9   For example, works such as Abdul R. JanMohamed and David Lloyd, eds., *The Nature and Context of Minority Discourse* (Oxford, 1990), or Mary Poovey's *Uneven Developments: The Ideological Work of Gender in Mid-Victorian England* (Chicago, 1988), explore the possibility of resistance and counterdiscourse. However, further examination will demonstrate that the production of hegemonic truths on the nature of criminals effectively preempted any negation in nineteenth-century social discourse. I will use "criminal" instead of "criminal man" in my own descriptions, but will refrain from "correcting" the inherently sexist language of the texts under study; therefore, I will spend most of my time discussing "criminal man," as this is the object of these discursive practices. I am grateful to Lesley Higgins and Timothy Reiss for their observations on these issues.

10   England and France provide a particularly appropriate framework for an analysis of discourse on "criminal man" as it was from there that the major attacks on the Italian School of Criminal Anthropology were launched. These countries equally saw the European emergence and rapid expansion of the realist and naturalist literary movements, of the detective novel, and of the press as a mass produced information medium.

11   Foucault, *Discipline and Punish*, p. 27.

12   Ibid., p. 194.

13   Timothy J. Reiss, "Project for a Discursive Criticism," in *The Uncertainty of Analysis: Problems in Truth, Meaning, and Culture* (Ithaca, N.Y., 1988), pp. 98–99.

14   Michel Foucault, *The Archaeology of Knowledge*, trans. A. M. Sheridan Smith (1969; London, 1972), pp. 162–65. This contradicts the often-held view that Foucault would have radically transformed his approach from an early structuralism to a post-1968 analysis of discursive practices. I agree with Hubert Dreyfus and Paul Rabinow when they state that *"There is no pre- and post-archaeology or genealogy in Foucault.* However, the weighting and conception of these approaches has changed during the development of his work." Hubert Dreyfus and Paul Rabinow, *Michel Foucault, Beyond Structuralism and Hermeneutics* (Chicago, 1982), p. 104. Original italics.

15   Dominique Maingueneau, of the French school of discourse analysis, thus argues that "the pertinent unit of analysis is not a single discourse but a space of exchanges between several judiciously chosen discourses . . . [as these] do not constitute themselves independently of one another to then interrelate, but rather are formed in

a regulated manner within the interdiscourse." *Genèses du discours* (Brussels, 1984), p. 11.

16 Bertrand Russell, "On Denoting," *Mind* 14 (1905).

17 Oswald Ducrot, *Dire et ne pas dire: Principes de sémantique linguistique* (Paris, 1972); and Irena Bellert, *On the Logico-Semantic Structure of Utterances* (Wroclaw, 1972).

18 Aristotle, *Topiques*, trans. Jacques Brunschwig (Paris, 1967), p. 2.

19 Marc Angenot, "Présupposé, Topos, Idéologème," *Etudes Françaises* 13/1–2 (1977): 11–34; "Fonctions narratives et maximes idéologiques," *Orbis Litterarum* 33 (1978): 95–110; and *La parole pamphlétaire: Contribution à la typologie des discours modernes* (Paris, 1982).

20 J.-H. Rosny Aîné, *Dans les rues: Roman de moeurs apaches et bourgeoises* (Paris, 1913), p. 24.

21 Dominique Maingueneau discusses this in *Nouvelles tendances en analyse du discours* (Paris, 1987), pp. 83–84.

22 Michel Foucault, *The History of Sexuality*, vol. 1, *An Introduction*, trans. Robert Hurley (1976; New York, 1978), pp. 94–95.

23 On the position of the subject, see Foucault, *The Archaeology of Knowledge*, pp. 92–96; on the great murmur of discourse, see the beginning of "The Order of Discourse" (1971), trans. R. Swyer in *Social Science Information* 10, no. 2 (April 1971); G. Deleuze discusses this in *Foucault*, trans. Seán Hand (1986; Minneapolis, 1988), p. 55.

24 Foucault, *Discipline and Punish*, pp. 27–28. Marc Angenot, a leading practitioner of discourse analysis, argues along the same lines when he states that social discourse must not be conceived as the empirical mass of all that is written, argued, and broadcast in a given society, but rather as the series of discursive and topical rules which organize the production of both the institutional and marginal forms of the sayable, the arguable, and the knowable of any society. See Angenot, "Le discours social: problématique d'ensemble," *Cahiers de recherches sociologiques* 2 (1984): 19–44; also *1889: Un état du discours social* (Longueuil, 1989), a pioneering work which analyses the totality of social discourse in France for the year 1889; and also on the position of the subject in knowledge production, see his *Critique de la raison sémiotique* (Montreal, 1985), pp. 67–70.

25 Foucault, *Discipline and Punish*, pp. 202, 177.

26 Ibid., p. 26. Italics mine.

27 Foucault, *The History of Sexuality*, 1:99–100.

28 This stance is opposed to Marx's famous determination of the object of historical materialism as being not what men say, but real men in their material conditions of existence. In Marc Poster, *Foucault, Marxism, and History* (Cambridge, 1984), Poster argues that Marx grounded historical materialism with a double maneuver which first divorced language from praxis and then subordinated the former to the latter (pp. 65–67). Discourse analysis, which considers language as a praxis, does not recognize this opposition. In his more recent work, Gareth Stedman Jones argues along the same lines when he states that "language disrupts any simple notion of the determination of consciousness by social being because it is itself part of social being. We cannot therefore decode political language to reach a primal and material expression of interest since it is the discursive structure of political language

which conceives and defines interest in the first place. What we must therefore do is to study the production of interest, identification, grievance and aspiration within political languages themselves" (*Languages of Class. Studies in English Working Class History. 1832–1982* [Cambridge, 1983], pp. 21–22).

Part I   Criminology

1   Karl Marx, *Grundrisse*, trans. Martin Nicolaus (1857–58; New York, 1973), p. 105.

1   Preconditions of Emergence: Crime and Criminality

1   Leon Radzinowicz, *Ideology and Crime* (New York, 1966), p. 15.
2   Clive Emsley, *Crime and Society in England 1750–1900* (London, 1987), pp. 115–16. For further discussion of the inscription of class interest in the penal code, see Michael Ignatieff, *A Just Measure of Pain* (London, 1978), pp. 16–17, 26.
3   This contradiction between theory and practice was studied by Marx in *On the Jewish Question*, in *Karl Marx: Early Writings*, trans. T. B. Bottomore (New York, 1964), p. 12.
4   Ysabel Rennie, *The Search for Criminal Man: A Conceptual History of the Dangerous Offender* (Lexington, 1978), pp. 14–15; and Leon Radzinowicz, *A History of English Criminal Laws and Its Administration from 1750*, vol. 1 (London, 1948).
5   Radzinowicz, *History*, 1:330.
6   Winifred A. Elkin, *The English Penal System* (London, 1957), p. 111. The motives for the landowners' resistance are clearly outlined in Douglas Hay, "Property, Authority and the Criminal Law," in Douglas Hay et al., *Albion's Fatal Tree* (London, 1975), p. 59.
7   Catherine Duprat, "Punir et guérir. En 1819, la prison des philanthropes," in Michelle Perrot, ed., *L'impossible prison. Recherches sur le système pénitentiaire au XIXe siècle* (Paris, 1980), p. 67.
8   Michel Foucault convincingly argues that prison was so readily accepted because it was prefigured in the ongoing establishment of the disciplinary process through which power is exercised in our modern Western societies in *Discipline and Punish: The Birth of the Prison* (New York, 1979).
9   André Normandeau, "Charles Lucas," in Hermann Mannheim, ed., *Pioneers in Criminology*, 2d ed. (Montclair, N.J., 1972), pp. 140–49. See also Patricia O'Brien, *The Promise of Punishment. Prisons in Nineteenth-Century France* (Princeton, N.J., 1982).
10   Elkin, *The English Penal System*, and Ignatieff, *A Just Measure*.
11   Charles Lucas, *Du système pénal et du système répressif en général, de la peine de mort en particulier* (Paris, 1827), pp. 276, 281–82; quoted in Normandeau, "Charles Lucas," p. 143.
12   G. M. A. Ferrus outlines the reinscription of the criminal in *Des prisonniers, de l'emprisonnement et des prisons* (Paris, 1850), pp. 161–62.
13   Gustave Bascle de la Grève, *Droit criminel à l'usage des jurés: Science morale, code et vocabulaire du jury* (Paris, 1854), p. 46.
14   Ibid., p. 324.
15   Foucault, *Discipline and Punish*, p. 29.
16   Julyan Symons, *Crime and Detection: An Illustrated History from 1840* (London, 1966).

17 Thomas W. Haycraft, *Executive Powers in Relation to Crime and Disorder, or Powers of Police in England. A Short Treatise on the Executive Powers which May Be Exercised by Private Citizens and Official Persons for the Pursuit of Crime and Maintenance of Public Order* (London, 1897).

18 O'Brien notes that in France, "most convicts, both men and women, were members of the laboring classes, from semiskilled and unskilled jobs" (*The Promise*, pp. 54, 58). Ignatieff states that 85 percent of arrests in the 1830s were "for vagrancy, prostitution, drunkenness, disorderly behavior, and common assault"; many prisoners were incarcerated "simply because they were poor" (*A Just Measure*, pp. 185–87).

19 In France, for example, La Société Générale des Prisons, founded in 1877, gathered together high officials from the prison, judicial, and government administrations; its journal, the *Revue Pénitentiaire et de Droit Pénal* produced 37 volumes until 1914.

20 Bertillonnage (1879) was a method for prisoner identification through multiple measurements, named after its inventor, Alphonse Bertillon.

21 Louis Chevalier, *Classes laborieuses et classes dangereuses à Paris pendant la première moitié du XIX siècle* (Paris, 1958), pp. 75–85, 98–105, 250–55. See also Peter Stallybrass and Allon White, *The Politics and Poetics of Transgression* (London, 1986).

22 The periodical *Les Annales d'hygiène publique et de médecine légale*, founded in 1829 by Parent-Duchatelet, Esquirol, Villermé, and others, described its hygiene program as particularly concerned with "the duality and cleanliness of comestibles; endemic and epidemic diseases; hospitals, lunatic asylums, lazarettos, prisons, cemeteries. But this research also has another future which is of a moral order. From the investigations of habits, professions, and all the nuances of social positions, it will draw reflexion and council. . . . It proposes to clarify morality and diminish the number of social infirmities. . . . Faults and crimes are the diseases of society which we must strive to cure, or at least to diminish." Quoted in Chevalier, *Classes laborieuses*, p. 30.

23 See *The Journal of the Statistical Society of London* 1 (1839), 3 (1840), 6 (1843), 11 (1848).

24 This new technique won wide approval throughout Europe; discussed in the meetings of statistical societies and of the British Association for the Advancement of Science, presented at the 1851 London Exhibition, it was adopted by several governments who began to produce criminal statistics, as well as by individual researchers such as Parent-Duchatelet, who used it in his *La Prostitution dans la ville de Paris* (1837). See Alfred Lindesmith and Yale Levin, "The Lombrosian Myth in Criminology," *The American Journal of Sociology* 42 (1936–37): 656–57.

25 L. A. Quételet, *A Treatise on Man and the Development of His Faculties*, trans. R. Knox (1835; Edinburgh, 1842; reprint, Westmeed, 1973), p. 6.

26 Henry Mayhew, *London Labour and the London Poor. A Cyclopedia of the Conditions and Earnings of Those that Will Work, Those that Cannot Work and Those that Will not Work*, 4 vols. (1851; reprint, enlarged ed. 1861–62, London, 1967), 1:1.

27 Ibid., 4:3. All above quotes are from the first three pages.

28 In his introduction to the 4th volume of *London Labour*, Reverend William Tuckniss counted no less than 530 charitable societies in London alone, spending close to £2 million a year (p. xvii).

29 David Owen, *English Philanthropy 1660–1960* (London, 1964), pp. 98ff.; and Gareth Stedman Jones, *Outcast London: A Study in the Relationship between Classes in Victorian Society* (Oxford, 1971), especially part 3, "Middle-Class London and the Problem of the Casual Poor."

30   See an enthusiastic *Times* review, September 3, 1888.

31   Michel Foucault, *Histoire de la folie à l'âge classique* (Paris, 1972), part 3, chapter 4.

32   P. Pinel, *Traité médico-philosophique* (Paris, An IX).

33   Pierre Grapin, *L'anthropologie criminelle* (Paris, 1973), p. 17.

34   H. Lauvergne, *Les forçats considérés sous le rapport physiologique, moral et intellectuel* (Paris, 1841), p. 72.

35   Prosper Lucas, *Traité philosophique et physiologique de l'hérédité naturelle dans les états de santé et de maladie du système nerveux* (Paris, 1850), p. 484.

36   Ibid., p. 515.

37   Ibid., p. 506.

38   Emile Zola, for example, used Lucas's theories in his Rougon-Macquart series.

39   Quoted by Videa Skultans in his introduction to *Madness and Morals: Ideas on Insanity in the Nineteenth Century* (London, 1975), p. 7.

40   Skultans outlines this historical shift and argues that economic and political factors played a major role in its development. Ibid., p. 21.

41   Henry Maudsley, *Responsibility in Mental Disease* (New York, 1874), pp. 29–30.

42   B. A. Morel, *Traité des dégénérescences physiques, intellectuelles et morales de l'espèce humaine* (Paris, 1857), p. vii.

43   Maudsley, *Responsibility in Mental Disease*, p. 32.

44   Ibid., p. 33.

45   Ibid., p. 26.

46   Quoted in Skultans, *Madness and Morals*, p. 18.

47   General Booth, *In Darkest England and the Way Out* (London, 1890), pp. 204–5.

2   Conditions of Emergence: Stakes and Positioning

1   *Actes du Deuxième Congrès International d'Anthropologie Criminelle, Biologie et Sociologie, Paris, 1889* (Lyon, 1890), p. 30.

2   Ibid., p. 31.

3   Ibid., p. 192: "On se consolera d'être un 'criminel-né' en songeant que l'on est honnête quand même."

4   Ibid., p. 492.

5   Ibid., p. 198.

6   Charles Mercier, *Crime and Criminals, being the Jurisprudence of Crime, Medical, Biological, and Psychological* (New York, 1919), p. ix: "I still think that common sense is the proper touchstone by which the validity of doctrines should be tested, especially those doctrines that have a direct bearing upon practice; and it is by the light of common sense that I have examined the subject of criminology."

7   Charles Goring, *The English Convict: A Statistical Study*, reprint of 1913 ed. (Montclair, N.J., 1972), p. 13.

8   Ibid., p. 15.

9   Thomas Kuhn, *The Structure of Scientific Revolutions*, 2d ed. (Chicago, 1970).

10   Ibid., pp. 18, 173.

11   For a description of such colonies, see Gareth Stedman Jones, *Outcast London: A Study in the Relationship between Classes in Victorian Society* (Oxford, 1971), pp. 303–14; and David Garland, *Punishment and Welfare: A History of Penal Strategies* (London, 1986), pp. 137–38.

12   Charles Létourneau, *Physiologie des passions* (Paris, 1868).

13   Gabriel Tarde, *La philosophie pénale*, reprint of 4th ed. (Paris, 1895), p. 320.

14   Charles Féré, *Dégénérescence et criminalité: Essai physiologique*, 2d ed. (Paris, 1895), pp. 90, 140.

15   Tarde, *La philosophie pénale*, p. 70.

16   Ibid., p. 183: "Mais le malfaiteur inné est incurable et incorrigible,—cas rare, du reste,—et il ne peut être question ni de le guérir, ni de l'amender."

17   Henri Joly, *Le crime: Etude sociale*, 2d ed. (Paris, 1888), p. 383.

18   Ibid., p. 384.

19   *Deuxième Congrès*, pp. 32, 279–80.

20   Goring, *The English Convict*, p. 370.

21   Ibid., p. 372.

22   Ibid., p. 371.

23   Ibid., p. 373.

24   Leon Radzinowicz, *In Search of Criminology* (Cambridge, 1962), p. 6.

25   Ibid., pp. 12–13.

26   Ibid., p. 77.

27   Ibid., p. 171.

28   Robert A. Nye, "Heredity or Milieu: The Foundations of Modern European Criminological Theory," *Isis* 238 (1976): 345–46, 352–53.

29   *Deuxième Congrès*, p. 63.

30   Ibid., p. 262.

31   Ibid., pp. 489–96.

32   Ibid., p. 35.

33   Roger L. Geiger, "The Institutionalization of Sociological Paradigms: Three Examples from Early French Sociology," *Journal of the History of the Behavioral Sciences* 11, no. 3 (1975): 235–45.

34   M. Geisert, *Le système criminaliste de Tarde* (Paris, 1935), pp. 15–18.

35   For example, the governments of Mexico, Paraguay, Peru, Hawaii, Romania, Serbia, Belgium, Brazil, the United States, France, Holland, Italy, Russia, and Sweden sent official delegates to the 1889 Congress. E. Magitot's preface to the proceedings of the second congress, warmly acknowledges state support (pp. xi–xii). The authority of the government was also well protected by the statutes of the congress: article 2 stated that "any political or religious discussion not directly related to criminal anthropology is strictly forbidden."

36   Radzinowicz, *In Search*, p. 172.

37   President's Commission on Law Enforcement and Administration of Justice, *The Challenge of Crime in a Free Society* (Washington, D.C., 1967), p. 273; quoted in Richard Quinney, *Class, State and Crime: On the Theory and Practice of Criminal Justice* (New York, 1977), p. 8.

38   Israel Drapkin and Emilio Viano, eds., *Victimology: A New Focus*, 5 vols. (Lexington, 1974), 1:xi.

39   The first quote on wickedness is in James Q. Wilson, *Thinking about Crime*, revised ed. (New York, 1985), p. 260. The utilitarian approach comes from Gary S. Becker, "Crime and Punishment: An Economic Approach," *Journal of Political Economy* 76 (1968): 176, and is quoted in Quinney, *Class, State and Crime*, p. 15. A *Sunday Times* (London) feature of March 4, 1973, could again invoke *atavism* to make sense of

American crime: "It is a new kind of crime which beleaguers the city—more accurately an ancient, crudely simple kind: an atavism perceived as a return to the dark ages." Quoted in Stuart Hall et al., *Policing the Crisis: Mugging, the State, and Law and Order* (London, 1978), p. 24.

40 Quinney, *Class, State and Crime*, p. 11.

3 Textual Construction: The Production of Scientific Truths

1 Cesare Lombroso, *Crime, Its Causes and Remedies*, trans. H. P. Horton from 1899 French ed. (Boston, 1911), pp. 1–3.

2 Gaston Bachelard, *La formation de l'esprit scientifique: Contribution à une psychanalyse de la connaissance objective*, 6th ed. (Paris, 1969), p. 213.

3 Cesare Lombroso, introduction to Gina Lombroso Ferrero, *Criminal Man According to the Classification of Cesare Lombroso* (New York, 1911), p. xv.

4 Linguists such as Roman Jakobson and Emile Benvéniste have described shifters as expressions whose referent can only be identified in relation to speakers: "I" and "you," "here" and "now" are prime examples. In this context the term is used to indicate that the meaning of criminological "discoveries" was entirely determined in reference to the speakers' universe of discourse: their signification was specified by the intertext.

5 Cesare Lombroso, *L'Uomo deliquente: In rapporto all' antropologia, alla giurisprudenza ed alla psichiatria*, 3 vols. 1 atlas. 5th ed. (1876; Turin, 1897), 1:412.

6 Lombroso, *L'Uomo deliquente*, 1:413–20; and Charles Féré, *Dégénérescence et criminalité: Essai physiologique* (Paris, 1895).

7 Cesare Lombroso, *Nouvelles recherches de psychiatrie et d'anthropologie criminelle* (Paris, 1892), p. 46.

8 Gabriel Tarde, *La criminalité comparée* (Paris, 1886), p. 21.

9 Ibid., p. 15.

10 Lombroso, *L'Uomo deliquente*, 1:189.

11 Ibid., 1:550.

12 J. Dallemagne, *Les théories de la criminalité* (Paris, 1896), p. 121.

13 Basically, logico-semantic presuppositions are identified by their resistance to interrogation and negation. The sentences "Moral atavism is not deduced from the comparison" and "Is moral atavism deduced from the comparison?" always presuppose "There exists [a phenomenon such as] moral atavism." See Oswald Ducrot, *Dire et ne pas dire* (Paris, 1972); and Irena Bellert, *On the Logico-Semantic Structure of Utterances* (Wroclaw, 1972).

14 Lombroso, *Nouvelles recherches*, p. 48, my italics.

15 Henri Joly, *Le crime: Etude sociale*, 2d ed. (Paris, 1888), pp. 31, 188, 175, 192.

16 Lombroso, *L'Uomo deliquente*, 1:321–26.

17 Lombroso, *Nouvelles recherches*, p. 1.

18 Joly, *Le crime*, p. 257.

19 Ibid., p. 157.

20 Tarde, *Criminalité comparée*, pp. 192–93.

21 *Actes du Premier Congrès International d'Anthropologie Criminelle, Biologie et Sociologie, Rome, 1885* (1886–87), pp. 166–67.

22 Ibid., p. 174.

23 Ibid., p. 201.

24 Indeed, Lombroso was beginning to have had enough *bouillon* over the years: "It is like the reproach which was made to me for not giving enough importance to social facts, this famous culture fluid Lacassagne spoke of in Rome and which has been rammed down our throats ever since. Did I not write a book entitled *Thoughts and Meteors?*" (ibid., p. 195).

25 A. Corre, introduction to Paul Aubry, *La contagion du meurtre: Etude d'anthropologie criminelle* (Paris, 1896), pp. 11–12.

26 *Actes du Deuxième Congrès International d'Anthropologie Criminelle, Biologie et Sociologie, Paris, 1889* (Lyon, 1890), p. 194.

27 Dallemagne, *Les théories*, p. 22.

28 Joly, *Le crime*, p. 76.

29 Lombroso, *L'Uomo deliquente*, 1:34.

30 Joly, *Le crime*, pp. 165–67.

31 Lombroso, *L'Uomo deliquente*, 1:20.

32 Ibid., 1:486.

33 Enrico Ferri, *Criminal Sociology*, trans. J. I. Kelly and J. Lisle, from 1905 French ed. (1884; Boston, 1917), p. 209.

34 Bachelard, *La formation*, p. 21.

35 See Michel Foucault, *Discipline and Punish: The Birth of the Prison*, trans. Alan Sheridan (1975; New York, 1979), pp. 191–92, for a discussion of examination procedures which "constitute the individual as effect and object of power, as effect and object of knowledge."

36 Paul Kovalevsky, *Psychopathologie légale*, 2 vols. (Paris, 1903), 1:358.

37 At the second congress, for example, E. Sciammana started his report as follows: "The study of criminal man had its origin in the purest love of science, in the most vivid desire for truth." Similarly, Manouvrier presented his critique as "made with the unique preoccupation for truth" (*Deuxième Congrès*, pp. 36, 28).

38 Lombroso, *L'Uomo deliquente*, 1:vii.

39 Ibid., 1:135.

40 Tarde, *Criminalité comparée*, p. 90.

41 Ferri, *Criminal Sociology*, p. 501.

42 Tarde, *Criminalité comparée*, p. 193.

43 Ferri, *Criminal Sociology*, pp. 259–71.

44 Achille Loria, *The Economic Foundations of Society*, trans. Lindley M. Keasley, from 2d French ed. (1899; New York, 1907), pp. 110–11.

45 Ibid., pp. 111–12.

46 Ibid., p. 380.

47 Lombroso, *Crime*, p. 276.

48 Ferri, *Criminal Sociology*, p. 245.

49 Ibid., p. 244.

50 Ibid., p. 245.

51 Zeev Sternhell, *La droite révolutionnaire 1885–1914. Les origines françaises du fascisme* (Paris, 1978); and Jean-Pierre Faye, *Théorie du récit: Introduction aux "Langages Totalitaires." Critique de/La Raison/l'Economie/Narrative* (Paris, 1972).

52 In the fifth edition of his *Sociologia criminale* (1929), Ferri wrote in a footnote: "the task of the social prevention of criminality was assumed and has begun to be real-

ized by the Fascist Government, which both in the Rocco Project of a Penal Code and in many special statutes, has accepted and is putting into effect some of the principles and the most characteristic practical proposals of the positive school" (1:11–12); quoted by Thorsten Sellin in his "Enrico Ferri," in Hermann Mannheim, ed., *Pioneers in Criminology*, 2d ed. (Montclair, N.J., 1972), p. 377. Ferri was nominated as a Fascist Senator in 1929, one month before his death, but his confirmation never occurred.

53   Tarde, *Criminalité comparée*, pp. 97–98; and Lombroso, *Nouvelles recherches*, pp. 123–24. See also Gustave Le Bon, *Les lois psychologiques de l'évolution des peuples* (Paris, 1894), pp. 3–4.

54   Lombroso, *L'Uomo deliquente*, 1:98.

55   Ibid., p. 582.

56   R. A. Nye, in his book entitled *The Origin of Crowd Psychology: Gustave Le Bon and the Crisis of Mass Democracy in the Third Republic* (London, 1975), p. 3, documents Le Bon's success: "It seems very probable that his *Psychologie des foules*, which is now in its 45th French edition and has appeared in at least 16 foreign languages, aside from helping set the foundations of social psychology itself, has been one of the best-selling scientific books in history."

57   Scipio Sighele, *Psychologie des sectes*, trans. Louis Brandin (1894; Paris 1898), pp. 36–37. My English.

58   Max Nordau, *Degeneration*, trans. from 2d German ed., 9th ed. (New York, 1902).

59   Raffaele Garofalo, *Criminology*, trans. R. W. Miller, from 1905 French ed. (1885; Boston, 1914), p. 97.

60   Philip Rieff has shown that Le Bon and Freud *identified* the crowd and the unconscious in "The Origin of Freud's Political Psychology," in Warren Wagar, ed., *European Intellectual History since Darwin and Marx* (New York, 1967), p. 95.

61   Sighele, *Psychologie des sectes*, p. 59. My English.

62   *Deuxième Congrès*, pp. 260–61, 383.

63   Kovalevsky, *Psychopathologie légale*, 1:23.

64   Charles Létourneau, *Physiologie des passions* (Paris 1868), p. 206.

65   Ibid., pp. 196–97.

66   Ibid., p. 67.

67   Ibid., pp. 73–74.

68   Luis Prieto, "Sur l'idéologie et sur le rôle des intellectuels dans le processus vers le socialisme." Unpublished article. These issues are further discussed in his *Pertinence et pratique. Essai de sémiologie* (Paris, 1975).

69   Following Noel McLachlan, W. R. Cornish made this point clear in his "Criminal Justice and Punishment": "Criminal justice was, most of the time, a neglected cause, in which reform proceeded snail-like, starved of funds and blighted by the expedience of the moment. Enthusiasts there were, and official inquiries offered them a special opportunity to have their principles and their plans minuted for posterity. What is less graphically recorded is the smallness of their number and the indifference and the parsimony with which their projects were often treated." W. R. Cornish, *Crime and the Law in Nineteenth-Century Britain* (Dublin, 1978), p. 13.

70   See Charles Goring, *The English Convict: A Statistical Study*, reprint of 1913 ed. (Montclair, N.J., 1972); and Henry Maudsley, *Responsibility in Mental Disease* (New York, 1874).

71 Gareth Stedman Jones, *Outcast London: A Study in the Relationship between Classes in Victorian Society* (Oxford, 1971), pp. 183–87, 193–96, and generally in part 2, "Housing and the Casual Poor," and part 3, "Middle-Class London and the Problem of the Casual Poor."

72 David Garland discusses these acts at length in *Punishment and Welfare* (London, 1986); the quote is from p. 224.

73 Garland's crucial book, *Punishment and Welfare*, analyzes these acts and correlates them to the social reform programs proposed by criminology, social work, and eugenics. He makes the point that the acts addressed the residuum problem (p. 228), and notes that there was no opposition to them by the socialist or labor groups (pp. 168–69). Garland insists that these acts mark the beginnings of a distinctly modern penal system, but Foucault's argument that it was established about a hundred years earlier is more convincing.

74 Ibid., p. 169. The same silence is noted in contemporary Britain in Stuart Hall et al., *Policing the Crisis: Mugging, the State, and Law and Order* (London, 1978), p. 33.

Part II The Press

1 Foucault notes the emergence of "the population" and the deployment of technologies of power that it made possible in *The History of Sexuality*, vol. 1, *An Introduction*, trans. Robert Hurley (1976; New York, 1978), pp. 25–26.

2 Parliamentary Papers, *Report of the Commissioners of the Poor Laws* (1834), XXXIV. Reply from Stiffkey, Norfolk, quoted in Patricia Hollis, *The Pauper Press: A Study in Working-Class Radicalism of the 1830s* (London, 1970), p. 295.

3 Eugen Weber, *Peasants into Frenchmen. The Modernization of Rural France 1870–1914* (Stanford, 1976), p. 326.

4 Quoted in Harold Herd, *The March of Journalism: The Story of the British Press from 1622 to the Present Day* (London, 1952; reprint, Westport, Conn., 1973), p. 98.

4 Preconditions of Emergence: Rising Mass Literacy

1 Letter to the *Gentleman's Magazine* (October 1797), pp. 819–20; reprinted in J. M. Goldstrom, comp. *Education, Elementary Education 1780–1900* (Newton Abbot, 1972), p. 22.

2 Patrick Colquhoun, *A New and Appropriate System of Education for the Labouring People* (London, 1806; reprint, Shannon, 1971), pp. 77–78.

3 W. Stanley Jevons, "The Rationale of Free Public Libraries," *Contemporary Review* 39 (1881): 385–402; quoted in Richard D. Altick, *The English Common Reader: A Social History of the Mass Reading Public, 1800–1900* (Chicago, 1957), p. 230. My indebtedness to Altick's pioneering work will be obvious throughout this section.

4 *Select Committee on Intoxication*, 1834, VIII, qu. 2054; in Patricia Hollis, *The Pauper Press: A Study in Working-Class Radicalism of the 1830s* (London, 1970), p. 10.

5 The National Society for Promoting the Education of the Poor in the Principles of the Established Church in England and Wales, founded in 1811, and the British and Foreign School Society, founded in 1813.

6 Civic instruction books printed by the government to propagate secular morality

were placed on the Index Librorum Prohibitorum. See Theodore Zeldin, *France 1848–1945* (1977; *Intellect and Pride*, Oxford, 1980), p. 179; and Françoise Mayeur, *L'enseignement Secondaire des Jeunes Filles Sous la Troisième République* (Paris, 1977).

7   M. Vaughan and M. S. Archer, *Social Conflict and Educational Change in England and France 1789–1848* (Cambridge, 1971), pp. 210–11.

8   Quoted in Zeldin, *France*, p. 150.

9   Richard Whateley, *Easy Lessons on Money Matters* (1833); reprinted in *Education, Elementary Education*, pp. 88–89.

10   Quoted in Eugen Weber, *Peasants into Frenchmen. The Modernization of Rural France 1870–1914* (Stanford, 1976), p. 331.

11   Ibid., p. 332.

12   The same insistence on moral virtue could be found in upper-class education as well. See Vaughan and Archer, *Social Conflict and Educational Change*, p. 208.

13   P. W. Musgrave, *Society and Education in England since 1800* (London, 1968), p. 30.

14   Quoted in G. A. Cranfield, *The Press and Society: From Caxton to Northcliffe* (London, 1978), p. 122.

15   Antoine Prost, *Histoire de l'enseignement en France, 1800–1967* (Paris, 1968), p. 113.

16   At mid-century Michelet estimated that a baker made six times more money than a teacher. Zeldin, *France*, p. 159.

17   Judith Ryder and Harold Silver, *Modern English Society: History and Structure 1850–1970* (London, 1970), p. 95.

18   Ibid., p. 96.

19   Quoted in Altick, *The English Common Reader*, pp. 156–57.

20   Patrick J. Harrigan, *Mobility, Elites, and Education in French Society of the Second Empire* (Waterloo, 1980), pp. 128–44. The criminal impact of *déclassés* on social organization is discussed in Bourget's novel *Le Disciple* (see chapter 9).

21   Among the most prominent religious agencies were the Religious Tract Society, the British and Foreign Bible Society, the Society for Promoting Christian Knowledge, and the French League for the Uplifting of the Masses and the Société de Saint-Vincent-de-Paul. See Altick, *The English Common Reader*, p. 103, on the littering effects of their propaganda.

22   Weber, *Peasants into Frenchmen*, p. 458.

23   Altick describes their success in detail, *The English Common Reader*, p. 75. The messages of hope are from Hannah More, *Cheap Repository Tracts*, vol. 2, *Turn the Carpet; Or the Two Weavers. A New Song* (1796); reprinted in *Education, Elementary Education*, pp. 23–24.

24   Cranfield, *The Press and Society*, p. 123.

25   Altick, *The English Common Reader*, pp. 76–77.

26   One of the most important English organizations in this field was the Utilitarian Society for the Diffusion of Useful Knowledge (SDUK), founded in 1826 by Henry Broughman, and which eventually covered the gamut of such activities. Besides involvement in the Mechanics' Institutes, the society published a Library of Useful Knowledge (1827) and a Library of Entertaining Knowledge (1829). Other SDUK publications included the British Almanach, intended to drive out the more popular superstitious or obscene kinds, and the *Penny Magazine* and *Penny Cyclopaedia* (1832–33), under Charles Knight.

27   R. D. Anderson, *Education in France, 1848–1870* (Oxford, 1975), p. 146. Altick gives

a history of the Mechanics' Institutes, and of their limited success in reaching their intended audience, *The English Common Reader*, pp. 189–92. For an account of working-class culture, see E. P. Thompson, *The Making of the English Working Class* (London, 1963).

28 Altick, *The English Common Reader*, p. 206.

29 Zeldin, *France*, p. 145.

30 The *Poor Man's Guardian* had "Liberty of the Press" and "Knowledge is Power" as mottos; within a couple of years several other illegal, unstamped papers were launched. See Thompson, *The Making of the English Working Class*, for vivid descriptions of these struggles.

31 Cranfield, *The Press and Society*, pp. 29–30.

32 Hollis, *The Pauper Press*, p. vii.

33 Altick, *The English Common Reader*, p. 282.

34 They were thus asking Bulwer-Lytton's question: "Is it not time to consider whether the printer and his types may not provide better for the peace and honour of a free state than the gaoler and the hangman—whether, in one word, cheap knowledge may not be a better political agent than costly punishment?" Quoted in Harold Herd, *The March of Journalism: The Story of the British Press from 1622 to the Present Day* (London, 1952; reprint, Westport, Conn., 1973), p. 148. Altick, *The English Common Reader*, p. 348, also argues that one of the more practical motives for the Cobdenites' involvement in the campaign against the taxes on knowledge was their desire to weaken the conservative press in general, and *The Times* in particular, in order to allow a provincial press to rise and give support to the Manchester school.

35 Altick, *The English Common Reader*, p. 354.

36 Claude Bellanger et al., *Histoire générale de la presse française* (Paris, 1969), 2:97.

37 In his *Memorandum on Popular Education* (London, 1868; reprint, New York, 1969), James P. Kay-Shuttleworth insisted that the recent extension of the franchise meant that there was then "a clear political necessity to fit the electors for the right exercise of their power," especially in the light of the "anti-social doctrines held by the leaders of Trades' Unions." Robert Lowe perhaps best expressed this view with his famous "I believe it will be absolutely necessary to compel our future masters to learn their letters."

38 See Jean-Pierre Séguin, *Canards du siècle passé* (Paris, 1969), for a sample of French nineteenth-century *canards*.

39 Marc Angenot, "La littérature populaire française au dix-neuvième siècle," *Revue Canadienne de littérature comparée* 9 (September 1982): 324–40. These close ties between the press and literature would be maintained through different forms throughout the century; it is interesting to note that the King Edward VII Chair in English Literature was established by Harold Harmsworth (the newspaper magnate, later Lord Rothermere), who gave the crown the responsibility of appointment.

40 Altick, *The English Common Reader*, pp. 344–45.

41 The first issue, for example, defined the most pressing social problem as discovering ways to provide the most happiness for the largest number. See Bellanger, *Histoire générale*, 2:117.

42 Angenot, "Littérature populaire," p. 332.

43 Marc Angenot, *Le roman populaire* (Montreal, 1975), p. 86.

44 Weber gives a vivid account of the paper: "The *Petit Journal*, splendid value for one sou, was a sort of *News of the World*: birth of quadruplets, bride gives birth a few hours after wedding, American abandons his bride and goes off with her dowry, sub-prefect falls off his horse. There was easy-to-understand coverage of happenings in Paris and the provinces that lent itself to comment and discussion around the kitchen table, news from abroad (sales of Cuban slaves, the chaining of Russian conscripts), court chronicles (elopements, confidence tricks, vendettas, crimes of passion), accounts of shows, debts, bankruptcies, current market prices (cattle, grain, etc.). One could not ask for more." *France*, p. 464.

45 René de Livois, *Histoire de la presse française*, 2 vols. (Lausanne, 1965), 2:276.

46 Ibid., 2:275.

47 See de Livois for an account of Millaud's enterprising and devious tactics.

48 Livois, *Histoire*, 1:326–27.

5 Conditions of Emergence: Running the Show

1 Raymond Williams, *The Long Revolution* (New York, 1961), pp. 193–94; and Claude Bellanger et al., *Histoire générale de la presse française* (Paris, 1969), p. xiii. For further details on this expansion, see A. J. Lee, *The Origins of the Popular Press in England, 1855–1914* (London, 1976); and René de Livois, *Histoire de la presse française* (Lausanne, 1965), vol. 2.

2 Francine Amaury, *Histoire du plus grand quotidien de la IIIe République: Le Petit Parisien (1876–1944)*, 2 vols. (Paris, 1972), 1:511.

3 Lee, *The Origins of the Popular Press*, p. 89, also notes that the owners of the *Daily Telegraph* and *Lloyds Weekly News* left estates worth more than £0.5 million.

4 Ibid., pp. 79–80.

5 Ibid., p. 180.

6 Bellanger, *Histoire générale*, 3:297.

7 Alfred Charles William Harmsworth (later Lord Northcliffe), for example, started his famous paper *Answers to Correspondents* in 1888, and eventually became the head of the largest publishing house in the world, owning the London *Evening News*, the *Daily Mail*, the *Daily Mirror*, *The Times*, and a host of specialized publications, a papermaking industry in Newfoundland, and specialized distribution networks. See Harold Herd, *The March of Journalism: The Story of the British Press from 1622 to the Present Day* (London, 1952; reprint, Westport, Conn., 1973), p. 249.

8 Williams, *The Long Revolution*, pp. 200–201.

9 Raymond Manevy, *La presse sous la IIIe République* (Paris, 1955), p. 19.

10 Arthur Raffalovitch, a prominent economist working in Paris, who wrote for distinguished publications such as *Le Journal des Débats*, at one time directed the financial journal *Le Messager de Paris*, and who was a member of the Institute and a *grand officer* of the Legion of Honor, described his basic strategy to the Russian minister of finance as follows: "It is important to have at one's disposal a few respected organs, such as *Le Journal des Débats* and *Le Temps*, or papers with a large circulation such as *Le Petit Parisien, Le Journal*, perhaps *L'Echo de Paris*. To have a pack of hired flatterers who very quickly transform themselves into blackmailers is a fool's trade in normal times" (in Bellanger, *Histoire générale*, 3:272).

11 Bellanger, *Histoire générale*, 3:272.

12   Ibid., 3:265–66.

13   Lee, *The Origins of the Popular Press*, pp. 89–103.

14   Jean Dupuy's career epitomizes this path: owner and director of *Le Petit Parisien* from 1888 to his death and president of the press association, he was senator for the Hautes-Pyrénées from 1891, minister of agriculture in the Waldeck-Rousseau cabinet, minister of commerce in 1909–10, and minister of public works in 1912– 13—there was talk of his candidacy for president in 1906 and in 1913. Dupuy usually bought or assured the support of regional papers when he or his sons ran for election. Senator for the Hautes-Pyrénées, he bought *Les Pyrénées* in Tarbes; he acquired *La France de Bordeaux* in 1901, and his son Pierre subsequently was elected deputy for the Gironde in 1902; the assured friendship of *La Dépêche* similarly helped the election of Paul, his other son, in Haute-Garonne in 1910. The launching of the weekly *L'agriculture nouvelle* in 1891 by Dupuy's electoral manager helped to consolidate his influential position: the owner of *Le Petit Parisien* (a paper with more than 75 percent of its sales in rural areas) became minister of agriculture a few years later. See Bellanger, *Histoire générale*, 3:307.

15   Bellanger, *Histoire générale*, 3:251; and Lee, *The Origins of the Popular Press*, p. 207.

16   The Havas news agency and *Le Temps* (which had its own foreign correspondents) are known to have rendered such services. See Lee, *The Origins of the Popular Press*, p. 214; and Bellanger, *Histoire générale*, 3:249.

17   Lee, *The Origins of the Popular Press*, p. 203, notes that the War Office routinely gave information to *The Times* before it was given to Parliament, so that the newspaper would have the time necessary to study the material and write careful reports.

18   Bellanger, *Histoire générale*, 3:259.

19   Quoted in Lee, *The Origins of the Popular Press*, p. 196.

20   Emile Zola, "La presse parisienne" (1877), *Etudes de Presse* 8 (1956): 262.

21   Description first given in *The Edinburgh Review*, quoted in Stanley Harrison, *Poor Men's Guardians: A Record of the Struggles for a Democratic Newspaper Press 1763–1973* (London, 1974), p. 41.

22   Herd, *The March of Journalism*, p. 231 n. 1.

23   Williams, *The Long Revolution*, p. 197.

24   Bellanger, *Histoire générale*, 3:299 n. 3, lists other examples as well.

25   Ibid., 3:299 n. 4; and Livois, *Histoire*, 2:377.

26   Livois, *Histoire*, 2:389.

27   Matthew Arnold, commentary in *Nineteenth Century* (1887); quoted in Lee, *The Origins of the Popular Press*, p. 118.

28   Examples of such novels would be *Le crime de la rue Marignan* and *Justice humaine*, published in the fall of 1888. The figures given by Williams in *The Long Revolution*, pp. 212–13, show that such a reading pattern certainly exists in our time, when the English upper class prefers the *Daily Express* (the closest to the tabloid format of any of the "popular" dailies) to *The Times* or the *Daily Telegraph*, and chooses the *Sunday Express* over the *Observer* or the *Sunday Times* for its weekend enjoyment.

29   Roland Barthes, "La censure et le censurable," *Communications* 9 (1967), quoted in Charles Grivel, "Les mécanismes de la censure dans le système libéral-bourgeois," *Pensée* 176 (1974): 89–105.

6   Textual Construction: Producing Information

1   Quoted in Claude Bellanger et al., *Histoire générale de la presse française* (Paris, 1969), 3:309. Present-day affirmations by newsbroadcasters confirm that such views are still acceptable. Walter Cronkite's famous "That's the way it is," and the classic "We don't make the news, we report it" pale beside the following statement made by R. S. Salant, president of CBS News: "Our reporters do not cover stories from *their* point of view. They are presenting them from *nobody's* point of view." Quoted in David L. Altheide, *Creating Reality: How T.V. News Distorts Events* (London, 1976), p. 17.

2   Quoted in G. A. Cranfield, *The Press and Society: From Caxton to Northcliffe* (London, 1978), pp. 206–7.

3   Quoted in Raymond Williams, *The Long Revolution* (New York, 1961), p. 174.

4   "Soyez em . . . bêtants, messieurs," quoted in Raymond Manevy, *La presse sous la IIIe République* (Paris, 1955), p. 213; the Millaud quote is in René de Livois, *Histoire de la presse française*, 2 vols. (Lausanne, 1965), 2:390.

5   Kennedy Jones, recorded in his book *Fleet Street and Downing Street*; quoted in Harold Herd, *The March of Journalism: The Story of the British Press from 1622 to the Present Day* (London, 1952; reprint, Westport, Conn., 1973), p. 238.

6   "Reviewing the files," wrote Burnham, "the honest biographer cannot dispute that the *Daily Telegraph* thrived on crime." Quoted in Williams, *The Long Revolution*, p. 196.

7   Quoted in Herd, *The March of Journalism*, p. 241.

8   Circulating conservative information was also favored by a growing unity of sentiment between the middle and upper classes from the 1850s to the end of the century, as described by Williams, *The Long Revolution*, p. 196: "In a period which saw the consolidation of sentiment from the middle class upwards—a unity of sentiment quite strong enough to contain constitutional party conflicts—most newspapers were able to drop their frantic pamphleteering, and to serve this public with news and a regulated diversity of opinion."

9   Luis J. Prieto in a lecture entitled "Théorie sémiologique de la pratique," given at the Université de Montréal on March 18, 1981.

10 Luis J. Prieto, *Pertinence et pratique: Essai de sémiologie* (Paris, 1975).

11 *The Times*, September 9, 1888. To ensure synchronic coherence, all newspaper quotes will be from 1888, unless otherwise indicated.

12 The value of this kind of reporting was outlined by Steven Box in his *Deviance, Reality and Society* (London, 1971), p. 40.

13 Douglas Hay, "Property, Authority and the Criminal Law," in Douglas Hay et al., *Albion's Fatal Tree: Crime and Society in Eighteenth-Century England* (London, 1975), p. 33.

14 J. M. Roberts, *Europe, 1880–1945* (London, 1967), p. 127.

15 This kind of sentencing made imprisonment with hard labor "one of the shared humiliations of the English poor," as noted by Michael Ignatieff in *A Just Measure of Pain: The Penitentiary in the Industrial Revolution, 1750–1850* (New York, 1978), p. 177. Ignatieff states that "there were tramps in the 1850s who could count the time they had spent on the 'shinscraper' [the treadwheel] in years of their lives."

16 Donald Bouchard notes that "decisive documents are those which articulate prac-

tical exigencies and imagination," in "For Life and Action: Foucault, Spectacle, Document," *The Oxford Literary Review* 4, no. 2 (1980): 20–28.

17   *Le Temps*'s front page could then reasonably and routinely carry news items such as: "Berlin, Nov. 11, 8:15. The Emperor, who has been hunting for the last few days in Wusterhausen with the King of Saxony, Prince George of Saxony, and the Duke of Coburg-Gotha, will go to Breslau on the 15 to attend new hunting expeditions in the vicinity. The municipality of Breslau has voted 30,000 marks for a reception for the sovereign."

18   Quoted in Roberts, *Europe*, p. 146.

19   *Le Petit Parisien* also had numerous reports on German spies, with large print titles like "UNPUNISHED SPIES," "GERMAN SPIES," or "ARREST OF A GERMAN" with "AN ODIOUS PERSONAGE" as subtitle—such articles, probably considered of dubious taste, were simply unheard of in the prestige press.

20   See Groupe μ, *Rhétorique générale* (Paris, 1970), p. 35ff., for a discussion of the notion of zero degree.

21   Similarly, daily reports of parliamentary debates which avowedly performed the neutral public service of linking the electorate to their representatives also served to valorize parliament and reinforce its acceptance as the essential institution of democracy, the great public forum, the indispensable political structure for the achievement of freedom, and so on. The work done in government commissions was thus overshadowed, and politics were reduced to infighting between individuals or parties vying for control—events much more amenable to "political gossip" (the title of the political column in the *Daily Mail*'s front page) than analysis.

22   Quoted in Francine Amaury, *Histoire du plus grand quotidien de la IIIe République: Le Petit Parisien (1876–1944)*, 2 vols. (Paris, 1972), 2:761.

23   See Altheide, *Creating Reality*, pp. 73–76, for a discussion of the angle in news stories.

24   "Faits Divers" column in *Le Temps*, September 9, 10, October 4, 10.

25   Gaston Leroux, *Le mystère de la chambre jaune* (1907; Paris, 1979), pp. 390–91.

26   I am here applying the model proposed by the Groupe μ, in their *Rhétorique générale*, pp. 106–13.

27   Ibid., p. 130.

28   The implications of the mass media for political, economic, and cultural relations are infinite, and have been the object of innumerable studies. The limited perspective which is taken here is that required by the theoretical premises of the study: if practice determines pertinence, how does pertinent knowledge then influence a particular practice in return?

29   For a recent study of the (minimal) retention of news coverage or understanding of basic news concepts by newspaper readers, even those who have received advanced education and read in order to keep informed, see Teun A. van Dijk, *News as Discourse* (Hove and London, 1988), pp. 154ff. Stories of individual crimes, accidents, and disasters are those which are most often remembered.

30   *Le Temps*'s column entitled "Life in Paris" exemplifies this type of report; its November 22 issue started with "You know that I trace here for you, day by day, the biography of the great and small characters on whom the kaleidoscope of public attention stops for an instant. Thus perhaps shall we finally draw the complete cal-

endar of Parisian types; but you are not at the end of your patience, nor I at the end of my labor."

31   Arthur Meyer, quoted in Livois, *Histoire*, 2:389. It is perhaps in this context that Girardin's definition of the press is best understood: "The true name of the press is forgetfulness" (ibid., 1:227).

32   "Moi je n'aime pas les grands journaux / Qui parl't de politique/ Qu'est-c'que ça m'fout qu'les Esquimaux / Aient ravagé l'Afrique. / Ce qui m'faut à moi c'est l'*Petit Journal* / La gazett', la croix de ma mère, / Tant plus qu'y a de noyés dans le canal, / Tant plus que c'est mon affaire." Quoted in Bellanger, *Histoire générale*, 3:298 n. 3.

33   Altick describes this taste for gothic horror in his *Victorian Studies in Scarlet* (New York, 1970), pp. 68ff. It is now generally recognized that there were five Ripper victims; all had their throats cut from ear to ear, suffered multiple cuts and wounds, most were disemboweled, some had organs removed, and the last victim was grossly mutilated in her room: her cheeks and face were severely cut, her throat was cut to the spinal column, her nose, ears, and breasts were cut off, and her organs taken out and placed on a nearby table.

34   The anti-German reporting of mass journalism in France and England illustrates these techniques. The out-group is identified spatially, not historically or dialectic-ally; economic, social, and political factors are fused into the single identification of an alien enemy group. The knowledge so generated could then be used to promote defensive nationalistic and militaristic state policies.

35   On September 14 *The Times* reported an inquest into the death of Alice Keeping, an eighteen-month-old child, which ended as follows: "Death was due to starvation. The jury returned verdict to that effect. The coroner remarked that Mrs. Keeping was a hard-working woman, and no blame attached to her." The police column of October 10 in *The Times* reported that John and Elizabeth Tobin were tried for "un-lawfully and willfully neglecting to provide adequate food, clothing, and medical aid for their child Daniel." There were five children being so neglected, left with very little food and clothing in a single room infested with vermin and "covered with human excrement." The parents were discharged. Through all these inci-dents, the message that laborers' children were dying of hunger and deprivation, whether their parents worked or not, was simply not registered. The cases fell into silence, and were thus, literally, insignificant.

36   The *Daily Telegraph* described the similar murder of Marie Aguétant (Prado's alleged victim) as of "the commonest kind," redeemed only by the murderer's most extraordinary personality (November 7).

37   Criminologists used the same tactic with their "penal substitutes" (see chapter 3).

38   One single letter of protest was published by the *Daily Telegraph*, on October 5. Call-ing the treatment Kelly had received in the hands of the police "inhuman to the very extreme," the author nevertheless ended his letter with pious thoughts rather than policy changes: "Would to God these poor creatures were treated kindly of every hand, and pointed to Christ, which is the only way to check them in their downward walk in life." The point was never mentioned again in the paper.

39   The *Daily Telegraph* eventually recognized that "It is not now believed that the un-happy woman belonged to the class from which the five other victims appear to have been selected. She has, on the other hand, the character of having been a decent woman, doing work whenever she could get it" (October 4). However, the

numerous descriptions of Kelly's good nature and struggle to survive in the East End recorded in the paper's reports of the coroner's inquest did not in any way prevent the publication of a leader article insisting on the separation of the sexes in the lodging-houses, and describing their inhabitants as "wild savages who detest every restraint and abhor order and law" (October 5).

40 Gareth Stedman Jones, *Outcast London: A Study in the Relationship between Classes in Victorian Society* (Oxford, 1971), p. 229.

41 Ibid., pp. 162–65, 200.

42 Judith R. Walkowitz, *Prostitution and Victorian Society: Women, Class, and the State* (Cambridge, 1980), especially chapter 10, pp. 210–13.

43 Stuart Hall et al., *Policing the Crisis: Mugging, the State, and Law and Order* (London, 1978), p. 37. For other examples of nineteenth-century views on crime in today's press, see ibid., pp. 91, 100–102, 112–15. Chapter 3 describes the "background assumption" of the consensual nature of society in newspaper reporting, ibid., pp. 55–57.

44 Jones concludes his *Outcast London* by showing that the accepted truths about the "lower orders" were maintained until the wartime economy absorbed available workers, emptying the workhouses and casual wards: "The casual poor were shown to have been a social and not a biological creation. Their life style had not been the result of some hereditary 'taint' but the simple consequence of the offer of poor housing, inadequate wages, and irregular work. Once decent and regular employment was made available, 'the unemployables' proved impossible to find. In fact they had never existed, except as a phantom army called up by late Victorian and Edwardian social science to legitimize its practice" (p. 336). Without the perspective of discourse analysis (which Jones began to adopt in his later work, *Languages of Class*), the historian is caught in the paradox of commissions which adopt false solutions in spite of available knowledge, and of sciences which produce "lies" or "phantoms"; this can lead to a mistaken view of power as conspiracy.

45 Jurgen Habermas, "The Genealogical Writing of History; On Some Aporias in Foucault's Theory of Power," trans. G. Ostrander, *Canadian Journal of Social and Political Theory* 10, nos. 1–2 (1986); Nancy Fraser, "Foucault on Modern Power: Empirical Insights and Normative Confusions," *Praxis International* 1, no. 3 (October 1981): 272–87; Tom Keenan discusses this issue at length in "The 'Paradox' of Knowledge and Power," *Political Theory* 15, no. 1 (February 1987): 5–37.

46 Michel Foucault, *The History of Sexuality*, vol. 1, *An Introduction*, trans. Robert Hurley (1976; New York, 1978), p. 96.

47 Michel Foucault, *The Order of Things: An Archaeology of the Human Sciences*, trans. Alan Sheridan (1966; New York, 1970), pp. 382–87; see also his *Raymond Roussel* (Paris, 1963), and his article on Blanchot, "La pensée du dehors," *Critique* 229 (1966): 523–46.

48 Michel Foucault, *Discipline and Punish: The Birth of the Prison*, trans. Alan Sheridan (1975; New York, 1979), pp. 191–94. Mark Seltzer notes this shift in Foucault's attitude toward literature in his *Henry James & the Art of Power* (Ithaca, N.Y., 1984), p. 176.

49 Charles Grivel, *La production de l'intérêt romanesque. Un état du texte (1870–1880) un essai de constitution de sa théorie* (Paris, 1973), pp. 344, 365–66.

50 D. A. Miller, *The Novel and the Police* (Berkeley, Calif., 1988), p. x. Franco Moretti

argues similarly in his essay "Clues," in *Signs Taken for Wonders. Essays in the Sociology of Literary Forms*. Trans. Susan Fischer, David Forgacs, and David Miller (London, 1983). Seltzer, while insisting on a "criminal continuity" between art and power, argues that "if one reads here not an intrinsic difference between literary and political practices but instead a certain alignment and alliance of tactics and interests, one should not simply 'write off' the difference between literary and political domains, but rather indicate the ways in which this difference itself may be made to work within a larger network of power-discourse relations" (*Henry James & the Art of Power*, pp. 131–32). My work is aligned with this strategy.

Part III   Literature

1   Priscilla P. Clark in her article "Stratégies d'auteur au XIXe siècle," *Romantisme* 17–18 (1977): 94, gives examples of such government pensions and positions.

2   By the end of the century national literatures were included in elementary and secondary school curriculum. The universities of Scotland and Ireland and the University of London established chairs of English literature ahead of Oxford, where English became a pass subject in 1873, and an honours subject in 1893. In France faculties of letters had been established in 1808 but their primary function was to grant the *baccalauréat*. Structured university studies were established in 1877, when students in sciences and letters were "created" with the provision of 300 *licence* scholarships (200 were added for the *agrégation* in 1880) and the hiring of "maîtres de conférences." The number of literature students went from 1,021 in 1882 to 2,358 in 1888, to 6,000–7,000 in 1914. University professors working between 1900 and 1914 came from social and economic backgrounds very similar to those of the swelling ranks of the novelists of the time: lower middle-class shopkeepers, artisans, and agricultural laborers together accounted for 60.8 percent of their numbers. See Richard D. Altick, *The English Common Reader: A Social History of the Mass Reading Public, 1800–1900* (Chicago, 1957), p. 161; Chris Baldick, *The Social Mission of English Criticism 1848–1932* (Oxford, 1983); Anne-Marie Thiesse and Hélène Mathieu, "Déclin de l'âge classique et naissance des classiques. L'évolution des programmes littéraires de l'agrégation depuis 1890," *Littérature* 42 (1981): 92–95; Antoine Prost, *Histoire de l'enseignement en France, 1800–1967* (Paris, 1968); and Victor Karady, "Recherches sur la morphologie du corps universitaire littéraire sous la Troisième République: Littéraires et scientifiques dans l'université au XIXe siècle," *Le Mouvement social* 96 (1976): 51–52.

3   This was perhaps best expressed by the nonconformist preacher who said: "There have been among us three great social agencies: the London City Mission; the novels of Mr. Dickens; the cholera." In Richard A. Levine, ed., *Backgrounds to Victorian Literature* (San Francisco, 1967), p. 173.

4   Traditional accounts of the history of crime stories usually identify landmark publications as the original sources of subgenres or noteworthy trends and techniques in crime fiction, to then situate them in a chain of writings forever stretching back in time, as aptly noted by John G. Cawelti: "Without exaggeration one can say that crime and literature have been in it together from the beginning" (*Adventure, Mystery, and Romance. Formula Stories as Art and Popular Culture* [Chicago, 1976],

p. 52). Thus, if Edgar Allen Poe is generally recognized as the father of detective fiction because of his Dupin stories (1841–45), Régis Messac in his pioneering study entitled *Le "detective-novel" et l'influence de la pensée scientifique* (Paris, 1929) went beyond Voltaire's *Zadig* and its source of inspiration, the French translation by the Chevalier de Mailly of the Italian work by Cristoforo Armeno, *Peregrinaggio di tri figlinoli del Re di Serendippo* (1557), allegedly borrowed from a Persian text, to various Arab, Hebrew, Hindu, and Sanskrit sources. A series of such firsts has thus been established: the first story to have been written backward (i.e., from the perspective of a dénouement which justifies the inclusion of previous narrative material) is said to be *Caleb Williams* (1794) by William Godwin. The title of first author of English detective novels is usually ascribed to Wilkie Collins, because of *The Woman in White* (1860) and *The Moonstone* (1868), although some historians contest this by pointing to Thomas Gaspey's *Richmond, or Scenes in the Life of a Bow Street Officer, Drawn Up from His Private Memoranda* (1827). The first French *roman policier* is said to be Emile Gaboriau's *L'affaire Lerouge* (1866), and Fortuné de Boisgobey is seen not only as his successful and prolific continuator, with *Le Forçat colonel* (1872) and many other works down to *La main froide* in 1889, but also as one of the prime sources of inspiration for Arthur Conan Doyle. Such information, however interesting, is of limited pertinence to this study, and will therefore not be pursued any further.

7   Preconditions of Emergence: The Promise of National Literatures

1   Christophe Charle, "L'expansion et la crise de la production littéraire (2e moitié du 19e siècle)," *Actes de la recherche en sciences sociales* 4 (1975): 50.

2   J. A. Sutherland, *Victorian Novelists and Their Publishers* (Chicago, 1976), p. 47.

3   Ibid., p. 43.

4   Ibid., p. 77.

5   Grant Allen, in his introduction to his novel, *The British Barbarians*; quoted in Darko Suvin, "The Social Addresses of Victorian Fiction: A Preliminary Enquiry," *Literature and Society* 8, no. 1 (1968): 23.

6   Richard D. Altick, *Victorian People and Ideas: A Companion for the Modern Reader of Victorian Literature* (New York, 1973), p. 145. For example, Hardy had to make Angel Clare carry Tess across a flooded stream in a wheelbarrow rather than in his arms, to satisfy the editor of the *Graphic*, then publishing *Tess of the D'Urbervilles* in serialized form.

7   W. H. Smith boycotted Hardy's *Jude the Obscure* and G. Moore's *A Modern Lover* and *A Mummer's Wife*, to name only three. Hardy ceased to write novels altogether after the boycott of *Jude*.

8   Altick, *Victorian People*, p. 196.

9   See Roger Bellet, "Une bataille culturelle, provinciale et nationale, à propos des bons auteurs pour bibliothèques populaires (janv.–juin 1867)," *Revue des sciences humaines* 34, no. 135 (1969): 453–73. In the case studied by Bellet, a petition sign by "the most respected citizens of Saint-Etienne" eventually reached the imperi. Senate. Signatories included "the President of the Conciliation Board, the Presi dent and past Presidents of the Associations of physicians, judges, engineers, the

Inspector of Elementary Schools . . . honorary and practicing notaries, lawyers, solicitors, merchants, bankers, surrogate Judges of the Peace . . . totalling 102, of which several were members of the Legion of Honor" (p. 467).

10   Suvin, "The Social Addresses of Victorian Fiction," p. 22.

11   Sutherland, *Victorian Novelists*, pp. 32–33; and Priscilla Clark, "Stratégies d'auteur au XIXe siècle," *Romantisme* 17–18 (1977): 97–98.

12   Roger Fayolle, *La critique littéraire* (Paris, 1964), p. 99; Sutherland, *Victorian Novelists*, p. 43; Michel Faure, "Le retour au jansénisme dans l'institution critique: le cas de Ferdinand Brunetière et de Jules Lemaître," *Littérature* 42 (1981): 66–67; and see also John Gross, *The Rise and Fall of the Man of Letters: Aspects of English Literary Life since 1800* (London, 1969).

13   Sutherland illustrates the general conviviality existing within publishing circles, *Victorian Novelists*, p. 85.

14   César Grana, *Bohemian versus Bourgeois: French Society and the French Man of Letters in the Nineteenth Century* (New York, 1964), p. 34.

15   Sutherland, *Victorian Novelists*, p. 52.

16   Ibid., p. 63.

17   Ibid., pp. 64, 13–14.

18   Richard D. Altick, *The English Common Reader: A Social History of the Mass Reading Public, 1800–1900* (Chicago, 1957), p. 309.

19   Christophe Charle, *La crise littéraire à l'époque du naturalisme: Roman, théâtre et politique. Essai d'histoire sociale des groupes et des genres littéraires* (Paris, 1979), p. 43: "During the second half of the 19th century, a complete mutation takes place. The circulation of certain successful novels represents the volume of the entire production of the first half of the century. . . . This quantitative mutation implies a complete transformation of the reading public."

20   Charle, "L'expansion et la crise," p. 45 n. 2.

21   Ibid., p. 50.

22   Lionel Gossman, "Literature and Education," *New Literary History* 13, no. 2 (1982): 357.

23   Chris Baldick, *The Social Mission of English Criticism 1848–1932* (Oxford, 1983); B. Doyle, "The Hidden History of English Studies," in P. Widdowson, ed., *Re-Reading English* (London, 1982); and T. Eagleton, *Literary Theory* (Minneapolis, 1983).

24   Pierre Martino, *Le Roman réaliste sous le Second Empire* (Paris, 1913), pp. 96–105. Similarly, the 1856 exam of the *Académie des sciences morales et politiques* required a review of "the influence that contemporary literature, and especially the novel, have had on the manners and morals in France." First prize was given to a magistrate's memoir which violently condemned novelists, including Balzac and Stendhal (p. 97).

25   Chris Baldick, *The Social Mission*, T. Eagleton, *Literary Theory*, and D. J. Palmer, *The Rise of English Studies* (Oxford, 1965).

26   For a concise account of the interrelation between the rise of literature in the modern sense and the nation, see Wlad Godzich and Nicholas Spadaccini, "Popular Culture and Spanish Literary History," in W. Godzich and N. Spadaccini, eds., *Literature among Discourses: The Spanish Golden Age* (Minneapolis, 1986), pp. 41–61.

27 Roland Barthes, *Le degré zéro de l'écriture suivi de Nouveaux Essais critiques* (Paris, 1953), p. 26. Italics mine.

28 Elizabeth Deeds Ermarth, *Realism and Consensus in the English Novel* (Princeton, 1983), p. 65. For a critique of Ermarth's position see N. N. Feltes, "Realism, Consensus and 'Exclusion itself'," *Textual Practice* 1, no. 3 (Winter 1987): 297–308.

29 D. A. Miller, *The Novel and the Police* (Berkeley, Calif., 1988), p. 92.

30 Ermarth, *Realism and Consensus*, pp. 85–86.

31 Miller, *The Novel and the Police*, p. 57. Miller is here discussing *The Moonstone*, but his argument extends to realist novels generally.

32 See Doyle, "The Hidden History of English Studies," for a discussion of this "quasi-professional" and "quasi-maternal" function assigned to women, especially the "surplus women" (neither wives nor mothers) revealed in the 1851 Census.

33 Gossman, "Literature and Education," p. 355; see also Palmer, *The Rise of English Studies*, p. 39.

34 Alice Durand-Gréville, *L'Instruction morale et civique des jeunes filles* (Paris, 1882); quoted in Linda L. Clark, *Schooling the Daughters of Marianne: Textbooks and the Socialization of Girls in Modern French Primary Schools* (Albany, 1984), p. 31.

35 *Réquisitoire* against Flaubert, reprinted in the 1972 Folio ed. of *Madame Bovary* (1856; reprint, Paris, 1972), p. 482.

36 Ibid., p. 501.

37 John Boyd-Kinnear, "The Social Position of Women in the Present Age," in *Women's Work and Women's Culture* (London, 1869), pp. 354–55; in Margaret Bryant, *The Unexpected Revolution: A Study in the History of the Education of Women and Girls in the Nineteenth Century* (London, 1979), p. 48. Boyd-Kinnear was arguing *against* this situation, and concluded, "do we not in truth reduce them to the mere slaves of the harem?" The second quote is by James Fitzjames Stephen, *Saturday Review* (July 4, 1857); quoted in Richard Stang, *The Theory of the Novel in England 1850–1870* (New York, 1959), p. 24.

38 F. D. Maurice, "Plan of a Female College for the Help of the Rich and the Poor," *Lectures to Ladies on Practical Subjects* (1855), p. 14, quoted in Baldick, *The Social Mission*, p. 68; and J. de Maistre, *Lettres et Opuscules inédits* (Paris, 1851), letter 41, quoted in Isabelle Bricard, *Saintes ou pouliches. L'éducation des jeunes filles au XIXe siècle* (Paris, 1985), p. 93.

39 Quoted in Aimé Guedj, "Le naturalisme avant Zola," *Revue des sciences humaines* 40, no. 160 (1975): 570. Eliot's *Scenes of Clerical Life* (1857), were described in similar terms by E. D. Forgues: "the scalpel which operates on the dead, after all, frightens us less between the hands of the disinterested naturalist than does this crystal lens with which we are, so to speak, dissected alive." Guedj, "Le naturalisme avant Zola," p. 569.

40 Letter to G. H. Lewes, November 1849, in Clement Shorter, *The Brontes: Life and Letters* (London, 1908), 2:80.

41 Emile Zola, "De la moralité," in *Le roman expérimental*, 4th ed. (Paris, 1880), especially pp. 279–80.

42 Philippe Hamon, *Introduction à l'analyse du descriptif* (Paris, 1981), pp. 31, 58.

43 Ferdinand Brunetière, "A propos de *Pot-Bouille*," in *Le roman naturaliste*, 7th ed. (1883; reprint, Paris, 1896), p. 296.

44   Ferdinand Brunetière, "La banqueroute du naturalisme," in *Le roman naturaliste*, p. 337.

45   Zola, "De la moralité," p. 284.

46   See above, chapter 3, "Knowledge and Power" section.

47   Michel Foucault, *The Order of Things: An Archaeology of the Human Sciences*, trans. Alan Sheridan (1966; New York, 1970), pp. 217–21, for a discussion of the epistemological shift allowing the recognition of man.

48   Ibid., pp. 313–14.

49   George Meredith, *Letters*, ed. W. M. Meredith (New York, 1912), 2:398; quoted in Stang, *The Theory of the Novel*, p. 34.

50   George Henry Lewes, in *Blackwood's Edinburgh Magazine* 86 (July 1859): 108; quoted in Stang, *The Theory of the Novel*, pp. 79–80. This view was maintained in the educational system, where literary texts were studied as illustrations of different aspects of human nature. See Antoine Prost, *Histoire de l'enseignement en France, 1800–1967* (Paris, 1968), p. 248.

51   Marc Angenot and Nadia Khouri, "The Discourse of Prehistoric Anthropology: Emergence, Narrative Paradigms, Ideology," *Minnesota Review* (Fall 1982), 112–31.

52   Rémy Ponton, "Naissance du roman psychologique: Capital culturel, capital social et stratégie littéraire à la fin du 19ᵉ siècle," *Actes de la recherche en sciences sociales* 4 (1975): 73.

53   Maurice Larkin, *Man and Society in Nineteenth-Century Realism: Determinism and Literature* (Totowa, N.J., 1977), p. 3.

54   Quoted in Alfred C. Proulx, *Aspects épiques des Rougon-Macquart de Zola* (The Hague, 1966), p. 136.

55   Questionnaire submitted by the *Revue illustrée* in 1892. Quoted in Martin Kane, *Zola's Bête Humaine: A Study in Literary Creation* (Berkeley, Calif., 1962), p. 101.

56   Quoted in Reba A. Soffer, "The Revolution in English Social Thought, 1880–1914," *The American Historical Review* 75 (December 1970): 1941.

57   Quoted in Maxime Leroy, *Histoire des idées sociales en France: D'Auguste Comte à P.-J. Proudhon* (Paris, 1954), p. 141.

58   Claude Bernard described the scientific experimenter as the "inquiring magistrate of nature": "only, instead of dealing with men who seek to trick him with untrue confessions or false testimonies, he must deal with natural phenomena that are for him characters whose languages and customs are unknown" (*Introduction à l'étude de la médecine expérimentale* [1865; reprint, Paris, 1966], p. 64). Zola approved of this vision and, echoing his mentor, stated "we novelists are the inquiring magistrates of men and their passions" (*Le roman expérimental*, p. 10).

59   Charles Grivel, *La production de l'intérêt romanesque. Un état du texte (1870–1880) un essai de constitution de sa théorie* (Paris, 1973), p. 187. D. A. Miller, in his *Narrative and Its Discontents. Problems of Closure in the Traditional Novel* (Princeton, 1981), describes the "narratable" as "the instances of disequilibrium, suspense, and general insufficiency from which a given narrative appears to arise. The term is meant to cover the various incitements to narrative, as well as the dynamic ensuing from such incitements, and it is thus opposed to the 'nonnarratable' state of quiescence assumed by a novel before the beginning and supposedly recovered by it at the end" (p. ix).

8 Conditions of Emergence: Disciplinary Limits

1   Claude Bernard, *Introduction à l'étude de la médecine expérimentale* (1865; reprint, Paris, 1966), pp. 125–26.

2   Richard A. Brooke, "The Development of the Historical Mind," in Richard A. Levine, ed., *Backgrounds to Victorian Literature* (San Francisco, 1967), p. 185.

3   G. M. Trevelyan later described this development as follows: "What was wrong with the historical reaction at the end of Victoria's reign, was not the positive stress it laid on the need for scientific method in weighing evidence, but its negative repudiation of the literary art, which was declared to have nothing whatever to do with the historian's task." See Brooke, "The Development of the Historical Mind," p. 186.

4   Bertrand Russell, *Our Knowledge of the External World as a Field for Scientific Method in Philosophy* (London, 1914), p. 27.

5   Quoted in Agathon, *L'esprit de la Nouvelle Sorbonne. La crise de la culture classique. La crise du français* (Paris, 1911), pp. 71–72.

6   Eliséo Véron, *La sémiosis sociale. Fragments d'une théorie de la discursivité* (Paris, 1987), pp. 43–44, 93.

7   Ibid., p. 79.

8   Marcelin Berthelot, *Science et morale* (Paris, 1896), p. 35. Berthelot was also president of the French Freethought societies, and served as minister of education in 1886–87 and minister of foreign affairs in 1895–96. On the importance of scientists in Third Republic politics, see John Eros, "The Positivist Generation of French Republicanism," *Sociological Review* 3 (December 1955): 255–73; and Harry W. Paul, "The Debate over the Bankruptcy of Science in 1895," *French Historical Studies* 5, no. 3 (1968): 299–327.

9   Edward A. Mackinnon, ed., *The Problem of Scientific Realism* (New York, 1972), pp. 19–20.

10   Timothy J. Reiss, *The Discourse of Modernism* (Ithaca, N.Y., 1982), pp. 41–42.

11   Gaston Bachelard, *Le nouvel esprit scientifique* (Paris, 1934), pp. 15, 16–17. Samuel Weber discusses these issues in the introduction to his *Institution and Interpretation* (Minneapolis, 1987).

12   Walter Besant, "The Art of Fiction" (Boston, 1884; reprinted in Eugene Current-Garcia and Walton R. Patrick, eds., *Realism and Romanticism in Fiction. An Approach to the Novel*, Chicago, 1962), p. 74.

13   Ibid., p. 72.

14   Ibid., pp. 74, 75, 76.

15   Ibid., p. 74.

16   Ibid., p. 85.

17   Ibid., pp. 77, 75.

18   Ibid., p. 82.

19   Henry James, "The Art of Fiction," *Longman's Magazine* 5 (September 1884); reprinted in Current-Garcia and Patrick, eds., *Realism and Romanticism in Fiction*, p. 91.

20   Ibid., p. 90.

21   Ibid.

22   Ibid., p. 95. Thus, Besant's national and class boundaries were difficult for James

to accept. His primary (and most natural) category, the "modern English novel," was "shadowy" for James, and judged to be the result of an "accidental confusion of standpoints" (p. 98); similarly, Besant's "remark about the lower middle-class writer and his knowing his place" struck James as "perhaps rather chilling" (p. 95).

23 Ibid., p. 93. Again on p. 105: "There is one point at which the moral sense and the artistic sense lie very near together; that is in the light of the very obvious truth that the deepest quality of a work of art will always be the quality of the mind of the producer."

24 Ibid., p. 97.

25 Ibid., p. 93.

26 Ibid., pp. 96, 97.

27 Ibid., p. 106.

28 Ibid., p. 101.

29 Robert Louis Stevenson, "A Humble Remonstrance," *Longman's Magazine* 5 (November 1884); reprinted in Current-Garcia and Patrick, eds., *Realism and Romanticism in Fiction*, pp. 111, 113–14.

30 Ibid., p. 115.

31 Ibid., p. 113.

32 The literary curriculum developed in the 1880s and 1890s reflected the same situation, as the production of literary history as the independent evolution of different periods or schools growing from one another effectively cut literature off from society and from virtually any and all material considerations. See Anne-Marie Thiesse and Hélène Mathieu, "Déclin de l'âge classique et naissance des classiques. L'évolution des programmes littéraires de l'agrégation depuis 1890," *Littérature* 42 (1981): 106–8.

33 Emile Zola, *Le roman expérimental*, 4th ed. (Paris, 1880), p. 29.

34 Ibid., p. 22.

35 Ibid., p. 24.

36 Wlad Godzich analyzes the instituting moment in "Religion, the State, and Post(al) Modernism," afterword to Weber, *Institution and Interpretation*, pp. 153–64.

37 Christophe Charle, "L'expansion et la crise de la production littéraire (2e moitié du 19e siècle)," *Actes de la recherche en sciences sociales* 4 (1975): 44–65; "Situation spatiale et position sociale. Essai de géographie sociale du champ littéraire à la fin du 19e siècle," *Actes de la recherche en sciences sociales* 13 (1977): 45–59; and "Situation du champ littéraire," *Littérature* 44 (1981): 8–20. See also Jacques Dubois, *L'institution de la littérature* (Paris, 1978), and his "Emergence et position du groupe naturaliste dans l'institution littéraire," in P. Cogny, dir., *Le naturalisme* (Paris, 1978), pp. 75–93.

38 Christophe Charle, *La crise littéraire à l'époque du naturalisme. Roman, théâtre et politique. Essai d'histoire sociale des groupes et des genres littéraires* (Paris, 1979), p. 66.

39 Brunetière at *La Revue des Deux Mondes*, France at *Le Temps*, Lemaître at *Le Journal des Débats*, and journalists in Madame Adam's *La Nouvelle Revue* supported the school, and attacked the naturalists. Many of the leading novelists of the school (which claimed descent from Taine and Renan, the recognized heads of the French intelligentsia) were supported by prestigious salons, where economic and political figures mingled with the publishing and theater circles. Loti was accepted in the *Académie* in 1891, Brunetière in 1894, Bourget in 1895, Lemaître and France

in 1896, Hervieu in 1900, and Barrès in 1906. See Rémy Ponton, "Naissance du roman psychologique. Capital culturel, capital social et stratégie littéraire à la fin du 19ᵉ siècle," *Actes de la recherche en sciences sociales* 4 (1975): 66–81; and his "Programme esthétique et accumulation de capital symbolique. L'exemple du Parnasse," *Revue française de sociologie* 14 (1973): 202–20.

40 Charles Grivel, *La production de l'intérêt romanesque. Un état du texte (1870–1880) un essai de constitution de sa théorie* (Paris, 1973), p. 366.

41 M. M. Bakhtin, "Discourse in the Novel," in *The Dialogic Imagination*, ed. M. Holquist, trans. C. Emerson and M. Holquist (1934–35; Austin, Tex., 1981), p. 278. Bakhtin notes that "the dialogic orientation of discourse . . . is a property of *any* discourse" (p. 279). However, whereas literary discourse displays this dialogical orientation, "extra-literary" discourses such as the human and social sciences or the press purported to be referring directly to external reality, as will be argued shortly.

42 Ibid., p. 262.

43 M. M. Bakhtin and P. M. Medvedev, *The Formal Method in Literary Scholarship. A Critical Introduction to Sociological Poetics*, trans. A. J. Wehrle (1928; Cambridge, 1985), pp. 133, 134.

44 Quoted in Tzvetan Todorov, *Mikhail Bakhtin: The Dialogical Principle*, trans. Wlad Godzich (Minneapolis, 1984), p. 54.

45 Ibid., p. 49.

46 Ibid., p. 54: "Isolated signs, linguistic systems, or even the text (as a semiotic entity) can never be true or false, or beautiful, etc."; "only the utterance can be accurate (or inaccurate, beautiful, just, etc.)."

47 Friedrich Nietzsche, *The Genealogy of Morals*, trans. Walter Kaufmann (1887; New York, 1969), p. 119. "Petit faitalisme" (Nietzsche's French), p. 151.

48 Arthur Jacobson, "Russell and Strawson on Referring," in E. D. Klemke, ed., *Essays on Bertrand Russell* (Urbana, Ill., 1970), p. 289.

49 Albert Einstein, "Remarks on Bertrand Russell's Theory of Knowledge," in *The Problem of Scientific Realism*, p. 175.

50 Gottlob Frege, "Über Sinn und Bedeutung" (1892), in P. Geach and M. Black, eds., *Translations from the Philosophical Writings of Gottlob Frege* (Oxford, 1952), p. 57.

51 Timothy J. Reiss, "Peirce and Frege: In the Matter of Truth," in Timothy J. Reiss, *The Uncertainty of Analysis: Problems in Truth, Meaning, and Culture* (Ithaca, N.Y., 1988), p. 31.

52 Saussure's complex and contradictory notion of *langue* provided the possibility of thinking the social production of knowledge, as did the work done on presuppositions by Frege and Russell, but this potential was neglected by all three researchers, and systematically denied by their followers. See M. M. Bakhtin and V. N. Volosinov, *Marxism and the Philosophy of Language*, trans. M. Ladislav and I. R. Titunik (Cambridge, Mass., 1973); Marc Angenot, "Bakhtine, sa critique de Saussure et la recherche contemporaine," *Etudes Françaises* 21, no. 1 (1984): 7–19; and Véron, *La sémiosis sociale*, and Reiss, *The Discourse of Modernism*, for discussions of this problematic.

53 See Reiss, *The Uncertainty of Analysis*, p. 41.

54 Quoted in ibid., p. 41.

55 *Collected Papers of Charles Sanders Peirce*, eds. C. Hartshorne and P. Weiss (reprint

of series published in 1868 in the *Journal of Speculative Philosophy* [Cambridge, 1931–58]), 1:541.

56   Peirce quote, ibid., 4:127. Reiss quote, *The Uncertainty of Analysis*, p. 41.

57   Peirce, *Collected Papers*, 2:149.

58   Nietzsche, *The Genealogy of Morals*, pp. 77–78. Marx analyzed at length the inter-relations between the production of "human nature" and the forces and relations of economic production. The following famous aphorisms summarize the issue well: "The class which is the ruling *material* force of society, is at the same time its ruling *intellectual* force": "the ideas of the ruling class are in every epoch the ruling ideas." Karl Marx and Frederick Engels, *The German Ideology* (1845–46; reprint, London, 1965), p. 60.

59   Reiss, *The Uncertainty of Analysis*, pp. 49, 52.

60   Godzich, "Religion, the State, and Post(al) Modernism," p. 164.

9   Textual Construction: Truth-Producing Fiction

1   Marin-Joseph Fenayrou was a pharmacist who, upon learning that his wife had had an affair with his shop assistant, agreed to forgive her only if she helped him murder her former lover (the affair had ended a year before the revelation and murder took place). Barrême was a government official, prefect of the Départe-ment de l'Eure, who was killed on a moving train, his body thrown out along the tracks; his murderer was never found, and there were suspicions that the affair had been hushed because Barrême's private life would cause scandal if revealed. Poinsot, a high-ranking judge, was found dead on a train; at first interpreted as a political crime, his murder was later rumored to be perpetrated by the brother of a young girl (a tenant's daughter) he had seduced. See Martin Kanes, *Zola's Bête Humaine: A Study in Literary Creation* (Berkeley, Calif., 1962), pp. 21–24.

2   1889 interview in the Rome *Tribuna*; Kanes, *Zola's Bête Humaine*, p. 24 n. 27.

3   Jacques Dubois, *L'Assommoir de Zola* (Paris, 1973), pp. 133–34.

4   Emile Zola, *La bête humaine* (1889; reprint, Paris, 1972), p. 58: " 'Dis vite: mon petit cadeau.' Lui riait aussi, en bon homme. Il se décida. 'Mon petit cadeau.' C'était un couteau qu'elle venait de lui acheter, pour en remplacer un qu'il avait perdu et qu'il pleurait, depuis quinze jours. Il s'exclamait, le trouvait superbe, ce beau couteau neuf, avec son manche en ivoire et sa lame luisante. Tout de suite, il allait s'en servir. Elle était ravie de sa joie; et, en plaisantant, elle se fit donner un sou, pour que leur amitié ne fût pas coupée." Future references to the novel will be to this edition, and page numbers will be indicated in the text.

5   Dubois, in *L'Assommoir de Zola*, pp. 133–34, discusses this pronoun use.

6   Jules Héricourt, " 'La bête humaine' de M. Zola et la physiologie du criminel," *Revue bleue* 45 (January 4, 1890): 714.

7   Cesare Lombroso, "La 'Bête humaine' et l'anthropologie criminelle," *Revue des revues* 4–5 (1892): 261; first published in *Fanfulla della Domenica*, June 15, 1890.

8   Ibid., p. 262.

9   Ibid., p. 263.

10   Ibid., p. 260.

11   See J. W. Scott, "Réalisme et réalité dans 'La Bête humaine.' Zola et les chemins de

fer," *Revue d'histoire littéraire de la France* 63 (1963): 635–43, for answers to questions of accuracy such as "Would Grandmorin's body have fallen at the post #153 if it had been thrown out immediately after the train came out of the tunnel?" Other critics held that problems arose not from the lack of accuracy but from the sheer quantity of technical details. One caricature of the times showed a railway superior admonishing an employee holding a flag in one hand and a book in the other, with the caption: "And above all, no mistakes in the signals!"—"Don't worry; I always have Zola's latest novel in hand."

12 Emile Zola, *Le roman expérimental*, 4th ed. (Paris, 1880), p. 25.

13 J. H. Rosny Aîné, *Dans les rues: Romans de moeurs apaches et bourgeoises* (Paris, 1913), p. 2. All references to the novel will be to this edition and page numbers will be indicated in the text.

14 As in the following dialogue and footnotes, p. 165: "—Sûr et certain. Le gonce est aspic[1] comme un chameau. Y ne briffe que de la barbaque[2] . . . y sort pas. . . ." "[1] Aspic, avare. [2] Barbaque, mauvaise viande."

15 Ferdinand de Brunetière, "A propos du *Disciple*," *Revue des Deux-Mondes* 94 (July 1, 1889): 216.

16 Paul Bourget, *Le Disciple* (Paris, 1889), p. 18. All references to the novel will be to this edition and page numbers will be indicated in the text.

17 Jacques Patin, "Paul Bourget au *Figaro*," *Le Figaro* (December 28, 1935); documented in René Dumesnil, *Le réalisme et le naturalisme* (Paris, 1955), p. 399.

18 Marc Angenot, "On est toujours le disciple de quelqu'un ou le Mystère du pousse-au-crime," *Littérature* 49 (1983): 62.

19 Brunetière, "A propos du *Disciple*," p. 220.

20 Anatole France, "La métaphysique devant la morale—M. Paul Bourget—M. Ferdinand Brunetière," in "La vie littéraire," *Le Temps* (July 7, 1889).

21 Anatole France, "M. Paul Bourget: *Le Disciple*," in "La vie littéraire," *Le Temps* (June 23, 1889).

22 Micheline Tison-Braun, *La crise de l'humanisme. Le conflit de l'individu et de la société dans la littérature française moderne* (Paris, 1958), pp. 112–14.

23 "Causerie bibliographique," *Revue scientifique* 44 (August 17, 1889): 213–15; quoted in Henry W. Paul, "The Debate over the Bankruptcy of Science in 1895," *French Historical Studies* 5, no. 3 (1968): 299–327.

24 *Séances et travaux de l'Académie des Sciences morales et politiques*, 134:5–29; documented in A. Feuillerat, *Paul Bourget* (Paris, 1937), p. 147.

25 Hippolyte Taine, *Correspondance*, 4:292.

26 See Feuillerat, *Paul Borget*, p. 146, for a description of the enthusiastic response to Bourget's novel.

27 Stephen Knight, *Form and Ideology in Crime Fiction* (Bloomington, Ind., 1980), p. 97.

28 John G. Cawelti, *Adventure, Mystery, and Romance. Formula Stories as Art and Popular Culture* (Chicago, 1976), p. 92.

29 Arthur Conan Doyle, "The Five Orange Pips," in *Adventures of Sherlock Holmes* (1892; reprint, New York, 1981), pp. 219, 217. All references to Sherlock Holmes stories and novels will be to this edition and page numbers will be indicated in the text when possible.

30 *A Study in Scarlet*, pp. 21–22.

31 Ashes and footprints in *The Sign of Four*, p. 91; tattoos in "The Red-Headed League," p. 177; secret writings in "The Adventure of the Dancing Men," p. 522; and hand types in *The Sign of Four*, p. 91.

32 "The Boscombe Valley Mystery," p. 205; "A Scandal in Bohemia," p. 169; and "The Boscombe Valley Mystery," p. 217.

33 "The Final Problem," p. 471.

34 Régis Messac, *Le "detective-novel" et l'influence de la pensée scientifique* (Paris, 1929), p. 587.

35 Latyschew, *Bulletin de la commission internationale pénitentiaire* (St. Petersburg, 1879), p. 209; documented in Cesare Lombroso, *Nouvelles recherches de psychiatrie et d'anthropologie criminelle* (Paris, 1892), p. 42.

36 Robert Louis Stevenson, *Strange Case of Dr Jekyll and Mr Hyde* (1886; reprint, Great Britain, 1979), p. 90. All references to the novel will be to this edition and page numbers will be indicated in the text.

37 For a brief outline of critical responses to the novel, see W. Veeder and Gordon Hirsch, eds., *Dr Jekyll and Mr Hyde: After One Hundred Years* (Chicago, 1988), p. ix–xi.

38 For an analysis of the homosexual desires in the novel, and of the absence of women in this tale, see W. Veeder, "Children of the Night: Stevenson and Patriarchy," in Veeder and Hirsch, *Dr Jekyll and Mr Hyde*, pp. 107–60.

39 From *A New Dictionary on Historical Principles* (Oxford, 1926); this dictionary also notes that in 1871, "troglodytic" could also mean "not interested or conversant with affairs."

40 The reference is probably to the well-known quatrain dedicated to Dr. Fell, eminent scholar and Dean of Christ Church College at Oxford: "I do not love thee Dr. Fell / The reason why I cannot tell / But this I know and know quite well / I do not love thee Dr. Fell."

41 For discussion of the names, and a bibliography of other such discussions, see Veeder and Hirsch, *Dr Jekyll and Mr Hyde*, pp. 107–60.

42 This is an application of the model proposed by Timothy J. Reiss for the Peircian sign as a triadic relation in "Peirce and Frege: In the Matter of Truth," in *The Uncertainty of Analysis: Problems in Truth, Meaning, and Culture* (Ithaca, N.Y., 1988).

43 Peter K. Garrett, "Cries and Voices: Reading *Jekyll and Hyde*," in Veeder and Hirsch, *Dr Jekyll and Mr Hyde*, pp. 59–72.

Conclusion

1 The trajectory, therefore, has been the reverse of that followed by Michel Foucault in *Discipline and Punish*, where an analysis of technologies of disciplinary power and fields of knowledge led to an understanding of the "ratio" of punishment.

INDEX

◆

Marie-Christine Leps is Associate Professor of English at York University.

Library of Congress Cataloging-in-Publication Data
Leps, Marie-Christine.
Apprehending the criminal : the production of deviance in nineteenth-century discourse / Marie-Christine Leps.
p.   cm.—(Post-contemporary interventions)
Includes bibliographical references (p.) and index.
ISBN 0-8223-1255-7 (acid-free paper).—
ISBN 0-8223-1271-9 (pbk. : acid-free paper)
1. Discourse analysis. 2. Crime in mass media—
History—19th century. 3. Criminology—History—
19th century. I. Title. II. Series.
P302.L46   1992
401'.41—dc20   92-7451 CIP